D0163216

American Public Service

Radical Reform and the Merit System

PUBLIC ADMINISTRATION AND PUBLIC POLICY

A Comprehensive Publication Program

1. *Public Administration as a Developing Discipline,* Robert T. Golembiewski
2. *Comparative National Policies on Health Care,* Milton I. Roemer, M.D.
3. *Exclusionary Injustice: The Problem of Illegally Obtained Evidence,* Steven R. Schlesinger
5. *Organization Development in Public Administration,* edited by Robert T. Golembiewski and William B. Eddy
7. *Approaches to Planned Change,* Robert T. Golembiewski
8. *Program Evaluation at HEW,* edited by James G. Abert
9. *The States and the Metropolis,* Patricia S. Florestano and Vincent L. Marando
11. *Changing Bureaucracies: Understanding the Organization before Selecting the Approach,* William A. Medina
12. *Handbook on Public Budgeting and Financial Management,* edited by Jack Rabin and Thomas D. Lynch
15. *Handbook on Public Personnel Administration and Labor Relations,* edited by Jack Rabin, Thomas Vocino, W. Bartley Hildreth, and Gerald J. Miller
19. *Handbook of Organization Management,* edited by William B. Eddy
22. *Politics and Administration: Woodrow Wilson and American Public Administration,* edited by Jack Rabin and James S. Bowman
23. *Making and Managing Policy: Formulation, Analysis, Evaluation,* edited by G. Ronald Gilbert
25. *Decision Making in the Public Sector,* edited by Lloyd G. Nigro
26. *Managing Administration,* edited by Jack Rabin, Samuel Humes, and Brian S. Morgan
27. *Public Personnel Update,* edited by Michael Cohen and Robert T. Golembiewski
28. *State and Local Government Administration,* edited by Jack Rabin and Don Dodd
29. *Public Administration: A Bibliographic Guide to the Literature,* Howard E. McCurdy

31. *Handbook of Information Resource Management,* edited by Jack Rabin and Edward M. Jackowski
32. *Public Administration in Developed Democracies: A Comparative Study,* edited by Donald C. Rowat
33. *The Politics of Terrorism: Third Edition,* edited by Michael Stohl
34. *Handbook on Human Services Administration,* edited by Jack Rabin and Marcia B. Steinhauer
36. *Ethics for Bureaucrats: An Essay on Law and Values, Second Edition,* John A. Rohr
37. *The Guide to the Foundations of Public Administration,* Daniel W. Martin
39. *Terrorism and Emergency Management: Policy and Administration,* William L. Waugh, Jr.
40. *Organizational Behavior and Public Management: Second Edition,* Michael L. Vasu, Debra W. Stewart, and G. David Garson
43. *Government Financial Management Theory,* Gerald J. Miller
46. *Handbook of Public Budgeting,* edited by Jack Rabin
49. *Handbook of Court Administration and Management,* edited by Steven W. Hays and Cole Blease Graham, Jr.
50. *Handbook of Comparative Public Budgeting and Financial Management,* edited by Thomas D. Lynch and Lawrence L. Martin
53. *Encyclopedia of Policy Studies: Second Edition,* edited by Stuart S. Nagel
54. *Handbook of Regulation and Administrative Law,* edited by David H. Rosenbloom and Richard D. Schwartz
55. *Handbook of Bureaucracy,* edited by Ali Farazmand
56. *Handbook of Public Sector Labor Relations,* edited by Jack Rabin, Thomas Vocino, W. Bartley Hildreth, and Gerald J. Miller
57. *Practical Public Management,* Robert T. Golembiewski
58. *Handbook of Public Personnel Administration,* edited by Jack Rabin, Thomas Vocino, W. Bartley Hildreth, and Gerald J. Miller
60. *Handbook of Debt Management,* edited by Gerald J. Miller
61. *Public Administration and Law: Second Edition,* David H. Rosenbloom and Rosemary O'Leary
62. *Handbook of Local Government Administration,* edited by John J. Gargan
63. *Handbook of Administrative Communication,* edited by James L. Garnett and Alexander Kouzmin
64. *Public Budgeting and Finance: Fourth Edition,* edited by Robert T. Golembiewski and Jack Rabin
65. *Handbook of Public Administration: Second Edition,* edited by Jack Rabin, W. Bartley Hildreth, and Gerald J. Miller
67. *Handbook of Public Finance,* edited by Fred Thompson and Mark T. Green
68. *Organizational Behavior and Public Management: Third Edition,* Michael L. Vasu, Debra W. Stewart, and G. David Garson
69. *Handbook of Economic Development,* edited by Kuotsai Tom Liou
70. *Handbook of Health Administration and Policy,* edited by Anne Osborne Kilpatrick and James A. Johnson
71. *Handbook of Research Methods in Public Administration,* edited by Gerald J. Miller and Marcia L. Whicker

72. *Handbook on Taxation*, edited by W. Bartley Hildreth and James A. Richardson
73. *Handbook of Comparative Public Administration in the Asia-Pacific Basin*, edited by Hoi-kwok Wong and Hon S. Chan
74. *Handbook of Global Environmental Policy and Administration,* edited by Dennis L. Soden and Brent S. Steel
75. *Handbook of State Government Administration,* edited by John J. Gargan
76. *Handbook of Global Legal Policy,* edited by Stuart S. Nagel
78. *Handbook of Global Economic Policy,* edited by Stuart S. Nagel
79. *Handbook of Strategic Management: Second Edition,* edited by Jack Rabin, Gerald J. Miller, and W. Bartley Hildreth
80. *Handbook of Global International Policy,* edited by Stuart S. Nagel
81. *Handbook of Organizational Consultation: Second Edition,* edited by Robert T. Golembiewski
82. *Handbook of Global Political Policy,* edited by Stuart S. Nagel
83. *Handbook of Global Technology Policy,* edited by Stuart S. Nagel
84. *Handbook of Criminal Justice Administration*, edited by M. A. DuPont-Morales, Michael K. Hooper, and Judy H. Schmidt
85. *Labor Relations in the Public Sector: Third Edition*, edited by Richard C. Kearney
86. *Handbook of Administrative Ethics: Second Edition,* edited by Terry L. Cooper
87. *Handbook of Organizational Behavior: Second Edition*, edited by Robert T. Golembiewski
88. *Handbook of Global Social Policy,* edited by Stuart S. Nagel and Amy Robb
89. *Public Administration: A Comparative Perspective, Sixth Edition,* Ferrel Heady
90. *Handbook of Public Quality Management*, edited by Ronald J. Stupak and Peter M. Leitner
91. *Handbook of Public Management Practice and Reform*, edited by Kuotsai Tom Liou
92. *Personnel Management in Government: Politics and Process, Fifth Edition,* Jay M. Shafritz, Norma M. Riccucci, David H. Rosenbloom, Katherine C. Naff, and Albert C. Hyde
93. *Handbook of Crisis and Emergency Management*, edited by Ali Farazmand
94. *Handbook of Comparative and Development Public Administration: Second Edition,* edited by Ali Farazmand
95. *Financial Planning and Management in Public Organizations*, Alan Walter Steiss and Emeka O. Cyprian Nwagwu
96. *Handbook of International Health Care Systems,* edited by Khi V. Thai, Edward T. Wimberley, and Sharon M. McManus
97. *Handbook of Monetary Policy,* edited by Jack Rabin and Glenn L. Stevens
98. *Handbook of Fiscal Policy,* edited by Jack Rabin and Glenn L. Stevens
99. *Public Administration: An Interdisciplinary Critical Analysis,* edited by Eran Vigoda
100. *Ironies in Organizational Development: Second Edition, Revised and Expanded,* edited by Robert T. Golembiewski

101. *Science and Technology of Terrorism and Counterterrorism*, edited by Tushar K. Ghosh, Mark A. Prelas, Dabir S. Viswanath, and Sudarshan K. Loyalka
102. *Strategic Management for Public and Nonprofit Organizations*, Alan Walter Steiss
103. *Case Studies in Public Budgeting and Financial Management: Second Edition,* edited by Aman Khan and W. Bartley Hildreth
104. *Handbook of Conflict Management,* edited by William J. Pammer, Jr. and Jerri Killian
105. *Chaos Organization and Disaster Management,* Alan Kirschenbaum
106. *Handbook of Gay, Lesbian, Bisexual, and Transgender Administration and Policy,* edited by Wallace Swan
107. *Public Productivity Handbook: Second Edition,* edited by Marc Holzer
108. *Handbook of Developmental Policy Studies,* edited by Gedeon M. Mudacumura, Desta Mebratu and M. Shamsul Haque
109. *Bioterrorism in Medical and Healthcare Administration,* Laure Paquette
110. *International Public Policy and Management: Policy Learning Beyond Regional, Cultural, and Political Boundaries,* edited by David Levi-Faur and Eran Vigoda-Gadot
111. *Handbook of Public Information Systems, Second Edition,* edited by G. David Garson
112. *Handbook of Public Sector Economics,* edited by Donijo Robbins
113. *Handbook of Public Administration and Policy in the European Union,* edited by M. Peter van der Hoek
114. *Nonproliferation Issues for Weapons of Mass Destruction,* Mark A. Prelas and Michael S. Peck
115. *Common Ground, Common Future: Moral Agency in Public Administration, Professions, and Citizenship*, Charles Garofalo and Dean Geuras
116. *Handbook of Organization Theory and Management: The Philosophical Approach, Second Edition,* edited by Thomas D. Lynch and Peter L. Cruise
117. *International Development Governance,* edited by Ahmed Shafiqul Huque and Habib Zafarullah
118. *Sustainable Development Policy and Administration,* edited by Gedeon M. Mudacumura, Desta Mebratu, and M. Shamsul Haque
119. *Public Financial Management,* edited by Howard A. Frank
120. *Handbook of Juvenile Justice: Theory and Practice,* edited by Barbara Sims and Pamela Preston
121. *Emerging Infectious Diseases and the Threat to Occupational Health in the U.S. and Canada,* edited by William Charney
122. *Handbook of Technology Management in Public Administration,* edited by David Greisler and Ronald J. Stupak
123. *Handbook of Decision Making,* edited by Goktug Morcol
124. *Handbook of Public Administration, Third Edition,* edited by Jack Rabin
125. *Handbook of Public Policy Analysis,* edited by Frank Fischer, Gerald J. Miller, and Mara S. Sidney
126. *Elements of Effective Governance: Measurement, Accountability and Participation,* edited by Kathe Callahan
127. *Handbook of Transportation Policy and Administration,* edited by Jeremy Plant

128. *Art and Practice of Court Administration,* Alexander B. Aikman
129. *Handbook of Globalization, Governance, and Public Administration,* Ali Farazmand and Jack Pinkowski
130. *Handbook of Globalization and the Environment,* edited by Khi V. Thai, Dianne Rahm and Jerrell D. Coggburn
131. *American Public Service: Radical Reform and the Merit System,* James S. Bowman and Jonathan P. West

Available Electronically

Principles and Practices of Public Administration, edited by Jack Rabin, Robert F. Munzenrider, and Sherrie M. Bartell

PublicADMINISTRATION*netBASE*

American Public Service

Radical Reform and the Merit System

James S. Bowman
Florida State University,
Tallahassee, USA

Jonathan P. West
University of Miami
Coral Gables, Florida, USA

CRC Press
Taylor & Francis Group
Boca Raton London New York

CRC Press is an imprint of the
Taylor & Francis Group, an informa business

CRC Press
Taylor & Francis Group
6000 Broken Sound Parkway NW, Suite 300
Boca Raton, FL 33487-2742

Printed in the United States of America on acid-free paper
10 9 8 7 6 5 4 3 2 1

International Standard Book Number-10: 0-8493-0534-9 (Hardcover)
International Standard Book Number-13: 978-0-8493-0534-4 (Hardcover)

Library of Congress Cataloging-in-Publication Data

American public service : radical reform and the merit system / edited by James S. Bowman, Jonathan P. West.
p. cm. -- (Public administration and public policy ; 131)
Includes bibliographical references and index.
ISBN 0-8493-0534-9 (alk. paper)
1. Civil service--United States. 2. Public administration--United States. I. Bowman, James S., 1945- II. West, Jonathan P. (Jonathan Page), 1941- III. Series.

JK692.A44 2006
352.6'30973--dc22 2006047550

Visit the Taylor & Francis Web site at
http://www.taylorandfrancis.com

and the CRC Press Web site at
http://www.crcpress.com

DEDICATION

To Loretta—JSB

For Colleen—JPW

CONTENTS

About the Editors xvii
Contributors xix
Acknowledgments xxi
Introduction xxiii

Part I Merit Systems in Flux 1

1 Changes in State Civil Service Systems: A National Survey 3
Steven W. Hays and Jessica E. Sowa
Introduction 3
Reforming the Personnel Function: Previous Research 4
Methodology 6
Findings: Current Trends in the Transformation of the Modern Civil Service 7
Decentralization (Reinvention) of HRM 10
The "Declassification" of Civil Servants 11
Restrictions on Due Process Rights 12
Activist Governors 14
Discussion and Conclusion 15
References 20
Appendix 22
HR Reform Interview Template 22

2 Framing Civil Service Innovations: Assessing State and Local Government Reforms 25
R. Paul Battaglio, Jr. and Stephen E. Condrey
Four Models of Human Resource Management Service Delivery 26
Radical Reform: The Case of Georgia 27
More Radical Reform: Florida and Service First 30
A Collaborative Approach: Modernizing the New York Civil Service 33

The Executive as Initiator of Strategic Reform: The Case of Louisiana 36
The Courts as an Initiator of Reform: The Unique Case of the Personnel Board of Jefferson County, Alabama 38
HRM in Chapel Hill, North Carolina: A Case for Best Practices 40
Conclusions and Implications 41
Acknowledgments 43
References 43

3 At-Will Employment: Origins, Applications, Exceptions, and Expansions in Public Service 47
Sally C. Gertz
Introduction 47
The Origin of Employment at Will 48
Exceptions to Employment at Will 50
Statutory Exceptions 51
Judicial Exceptions 51
Applications of Contemporary Employment at Will: Criticisms, Defenses, Reforms 54
Criticisms 54
Defenses 57
Reforms 59
Expanding Employment at Will to Classified Civil Servants: The Constitutional Issues 61
Procedural Due Process and Taking Claims 61
Impairment of Contract 62
Substantive Due Process, Equal Protection Clause 63
Expanding Employment at Will to Classified Civil Servants: Reducing the Transparency of Government by Eliminating Due Process 63
Conclusion 65
Acknowledgments 70
Endnotes 70

Part II Is Patronage a Problem? 75

4 Bringing Back Boss Tweed: Could at-Will Employment Work in State and Local Government and, if So, Where? 77
Robert Maranto and Jeremy Johnson
Introduction 77
The Case for Reforming the U.S. Civil Service 78
Why What Works in Washington May Not Play in Philadelphia: A Political Theory of State Public Personnel Reform 80
Patronage Demand Variables 81
Political Environmental Variables 82
Bureaucratic Capacity 82

The Best and Worse States for Civil Service Reform 83
Patronage Demand Variables 83
Political Environmental Variables 86
Summary Measures: Which States Rank Where? 87
Discussion 92
Acknowledgments 97
References 97

5 The Demonization of Patronage: Folk Devils and the *Boston Globe*'s Coverage of the 9/11 Terrorist Attacks 101
Domonic A. Bearfield
Introduction 101
Folk Devils and Moral Panics 102
The Patronage Folk Devil 103
Boston and Patronage 104
Moral Panic: Massport and the *Boston Globe*'s Coverage after 9/11 105
The Case of the Convenient Whipping Boy 106
Analysis 109
Conclusion 114
Acknowledgments 116
Endnotes 116

Part III State Cases of Civil Service Reform 121

6 Ending Civil Service Protections in Florida Government: Experiences in State Agencies 123
James S. Bowman and Jonathan P. West
Introduction 123
Scholarly Literature and Background Material 124
Scholarly Literature 124
Background Material 125
Methodology 127
Findings 129
Transportation 129
Environmental Protection 134
Department of Children and Families 138
Comparing Survey and Case Data 141
Conclusion 142
Endnotes 144
Appendix 1 147
Department of Transportation Terminations 147
Appendix 2 148
Human Resource Unit in Transition at the Department of Environmental Protection 148
Appendix 3 149
Terminations at Department of Children and Families 149

7 At-Will Employment in Government: Its Impact in the State of Texas 151
Jerrell D. Coggburn
Introduction 151
HR in Texas State Government 153
Survey of State HR Directors 154
Findings and Analysis 154
Discussion 167
Implications of Survey Findings 167
Additional Perspectives 168
Conclusion 170
References 171
Endnotes 173

8 The Attraction to at-Will Employment in Utah Governments 175
Richard Green, Robert Forbis, Jennifer Robinson, Stephen Nelson, Jennifer Seelig, and Angela Stefaniak
Introduction 175
Methodology 177
Findings and Analysis 178
Understanding at-Will Public Employment 181
Accountability and at-Will Employment 182
Discipline and Dismissal 183
The Role of Employee Motivation 185
Views on Expanding at-Will Employment in Utah 187
Conclusion 188
Endnotes 191
References 191

Part IV Future Reform Issues 193

9 Dissin' the Deadwood or Coddling the Incompetents? Patterns and Issues in Employee Discipline and Dismissal in the States 195
Richard C. Elling and Lyke Thompson
Introduction 195
Employee Dismissal Evidence 196
Patterns of State Employee Dismissal: The 20-State Study 197
Dealing with Problem Employees: The Views of State Managers 201
Determinants of Dismissal Rates and the Severity of Dismissal as a Management Impediment 203
Civil Service Coverage and Dismissal Rates 203
Simplification of the Disciplinary Process and Dismissal Rates 204
Collective Bargaining and Dismissal 205
Implications for Dismissal Practices and Civil Service Reforms 207

The Dilemmas of at-Will Employment........ 210
Endnotes........ 214

10 At-Will Employment and Racial Equality in the Public Sector: The Demise of a Niche?........ 219
George Wilson
Introduction........ 219
The Public Sector as a Niche for African Americans........ 220
The Nature and Benefits of Work in the Public Sector........ 223
Working in the Public Sector........ 223
Benefits of Working in the Public Sector........ 224
The Rise of at-Will Employment in the Public Sector........ 225
Disproportionate Impact of at-Will Employment Policy by Race........ 226
At-Will Employment and Job Dismissals........ 226
At-Will Employment and Social Psychological Benefits........ 228
Conclusion........ 228
Acknowledgments........ 229
References........ 229

11 Federal Labor-Management Relations under George W. Bush: Enlightened Management or Political Retribution?........ 233
James R. Thompson
History of Labor-Management Relations in the Federal Government........ 234
Creating a New Personnel System for the Department of Homeland Security........ 237
Creating a New Personnel System for the Department of Defense........ 239
Unions and Organizational Performance........ 240
High-Performance Work Systems and Unions........ 241
The Clinton Management Strategy........ 243
The Bush Management Strategy........ 244
"Taking Charge of Federal Personnel"........ 245
Outcomes of the Bush Labor Relations Strategy........ 246
Problematic Program Implementation........ 247
Hostile Labor-Management Environment........ 247
Increased Litigiousness........ 248
Conclusion........ 250
Endnotes........ 250

Index........ 255

ABOUT THE EDITORS

James S. Bowman is professor of public administration at the Askew School of Public Administration and Policy, Florida State University. His primary area is human resource management. Noted for his work in ethics and quality management, Dr. Bowman also has done research in environmental administration. He is author of nearly 100 journal articles and book chapters as well as editor of five anthologies. Bowman coauthored, with Berman, West, and VanWart, *Human Resource Management: Paradoxes, Processes and Problems* (2nd ed., Sage) in 2006, and *The Professional Edge: Competencies in Public Service* (Sharpe) in 2004. He is editor-in-chief of *Public Integrity*, a journal sponsored by the American Society for Public Administration, and four other professional associations. A past National Association of Schools of Public Affairs and Administration fellow as well as a Kellogg Foundation fellow, he has experience in the military, civil service, and business.

Jonathan P. West is professor of political science and director of the graduate public administration program in the School of Business Administration at the University of Miami. His research interests include human resource management, productivity, local government, and ethics. Professor West has published nearly 100 articles and book chapters. His most recent books are *The Ethics Edge*, coedited with Evan M. Berman (ICMA, 2007), *Human Resource Management: Paradoxes, Processes and Problems* (2nd ed., Sage, 2006), *The Professional Edge* (Sharpe, 2004), both coauthored with Berman, Bowman, and VanWart, and *American Politics and the Enviornment* (Longman, 2002), coauthored with Sussman and Daynes. He is the managing editor of *Public Integrity*. He taught previously at the University of Houston and University of Arizona, and served as a management analyst in the U.S. Surgeon General's Office, Department of the Army, Washington, D.C.

CONTRIBUTORS

R. Paul Battaglio Jr., Department of Public Administration, University of Nevada, Las Vegas

Domonic A. Bearfield, The George Bush School of Government and Public Service, Texas A&M University, College Station

James S. Bowman, editor-in-chief of *Public Integrity*, and Askew School of Public Administration and Policy, Florida State University, Tallahassee

Jerrell D. Coggburn, Department of Public Administration, The University of Texas at San Antonio

Stephen E. Condrey, Carl Vinson Institute of Government, The University of Georgia, Athens

Richard C. Elling, Department of Political Science, Wayne State University, Detroit, Michigan

Robert Forbis, Department of Political Science, University of Utah, Salt Lake City

Sally C. Gertz, Florida State University College of Law, Tallahassee

Richard Green, Center for Public Administration and Policy, University of Utah, Salt Lake City

Steven W. Hays, Department of Political Science, University of South Carolina, Columbia

Jeremy Johnson, Department of Political Science, Brown University, Providence, Rhode Island

Robert Maranto, Political Science Department, Villanova University, Villanova, Pennsylvania

Stephen Nelson, Department of Political Science, University of Utah, Salt Lake City

Jennifer Robinson, Department of Political Science, University of Utah, Salt Lake City

Jennifer Seelig, Department of Political Science, University of Utah, Salt Lake City

Jessica E. Sowa, Department of Political Science, Cleveland State University

Angela Stefaniak, Department of Political Science, University of Utah, Salt Lake City

James R. Thompson, Graduate Program in Public Administration, University of Illinois at Chicago

Lyke Thompson, The Center for Urban Studies and Department of Political Science, Wayne State University, Detroit, Michigan

Jonathan P. West, Department of Political Science, University of Miami, Coral Gables, Florida

George Wilson, Department of Sociology, University of Miami, Coral Gables, Florida

ACKNOWLEDGMENTS

Many people contributed to *American Public Service: Radical Reform and the Merit System*. First, of course, gratitude is extended to the chapter authors, who educated us with their thoughtful papers. They worked to produce a book representative of contemporary thinking on this essential topic. Their readiness to revise and resubmit their initial manuscripts attests to their respect for the subject matter and their skill in mastering it.

The task was facilitated by the thorough, insightful, and prompt reviews of draft chapters by the referees for this project, who included each of the volume's contributors as well as Douglas Goodman (Mississippi State University), George Sulzner (University of Massachusetts Amherst), and Richard Kearney (East Carolina University). We also appreciate the work of Claire Connolly, who assisted in readying the manuscript for publication. Finally, many thanks are due to our families for their support.

INTRODUCTION

The public service is being transformed as reform is occurring at all levels of government both here and abroad. Although some of the changes address narrow, specific issues, increasingly more radical innovations are commonplace. A key example is the effort to modify or eliminate the distinguishing characteristic of the merit system: safeguarding the independence of the public servant corps from political influence. [1] The ensuing debate over attempts to alter the balance between professional expertise and political responsiveness has included the private sector doctrine of at-will employment, whereby employees can be dismissed for any or no reason. Ironically, this policy is being enacted in the public sector despite its historic abuse during the spoils system of the 19th century [2] and when its use is questioned in the private sector. [3]

A priceless asset in American governance, a nonpartisan public service acts as a vital link between governmental institutions and the populace. Understanding the effects of radical change on public personnel systems is critically important both now and in the future to all those interested in the quality of American democracy: elected officials, political appointees, civil servants, and most of all the citizenry. The current status of reform at the state and national levels is briefly summarized below, followed by a literature review, [4] and then a précis of each chapter in the book.

Fueled by entrepreneurial strategies, budget cutbacks, and devolution, the contemporary reform movement [5] has gained exemptions from federal and state merit systems by augmenting management prerogatives and restricting employee rights. [6] At the state level, major reform examples exist: Texas nullified its merit system in 1985 (making all state employees at-will), a 1996 Georgia law mandated that all new civil servants be hired on an at-will basis, and in 2001 Florida eliminated job tenure for most incumbent middle managers. [7]

As Steven W. Hays and Jessica E. Sowa report in Chapter 1, South Carolina and Arkansas recently abolished their merit systems; less dramatically, many states (e.g., Indiana, Delaware, and Kansas) are reclassifying career service positions to unclassified ones as a consequence of reorganizations, reductions in force, or attrition. Such strategies are often mutually reinforcing in a manner that promotes the ongoing deterioration of career public service; the effect is that the status of the public employee today is comparable to that of the business worker. Indeed, Hays and Sowa believe that civil service systems are "entering a new and disquieting phase of vulnerability." In Chapter 4, Robert Maranto and Jeremy Johnson, advocates of ending federal employee tenure, observe that "many and perhaps most states" are not ready for civil service reform based on state corruption rankings, traditional party organizations, media capacity, electoral competition, and bureaucratic capacity.

At the federal level, a variety of agencies (e.g., the Federal Aviation Administration, Internal Revenue Service, General Accountability Office, and National Aeronautics and Space Administration) have received full or partial waivers from Title 5 of the U.S. Code, which defines the merit system. In the wake of the September 11, 2001 attacks, the Transportation Security Agency established at-will employment for its personnel, and subsequently the Departments of Homeland Security and Defense were authorized to create new human resource management systems that strengthened administrative discretion and diminished employee protections. The Bush administration is currently seeking congressional approval to use these new approaches as templates for government-wide change.

Despite the lack of "readiness" in state governments and the use of untested strategies in federal departments, fundamental reformation of civil service systems is nevertheless underway. Policy makers have acted to erode tenure protections with little evidence documenting job security as a major problem and few facts regarding the efficacy of changes. [8] In the process, both the legal and psychological contracts between public employees and their employers have been substantially altered. Clearly the American public service confronts a turbulent environment, the outlines of which are described by the existing literature.

LITERATURE REVIEW

A useful body of civil service reform literature has emerged in the last decade. Kettl and his colleagues [9] outlined many of the themes—decentralization, performance measurement, contracting out, and civil service deregulation—echoed in subsequent work. For instance, Ingraham and her coauthors [10] offered a vision for 21st-century public service, and Denhardt and Denhardt [11] contrasted components of the "new public service" with those of New Public Management and "old public administration." Schultz and Maranto [12] provided a history of the nation's civil service reforms (see also [13, 1]). Condrey and Maranto [5] presented historical, comparative, and point-counterpoint material on radical reform; and Thompson [14] examined institutional consequences of civil service disaggregation during the Clinton years.

West [15] edited a journal symposium on Georgia's legislation, Bowman [8] critiqued Florida's changes, Walters [7] described changes in three states, Maranto [16] maintained that opposition to reform was based on misconceptions about political appointees as well as careerists, West and Bowman [17] investigated Florida's initiative using stakeholder analysis, and Kellough and Nigro [6] collected studies in 2002 on state-level reforms.

Overall, this work is theoretical, descriptive, and normative, as it posits frameworks to understand change, describes those reforms, and develops arguments about them. There is, however, a paucity of evaluative research in most jurisdictions. Little systematic data exists, although there are several examples of empirical research. Nigro and Kellough [18] found that Georgia employees had reservations about the purpose of reform and its daily administration, but the system "had little of the desired impact on agency performance beyond redefining workers' . . . job security" (p. 17). The results from an examination of one agency in the same state revealed that the impact of change on employment commitment and loyalty has not been significant. [19] Condrey's [20] assessment of Georgia's reform found many departments unprepared for their new roles under decentralization and found that cronyism was influencing personnel actions in some agencies. Bowman et al. [21] surveyed affected Florida personnel and found that respondents doubted assumptions made by both reformers and their critics, were concerned about downsizing, and rejected claims made by change advocates about the effects of at-will employment on productivity, morale, and pay.

With few exceptions, then, there is little research on the impact of at-will employment on career employees. The present volume, therefore, examines the impact of at-will employment in civil service systems. The significance of this subject cannot be understated: the keystone of the merit system is safeguarding career personnel from political interference. The following section provides an overview of the chapters.

BOOK CHAPTERS

As discussed above, there is a variety of interesting literature on contemporary civil service reform. Until now, however, no single reference has offered a comprehensive, empirical selection of the latest work on radical reform and the merit system. This collection of original studies is the product of a 2004 nationwide call for papers, and the resulting *Review of Public Personnel Administration* and *International Journal of Public Administration* symposia. This volume, then, offers fresh insights into a common phenomenon: the effects of merit system changes on employees. The selections proceed by introducing their respective subject matter, providing necessary background material, developing pertinent topics, and concluding with a discussion of the implications of the findings.

The volume consists of four parts: (1) "Merit Systems in Flux," (2) "Is Patronage a Problem?" (3) "State Cases of Civil Service Reform," and (4) "Future Reform Issues." Part 1 presents a portrait of contemporary reforms from across the country and concepts to interpret that data. Steven W. Hays and Jessica E. Sowa in "Changes in State Civil Service Systems: A National Survey" reveal a very dynamic environment that is fundamentally redefining the role of public servants—how they are recruited, managed, and retained. These changes range from sweeping transformations in the terms and conditions of employment to more modest, yet significant, modifications in the employment relationship. The authors find, "Under the banners of 'decentralization,' 'accountability,' and 'flexibility,' the due process rights of many civil servants are eroding and at-will employment is affecting greater segments of the public labor force." They identify four interrelated trends: decentralization of human resource authorities, expanded managerial discretion over conversion of protected classified personnel to at-will status, the decline of grievance procedures, and the growing involvement of governors intent on "running government like a business." Their conclusion: civil service systems are undergoing a house-cleaning as many public servants today work in settings not too different from their private sector counterparts.

Chapter 2, "Framing Civil Service Innovations: Assessing State and Local Government Reforms," by R. Paul Battaglio, Jr. and Stephen E. Condrey, uses a comparative model comprised of competing approaches to human resources to analyze the diffusion of reform. They examine four states and two localities, and the diverse strategies that these jurisdictions used to undertake reform: radical, collaborative, court-ordered, executive-led, and best-practice change. "Those seeking an effective human resource system," the authors write, "should not look to the latest management fad or 'quick fix' but rather should concentrate on the proper resources (both monetary and human) and buy-in of the organization's major stakeholders."

Chapter 3, "At-Will Employment: Origins, Applications, Exceptions, and Expansions in Public Service," by Sally C. Gertz, examines the root of many reforms: the business-inspired employment at-will doctrine. The chapter describes the development of the concept in American law and the creation of statutory and judicial exceptions to it. Legal scholarship defending and criticizing the doctrine is contrasted. Against this backdrop, the expansion of at-will employment to the civil service is discussed. The analysis concludes that constitutional objections to the expansion will not succeed, and the resulting trend will have a detrimental effect on the transparency of government operations.

Selections in Part 2, "Is Patronage a Problem?" address whether the relaxation of civil service protections against partisan intrusion will result in corruption. Robert Maranto and Jeremy Johnson, in "Bringing Back Boss Tweed: Could at-Will Employment Work in State and Local Government and, If So, Where?" believe that there is little problem at the national level because the mass media, party competition, and ethics regulation protect against the emergence of a modern-day spoils system. Such conditions, however, may not hold for state governments. To test this supposition, they develop indices based on media scrutiny, party organization, corruption levels, administrative capacity, and minority party strength. They then predict which states are the best candidates for successful, corruption-free reform; states least prepared to implement change effectively are among those most likely to engage in reform.

In "The Demonization of Patronage: Folk Devils and the *Boston Globe*'s Coverage of the 9/11 Terrorist Attacks," Domonic A. Bearfield also raises questions about criticisms leveled at the contemporary reform movement. He argues that patronage has become a "folk devil," employing the theory of "moral panics" to understand its use. Following the terrorist attacks of 9/11, the *Boston Globe* made use of the patronage folk devil, provoking a moral panic that distracted policy makers from more relevant systemic, societal, and bureaucratic problems. Folk devils can pose an obstacle to civil service reform by engendering emotional responses that can result in unjustified damage to administrator and agency reputations. Bearfield contends, as a result, that such distractions inhibit a more analytical approach to the study of patronage.

Part 3, "State Cases of Civil Service Reform," provides examples of ongoing change. "Ending Civil Service Protections in Florida Government: Experiences in State Agencies," by James S. Bowman and Jonathan P. West, ascertains the extent to which the elimination of the defining characteristic of the merit system—job protection against partisan mischief—has affected employees in three departments. Middle managers converted from career service to at-will status—officials occupying linchpin roles in their agencies—have a much more pronounced, negative assessment of the changes than do human resource managers. Whereas some interviewees perceived modest change, many others saw the independent civil servant being neutralized and service jeopardized by the reluctance to "speak truth to power" as a result of reform.

Jerrell D. Coggburn, in the next chapter, analyzes survey data from state personnel managers. In "At-Will Employment in Government: Its

Impact in the State of Texas," respondents agree that the at-will doctrine enhances employee responsiveness and believe that the legal environment serves as a constraint on agency use of at-will terminations. The findings show mixed views on at-will employment's effects on employee behavior (e.g., risk taking, whistle-blowing, decision making, and sensitivity to fairness issues) and agency performance. The author calls for governments to take a more holistic view of at-will employment when considering adoption.

Chapter 8, "The Attraction to at-Will Employment in Utah Governments," reports the results of an exploratory study of officials who are considering, or have already established, at-will relationships in one or more units of their agencies. Richard Green and his colleagues discuss the reasons given for using at-will employment, the extent to which respondents wish to have it in their departments or jurisdictions, and the means used to implement change. The problems with existing personnel systems and the expected advantages of change are discussed. They find that the at-will doctrine is not well understood, and the tension between political responsiveness and managerial effectiveness is downplayed. The authors conclude that "the dismissive attitude among many of the interviewees about possible political manipulation under at-will employment relations is one of the more remarkable and worrisome findings of this study." Any reform debate, they maintain, must anticipate the presence of an impatience with merit systems as well as the inherent "politicality" of public management.

The controversies over civil service have spawned a variety of significant ramifications and implications of reform. Therefore, Part 4, "Future Reform Issues," identifies a variety of key issues. No image of the supposed shortcomings of civil service is more popular than the existence of "deadwood" in its ranks. As Richard C. Elling and Lyke Thompson suggest in "Dissin' the Deadwood or Coddling the Incompetents? Patterns and Issues in Employee Discipline and Dismissal in the States," a plethora of factors are associated with effective job performance. Accordingly, empirical findings from 20 states are brought to bear on adverse action data over three time periods to suggest how the past might inform the future. The authors report, "Even if one ignores the potential for political abuse of the firing process inherent in [the at-will model], those who endorse it must understand that the ability of a jurisdiction to attract employees is a function of a number of factors, including whether applicants believe they have a reasonable chance of remaining with the jurisdiction. The greater job security of public employment has traditionally been seen as compensating for lower pay." A preoccupation with at-will employment arrangements, they argue, is shortsighted, as employee termination cannot be considered in isolation from other characteristics of a jurisdiction's personnel system.

The following chapter, George Wilson's "At-Will Employment and Racial Equality in the Public Sector: The Demise of a Niche?" identifies the likely impact on racial inequality of moving from a protected class employment status to an unprotected at-will relationship. Such a change negatively affects the long-standing labor market "niche" for African Americans. Enhanced employer discretion, he indicates, will result in increased discrimination and damage the social and psychological benefits associated with government employment. Such consequences must be carefully considered prior to change.

Chapter 11, "Federal Labor-Management Relations under George W. Bush: Enlightened Management or Political Retribution?" chronicles recent developments in employment relations in the national government. James R. Thompson outlines the design of the new personnel systems for the Departments of Homeland Security and Defense, which together comprise a large portion of the federal workforce. The discussion analyzes the nature of those changes, focusing on whether or not they are based on a coherent management strategy or, alternatively, stem from political motivations. Thompson is concerned about reforms that, although short of implementing at-will employment, greatly strengthen managerial control on the premise that it promotes high performance. This assumption runs counter to practical experience and scholarly literature, he argues, and as a result reforms portend a contentious workplace in the future.

To summarize, contributors to this volume bring a diversity of perspectives and experiences to the subject. As noted, the variety of approaches found here includes survey research, legal analysis, case work, model building, and theory testing. A combination of quantitative and qualitative approaches is used. The academic backgrounds of the authors include political science, public policy and administration, law, and sociology. A number of them have substantial government experience, and many have been involved in public service training. Each author draws conclusions based on the analysis that contain lessons for policy makers, managers, scholars, and citizens interested in civil service reform and at-will employment. Overall, then, the book provides a baseline of data on reforms, as well as an account of their current promise and pitfalls.

CONCLUSION

Throughout, the collection offers an examination of the innovations, strategies, and issues found in the contemporary civil service reform debate. As such, it represents the state of the art and suggests directions for how to proceed in the future. In so doing, the volume contributes to understanding the ethos of government management in democracy. Certainly no single compendium of current work in a multidisciplinary field such as public administration can or should be complete. Yet a timely study of reform issues can be found in these pages. The role of the merit system in American democracy is a critical subject for inquiry. As a presentation of recent advances on this vital topic, this book will have achieved its purpose if greater reflection on the character of reform occurs in the future than has occurred in the past.

In the end, an important obligation of government is to be a model employer in society, to set a high standard that others can aspire to achieve, and to offer work that honors fairness in employer-employee transactions. Two home-growth cultures—political exchange and civil value [22]—coexist in varying degrees and at different times in American government. The first is premised on contracts, favors, and jobs in exchange for campaign contributions; it is susceptible to corruption because it nurtures an environment of cronyism, favoritism, and waste. In contrast, the civil culture is one in which the commonweal is the central value; it is based on universally applicable rules, equal treatment, and professional stewardship of public resources. How the civil service reform debate is finally resolved, and which culture predominates, will affect the quality of American democracy in the years ahead.

James S. Bowman
Jonathan P. West

NOTES

1. Ingraham, P., *The Foundation of Merit: Public Service in American Democracy*, Johns Hopkins University Press, Baltimore, 1995.
2. Freedman, A., *Patronage: An American Tradition*, Nelson Hall, Chicago, 1994.
3. Werhane, P. H., Radin, T., with Bowie, N., *Employment and Employee Rights*, Blackwell, Malden, MA, 2004.
4. Parts of that discussion are drawn from Bowman et al. [20].
5. Condrey, S., and Maranto, R., eds., *Radical Reform of the Civil Service*, Lexington Books, New York, 2001.
6. Kellough, J., and Nigro, L., eds., *Civil Service Reform in the States*, State University of New York Press, Albany, 2006.
7. Walters, J., Life after Civil Service Reform: The Texas, Georgia, and Florida Experiences, Washington, D.C.: The Center for the Business of Government, 2002.
8. Bowman, J., At-will employment in Florida: A naked formula to corrupt public service, *WorkingUSA*, 6, 90, 2000.
9. Kettle, D., Ingraham, P., Sanders, R., and Horner, C., *Civil Service Reform: Building a Government That Works*, Brookings Institution, Washington, DC, 1996.
10. Ingraham, P., Selden, S., and Moynihan, D., People and performance: Challenges for the future of public service—the report from the Wye River Conference, *Public Administration Review*, 60, 54, 2000.

11. Denhardt, R., and Denhardt, J., *The New Public Service: Serving, Not Steering*, Sharpe, Armonk, NY, 2002.
12. Schultz, D., and Maranto, R., *Politics of Civil Service Reform*, Lang, New York, 1998.
13. Light, P., *The Tides of Reform: Making Government Work 1945–1995*, Yale, New Haven, CT, 1997.
14. Thompson, J., The civil service under Clinton: The institutional consequences of disaggregation, *Review of Public Personnel Administration*, 21, 87, 2001.
15. West, J., Georgia on the mind of radical civil service reformers, *Review of Public Personnel Administration*, 21, 79, 2002.
16. Maranto, R., Praising civil service but not bureaucracy: A brief against tenure in the U.S. Civil Service, *Review of Public Personnel Administration*, 22, 175, 2002.
17. West, J., and Bowman, J., Stakeholder analysis of civil service reform in Florida: A descriptive, instrumental, normative human resource management perspective, *State and Local Government Review*, 36, 20, 2004.
18. Nigro, L., and Kellough, J., Civil service reform in Georgia: Findings of a survey of state employees' views about GeorgiaGain and Act 816, unpublished paper, Georgia State University, 2001.
19. Gossett, C., The changing face of Georgia's merit system: Results from an employee survey in the Georgia Department of Juvenile Justice, *Public Personnel Management*, 32, 267, 2003.
20. Condrey, S., Georgia's civil service reform: A four-year assessment, in *Radical Reform of the Civil Service*, Condrey, S., and Maranto, R., eds., Lexington, New York, 2001, 177.
21. Bowman, J., Gertz, M., Gertz, S., and Williams, R., Civil service reform in Florida state government: Employee attitudes one year later, *Review of Public Personnel Administration*, 32, 286, 2003.
22. Rosenbloom, D., *Understanding Public Administration: Management, Politics, and Law in the Public Sector*, McGraw-Hill, New York, 1998.

PART I

MERIT SYSTEMS IN FLUX

1

CHANGES IN STATE CIVIL SERVICE SYSTEMS: A NATIONAL SURVEY

Steven W. Hays
University of South Carolina

Jessica E. Sowa
Cleveland State University

INTRODUCTION

Over the past 20 years, deregulation of the personnel function in government has become more and more prevalent in the United States, leaving the management of human resources in a state of transition. [3] Across the 50 states, numerous officials are challenging traditional models of human resource management (HRM), with the focus of this challenge often placed on fundamentally redefining the nature of the public employee relationship with government. Although this movement toward decentralization of the HRM responsibilities associated with more centralized civil service systems to individual agency control has promised to produce significant rewards for the public sector, it can be argued that the verdict is still pending on the long-term impact. Indeed, we know little about the ramifications of this sea change in the way public employees are recruited and managed. More dialogue is required to understand what remains of the personnel as we know it in the public sector and whether these changes serve the greater good of governance in the United States.

This chapter presents exploratory findings on the current state of human resource management in state government in the United States, with a focus on the impact of reform on what can be considered the primary unit of analysis in HRM—the employee. The practical repercussion of the implementation of deregulation and decentralization across the states has been the redefinition of the status and role of the public employee, a redefinition that has significant implications for the practice of public sector human resource management and administration. Many of the securities that were afforded to public employees, securities that were to substitute for the higher levels of extrinsic rewards available in the private sector, are gone or have been redefined. This redefinition has left public employees unsure of their status and aware that change is definitely here, for good or ill. Public employees and HRM scholars acknowledge that the times are changing in the management of human resources in government and that this change may represent some grim realities for those currently involved in or seeking to enter public employment.

REFORMING THE PERSONNEL FUNCTION: PREVIOUS RESEARCH

In exploring the research on personnel reform in the United States, one must start with the question of what is wrong with the civil service that requires fundamental reform. As with most systems involved in the administration of government in the United States, personnel systems have been the subject of almost continuous debate concerning their efficacy. The modern civil service system, designed to combat challenges surrounding the politicization of public service employment and the associated inefficiencies, has been argued to suffer from numerous dysfunctions requiring the continued attention of reformers. These dysfunctions, according to critics of the civil service system, include (but are not necessarily limited to) crushing amounts of red tape in executing personnel functions, severe delays associated with all personnel functions (from hiring to firing), and the failure of the system to promote high performance from employees or to punish poor performance. [12, 13] Therefore, a system that was designed to rationalize public employment and ensure that those employees were competent has been argued to have developed into an inefficient and often irrational quagmire. [14] As a result of the perceived dysfunctions in civil service systems, state governments, often the laboratory of public administrative change, have been engaging in a variety of reforms to improve public employment and overall performance in government. These reforms in turn have produced research focused on exploring and understanding how these reforms or changes have impacted government in the states.

Previous research on human resource management change in the states has generally adopted two approaches: examining the impact of HRM change on the structure, processes, and individuals involved in the management of people in state government; or exploring the experiences of particular state governments that have radically changed their existing personnel structure. One primary focus of this research has been on the relative placement of personnel responsibility or authority in state governments, exploring the implications of various forms of centralization and decentralization of the personnel function. Hou et al. [8] discussed the movement from personnel centralization in a central office, such as a civil service commission or office of human resources, to decentralization with responsibility for personnel actions placed under the individual control of department managers. Using data from the Government Performance Project, these scholars found that states with higher service demands, defined as the myriad of services that are required by the population of a state, are more likely to decentralize their HRM authority from a central personnel office to functional agencies. In addition, when states have central personnel offices that report directly to the governor of a state, they are also more likely to decentralize HRM responsibilities. [8]

With reference to the factors that limit deregulation and reform of HRM functions, states with politically charged state governments, defined as those with divided governments between the governor and the legislature, and states with a high presence of union activity are less likely to decentralize HRM responsibilities to lower agency control. [8] In studying personnel reform in the states, Kellough and Selden [10] also found that public employee unionization had a negative effect on the implementation of HRM reform. Finally, in terms of the negative effects of personnel reform, Coggburn [2] concluded that deregulation of public personnel also has led to an increase in the number of part-time employees, suggesting a relationship between personnel deregulation and the job security of public employees in the states.

Other scholars have explored the experiences of individual state governments that are generally identified as having fundamentally restructured or "demolished" their existing centralized civil service systems. The State of Georgia, with the 1996 Merit Systems Reform Act, fundamentally changed the structure of its HRM system, promoting the need to give managers the right to manage. [5] However, the degree to which this managerial authority has led to increased productivity or has improved the ability of the government to serve the people is not fully tested. In addition, studies of certain facets of this reform, such as GeorgiaGain, found that employees were highly critical of much of the reform package, questioning the effectiveness of the reform and generally voicing concern over the primary motives behind the reform. [9, 11] GeorgiaGain is best known as the reform that created a totally unclassified labor force and introduced "pay for performance" as a substitute for standard salary practices, such as automatic longevity increase. Scholars studying the reform of the civil service system in Florida discovered similar concerns among state employees; many of them responded negatively to the question of whether Florida's reform, Service First, would increase the productivity of the government. [1]

Scholars studying public personnel reform have identified factors that contribute to the implementation (or lack thereof) of particular reforms, those focused on decentralization and deregulation of the personnel function. In addition, researchers examining the implementation of these reforms in individual states have shown that the proposed "benefits" of reform are far from clearly proven and in fact have produced some negative externalities on state employees. The question then remains as to what the current picture of HRM practices reflects in state governments today and what the impact of this picture is on public employees.

METHODOLOGY

The primary purpose of this study was to determine if the wholesale changes in the terms and conditions of public employment that are evident in a few states (e.g., Florida and Georgia) are prevalent elsewhere. To that end, a telephone survey of state offices of human resource management (OHRs) was conducted. Using a patterned interview template (see the appendix at the end of this chapter), representatives from all 50 states were contacted during a 15-week period from mid-January through late May 2005. Respondents consisted of agency directors in many cases, but also included deputy directors and other subordinates. Five HR directors responded in writing, and, in four instances, the status of state HR systems was probed through interviews with university faculty members in the respective states. A critical consideration in the identification of respondents was that the individual(s) interviewed in each state be well versed in the content and operation of the relevant state civil service system. In many cases, this required that two or more respondents be interviewed in each state. Similarly, a number of the respondents begged off from answering certain questions, and either referred the researchers to other individuals or followed up with written additions to their oral responses. Although it is impossible to assert that a complete and accurate picture was obtained from every interviewee, the researchers are satisfied that all respondents were reliable, highly informed, and well-placed sources of information on their respective state personnel systems.

The interviews focused primarily on the recent changes in the states' personnel systems, especially those involving reinvention and accountability measures, the means by which HR services are provided, the array of procedural protections available to civil servants, and any attempts to remove workers from the classified ("career") service or to change the nature or definition of their positions. Information gleaned from interviews was supplemented with written documentation such as OHR annual reports, workforce profiles, and other sources of data that are available both on the Internet and through more traditional sources.

Although an effort has been made to standardize the response patterns among the states, differences in terminology and data availability represented a major challenge. In some states, for example, no one was able to provide even an estimate of the number of employees subject to direct appointment and removal by the governor. Additionally, the recent gubernatorial elections—along with very fluid political situations in a large number of states—have produced very dynamic environments. Many states stand at the threshold of sweeping HRM changes, but the ultimate outcome of these initiatives will not be determined until long after the end of the current legislative sessions and are therefore beyond the scope of this chapter. Another delimiting factor was the reluctance of many individuals to be quoted directly. Approximately 25 percent of the respondents expressed concern about maintaining their anonymity or requested specifically that their observations be disguised.

FINDINGS: CURRENT TRENDS IN THE TRANSFORMATION OF THE MODERN CIVIL SERVICE

Exploration of the data collected in this study confirms almost without question that reinvention of HRM is proceeding at a rapid pace and that many facets of this movement represent what can be considered attacks upon the professional public service. Under the banners of "decentralization," "accountability," and "flexibility," the due process rights of many civil servants are eroding and at-will employment is affecting greater segments of the public labor force. Although there are very few instances of the pronounced changes that occurred in Florida and Georgia—and only one example of the extreme absence of career protections that prevails in Texas—there is a discernable drift (and in some cases a tidal wave) in the direction of at-will employment. This fact is evident in four interrelated trends that emerge from the data: the continuing decentralization of HRM authority, coupled with expanded supervisory influence over public workers' terms of employment; a widespread increase in the number of positions that are being declassified or "uncovered" from civil service guidelines; a reduction in the employees' ability to grieve supervisory decisions; and the involvement of a growing legion of activist governors who are intent upon imposing "business practices" in public agencies, regardless of whether or not these "business practices" have a proven effectiveness standard. (See Table 1.1.)

Table 1.1 General Summary of Interview Findings: Snapshot of Current Conditions in the States' Personnel Systems

State	*Level of HR Decentralization*	*Expansion of At-Will Employees*	*Range of Grievable Issues*	*Activist Governor*	*"Decline in Job Security"*
Alabama	Partial	No	Agency Specific	No	Yes
Alaska	Centralized	No	Restricted	Yes	No
Arizona	Partial	Yes	Restricted	Yes	Yes
Arkansas	Significant	Yes	Restricted/Agency Specific	No	Yes
California	Partial	No	Expansive	Yes	Yes
Colorado	Significant	Yes	Restricted	Yes	Yes
Connecticut	Partial	No	Expansive	No	No
Delaware	Partial	Yes	Expansive	No	No
Florida	Significant	Yes	Restricted	Yes	Yes
Georgia	Significant	Yes	Restricted	No	Yes
Hawaii	Centralized	No	Expansive	No	No
Idaho	Partial	Yes	Agency Specific	No	Yes
Illinois	Partial	No	Expansive	No	Yes
Indiana	Recentralizing	Yes	Restricted	Yes	Yes
Iowa	Significant	Yes	Expansive	No	No
Kansas	Significant	Yes	Expansive/Agency Specific	Yes	Yes
Kentucky	Centralized	Yes	Expansive	Yes	No
Louisiana	Partial	No	Restricted	No	Yes
Maine	Recentralizing	No	Expansive	Yes	Yes
Maryland	Partial	No	Expansive	No	No
Massachusetts	Partial	Yes	Expansive	Yes	Yes
Michigan	Partial	No	Expansive	No	Yes
Minnesota	Partial	No	Expansive	No	Yes

Mississippi	Partial	Yes	Restricted	Yes	Yes
Missouri	Significant	Yes	Agency Specific	Yes	Yes
Montana	Partial	No	Restricted	No	No
Nebraska	Centralized	Yes	Restricted	No	Yes
Nevada	Partial	No	Expansive	No	No
New Hampshire	Partial	No	Expansive	No	No
New Jersey	Partial	Yes	Expansive	No	Yes
New Mexico	Centralized	No	Expansive	No	No
New York	Partial	No	Expansive	No	No
North Carolina	Significant	Yes	Restricted	No	Yes
North Dakota	Significant	No	Restricted	No	No
Ohio	Partial	Yes	Restricted	No	No
Oklahoma	Significant	Yes	Restricted	No	Yes
Oregon	Partial	Yes	Expansive	Yes	Yes
Pennsylvania	Significant	No	Expansive	No	No
Rhode Island	Centralized	Yes	Expansive but Not Utilized	Yes	Yes
South Carolina	Significant	Yes	Restricted	Yes	Yes
South Dakota	Centralized	No	Expansive	No	No
Tennessee	Centralized	No	Restricted	No	No
Texas	Complete	Yes	Not Applicable	No	Yes
Utah	Partial	Yes	Expansive	Yes	No
Vermont	Significant	Yes	Restricted	Yes	Yes
Virginia	Significant	No	Restricted	No	Yes
Washington	Significant	Yes	Restricted	Yes	Yes
West Virginia	Partial	Yes	Restricted	Yes	Yes
Wisconsin	Partial	No	Expansive	Yes	Yes
Wyoming	Partial	Yes	Restricted	No	No

Decentralization (Reinvention) of HRM

Reform of HRM was originally marketed to public administrators as a means to increase administrative flexibility, add responsiveness, and expedite hiring and other important supervisory decisions. These were admirable goals when examined in the context of intractable personnel systems, systems in which supervisors were virtually powerless to discipline problem employees or quickly hire and promote deserving achievers. This reform was to be the answer to all of the problems that had arisen within the traditional civil service systems, but like any change that promises to be "the answer," this answer was not without serious repercussions.

An unanticipated (or, perhaps, very predictable, depending on one's point of view) consequence of decentralization has been the dismantling of police functions governing employee rights and the bestowal of vast new supervisory powers upon agency personnel. Of the 50 responding states included in this study, 16 report massive decentralization, whereas another 24 are making moves in that direction. Table 1.1, column 1, provides a breakdown of heavily decentralized (labeled *significant*) states and those that are only "partially" decentralized. In some extreme cases—such as Arkansas, Missouri, North Dakota, Oklahoma, and South Carolina—the old merit system has been effectively abolished. Centralized testing and review of applicants have virtually disappeared from reinvented states, and control over classification, compensation, job assignments, performance appraisals, and other conditions of employment has been vested in agencies. Only eight states retain a more or less classical (centralized) merit system, and two (Indiana and Maine) are *recentralizing* in an effort to regain control over their HR systems.

Several states that have recently decentralized used South Carolina as their model. Kansas, Virginia, and Washington, for instance, adopted the consultative format employed in South Carolina, a model of HRM in which the central OHR provides technical support to agencies with few or no audit or control responsibilities, in a sense operating as an HRM consultant rather than engaging in governance or monitoring of behavior. Although this model provides agency-level supervisors with more flexibility and control over personnel functions, the implications for the employees themselves are more ominous. This is a "hope for the best" strategy in which employees are left to the tender mercies of their agency supervisors (a situation that will vary wildly, depending upon both the technical capacities and good intentions of the agency managers). Therefore, the consultative model represents a change in HRM that may leave employees particularly vulnerable to capricious decisions on the part of agency managers with very little recourse.

The "Declassification" of Civil Servants

Perhaps the most dramatic phenomenon uncovered by this study is the extent to which a majority of states are moving employees from the classified to the unclassified service. Also referred to as *uncovering*, the trend is apparent to greater or lesser degrees in 28 of the responding states (Table 1.1, column 2). Some of the changes are relatively minor, such as those in which a single agency has been targeted for conversion. This occurred in Delaware (180 workers in the Office of Information Systems were "made exempt"), Idaho (the entire Workers Compensation Agency was declassified), Iowa (300 employees in the Economic Development Office were "converted," and further conversions are planned), Nebraska (the career protections of 200 employees in the Department of Corrections were eliminated in 2004), and Vermont (affecting 300 workers in the Department of Corrections).

In stark contrast to the gradual process of declassification that exists in many states is the Mississippi example. Pending legislation in that state would suspend all employee property rights for a 12-month period. Under the property rights concept, full-time civil servants retain legally protected (14th Amendment) rights which translate into a virtual shield against removal exept for causes such as gross incompetence or criminal conduct. If adopted, every state worker would instantaneously become an at-will employee, thereby allowing the governor (at this writing, Haley Barbour) to reorganize, consolidate, hire, fire, and otherwise alter state government without the messiness of employee grievances and lawsuits. This effort failed to gain legislative approval in both 2005 and 2006, but the governor has vowed to keep trying.

Less startling (but still interesting) examples of such activities appear in additional states, including Arizona, Kansas, Missouri, Nevada, and South Carolina. Arizona is moving to uncover classified workers at the rate of 1 percent per year. This is a concentrated policy that is trumpeted in the OHR's annual report (along with proud assertions that the state ranks 49th in its ratio of state workers to population). The situation in Kansas is less concrete, but nonetheless fascinating. Under its new governor, Kathleen Sebelius, every "top level position" that is vacated by retirement, promotion, or other means immediately becomes an at-will appointment, thereby perhaps providing little incentive to expeditiously fill positions with employees from within the current government system. Another 800 or more positions are targeted for uncovering in that state. Missouri, meanwhile, is undergoing a housecleaning in which many workers in a variety of agencies have lost their career protections. Through both formal and informal means, the most heavily impacted agencies include Health and Human Services, the Department of Social Services, the Department of Juvenile Justice, and the Department of Aging. The

Nevada situation is somewhat murkier, in that it rests on pending legislation that would increase the governor's appointment power fourfold. The catalyst for this proposal is the need to increase accountability and responsiveness to elected officials. Within this context, it is important to note that only about 150 executive department positions in Nevada are currently under the governor's direct or indirect control (compared to nearly one-third of all employees in some states, and even larger percentages in Florida, Georgia, and Texas).

South Carolina's experiment with declassification is more mature than the examples described in the previous discussion. Under the administration of Governor Carroll Campbell during the early 1990s, the Governmental Accountability Act of 1993 decentralized the personnel system, immediately eliminated the career protections from 220 high-level employees ("deputy directors"), opened the door for continued conversion of career civil servants to at-will appointments, and drastically reduced the already limited range of grievable issues. Since that time, further reforms centering on the expansion of the governor's cabinet have continually increased the number of at-will appointees. As an interesting sidebar to this drama, South Carolina has repeatedly been celebrated by *Governing* magazine as a paragon of civil service reform. For many of the career civil servants who toil in the trenches of state government, this designation is viewed with considerable irony.

One additional trend in declassification that warrants a brief mention is that the university systems in several states are seeking exemptions from the classified service. To provide themselves with greater flexibility, universities in Arizona, Colorado, Kansas, and Virginia are seeking authority to remove their classified workers from the career civil service. This would allow them to hire and fire non-fault workers without restraint, and to (potentially) outsource their duties, consolidate positions, or otherwise explore money-saving options. Additional state university systems are reportedly making plans to emulate this pattern. To date, two states (Arizona and Colorado) have made "progress" in this area.

Restrictions on Due Process Rights

Of all the myths surrounding public employment, the most questionable is probably the notion that civil servants are immune from termination or other disciplinary actions. This perception is probably attributable to federal General Schedule workers (at least before Homeland Security), and to stories arising from highly unionized settings such as California and Connecticut. In the vast majority of states—even those with heavy union representation—the range of managerial prerogatives can be large.

The specific terms governing labor-management relations are articulated either in statute within nonunionized states or in negotiated agreements where collective bargaining exists. However, an often-overlooked fact is that most states reserve large areas of discretion for their managers. Generally speaking, the vast majority of employee complaints are settled within their agencies and only the most severe cases of property right invasions can be taken to a higher authority. If a supervisor truly wants to pursue a disciplinary action against a worker, the requisite tools are often in place to successfully prosecute a dismissal or other adverse action. [6] Therefore, the perception that government workers cannot be removed without a major expenditure of time and expense is more myth than reality.

Weakening job security is becoming even more pronounced due to the attrition of due process rights that has accompanied the accountability movement. In over half the states, grievance rights are "restricted" (Table 1.1, column 3). This means that supervisors enjoy considerable flexibility in the range of decisions that they can make vis-à-vis their subordinates and that employees are able to grieve fewer and fewer matters. In some cases, the array of grievable issues is strictly limited by statute. Managerial prerogative was noted as being a preeminent concern in almost all right-to-work states, and in those without formal collective bargaining laws. Some states (e.g., Colorado and Louisiana) make a distinction between a formal grievance and a complaint or appeal. In Colorado, complaints involve any condition of employment that does not involve a property right (termination or demotion, for the most part); these are all heard at the agency level. Only grievances—cases involving clear property right invasions—are eligible for review before an external body. The same situation exists in Louisiana, except that the term *appeal* is used to describe claims of discrimination or violations of civil service rules (both of which are subject to external review). All other matters—including reassignments, reclassifications, compensation, transfers, and the like—are either non-grievable or eligible only for internal review. Many respondents claimed that their success rate in formal grievances is high (i.e., supervisors prevail over subordinates), and that formal employee complaints are becoming rarer due to changes in law or the political environment.

Hopefully, a few of the specific changes that have occurred in recent years will clarify this situation. In Alaska, for example, the state supreme court recently ruled that reclassifications and similar decisions are subject to managerial discretion despite the existence of union contracts specifying the opposite. Arkansas, meanwhile, has given its supervisors "absolute authority" over all human resource management issues short of discrimination and retaliation. Other states, such as Nebraska and Utah, have placed wording such as "legitimate business need" and "no longer meets the needs of the position" as sufficient justification to terminate workers.

In other settings, a higher burden of proof has been established for classified workers grieving anything other than property right invasions. West Virginia law, for example, states that the employee has the burden of proof and persuasion when grieving actions such as reassignments, performance appraisals, and classification. Finally, there is at least one instance in which grievances have been removed from employees' arsenal of due process protections. The State of Oklahoma's Uniform Employee Grievance Procedure was revoked within the past two years. (This occurred at about the same time that the Oklahoma legislature implemented a right-to-work law as a catalyst for economic development.)

Although an aggressive employee union can counter the attrition of employee due process protections, the existence of powerful unions does not automatically guarantee that workers will exercise their rights. The respondent from Rhode Island, for instance, noted that employees are keeping their heads low and *not* filing grievances because they do not want to further anger an already moody group of politicians.

In essence, the core lesson from this review of due process protections is that many public servants today work in settings that are not too different from those of their private sector counterparts. Those inside the "protected" service enjoy some due process rights, but nowhere near the number that is commonly believed. In addition, because supervisory discretion can be quite pronounced, these public workers are potentially vulnerable to pressure tactics or other strategies intended to force them out of office. The "lean on them 'til they break" strategy of managing public employees has existed as long as merit systems, and its usage may well be on the upswing thanks to reinvention and deregulation.

Activist Governors

The trends that have just been discussed are fueled in part by the election of activist governors in at least 20 states (Table 1.1, column 4). Almost all of these individuals campaigned on the equivalent of a business platform ("economy and efficiency"), and most promised some type of housecleaning of their state bureaucracies upon election. Many have been true to their word, with the most famous example being that of California, where the new governor has reportedly cleaned house through appointments and is trying to expand his influence by reorganizing and consolidating agencies (strategies that often uncover protected employees and expose them to layoff or termination). Arnold Schwarzenegger has also picked a major fight with the powerful public employee unions by pressing for a replacement of the state's generous defined benefit retirement system with a defined contribution plan.

Although Schwarzenegger captures the most publicity, the real reformists are not located in California. More sweeping changes have been instituted by relatively anonymous governors in states such as Arizona, Colorado, Indiana, Kansas, Mississippi, Missouri, Rhode Island, Vermont, and West Virginia. As noted, the Arizona governor has been expanding her appointment power by uncovering 1 percent of the classified service per year, while also trying to outsource jobs and further reduce the absolute size of government. Many of the changes taking place in Colorado's HR system were triggered by Governor Bill Owens, an individual who is pushing for far greater appointment authority and who led a successful effort to repeal the union dues checkoff. Indiana offers the most stunning example of a governor hitting the ground running. In his first official act upon inauguration in January 2005, Indiana Governor Mitch Daniels signed an executive order abolishing all public unions and negating existing labor contracts. Kentucky Governor Ernie Fletcher engineered a similar coup by ordering the elimination of all labor-management negotiations. This general anti-union theme is being repeated in Missouri, where Governor Matt Blunt is attempting to repeal collective bargaining provisions and eliminate the dues checkoff. Oregon's governor, Ted Kulongoski, is more focused on outsourcing and requiring every civil servant to justify his or her position, and Rhode Island Governor Donald Carcieri has expressly engaged in a battle of disincentives. Unable to remove workers ex cathedra due to the strong union influence in his state, he has embarked on a "starve them out" strategy consisting of wage freezes (and even cuts), reductions in benefits, and other measures intended to force out senior bureaucrats to open up their positions for his appointees. However, these moves will pale in comparison if Haley Barbour is ever successful in his attempt in Mississippi to denude the public workforce of all due process protections for one calendar year.

The mere fact that so many governors appear to be waging war with their career civil servants is troubling enough, but the extent to which many appear to be winning the battle is particularly worrisome. Professional civil servants are clearly under attack on many fronts. Some of the potential consequences and implications of these disturbing trends are discussed in the next section.

DISCUSSION AND CONCLUSION

The most succinct way to summarize the findings of this study is to conclude that current trends are sobering (at the risk of gross understatement). The project was launched with the expectation of finding a handful of states in which the Florida and Georgia models are being emulated. Instead, the phenomenon is relatively common. Conversions of classified workers to at-will status are not taking place with the passion and vigor exhibited in Florida, Georgia, and Texas, but the general trend is evident in at least a majority of the 50 states. Some HR executives asserted that *merit system* is an outdated expression and that it is no longer relevant to contemporary public management. Adding to the gloom are ubiquitous employee layoffs, efforts to diminish fringe benefit packages, and other moves that can roughly be characterized (in words once used enthusiastically by Margaret Thatcher in the same general context) as "the deprivileging of the civil service." [7]

Depending upon one's devotion to the concept of a competent and professional government workforce, these developments will undoubtedly be viewed differently based on the reader's position in the political spectrum. Accountability and responsiveness are certainly important qualities for any civil service, and the citizenry appears to be sympathetic to public executives' cries for greater control over bureaucracy. And, to be fair, the number of positions that *some* governors can appoint (directly or indirectly) remains surprisingly insignificant. Respondents in a few states report the percentage of at-will employees to be around 5 percent (e.g., Tennessee), and a larger group of states limit their at-will employment levels to between 10 and 15 percent (e.g., Connecticut, Delaware, Kentucky, Massachusetts, Minnesota, Montana, and New Hampshire). Notably, several of these states have already been discussed as hotbeds of reform, however defined.

On the opposite side of the ledger are states in which at-will employment covers *100 percent* (Texas) of the workers, and those in which the percentages are smaller yet still quite substantial (about 72 percent in Georgia, 48 percent in Idaho, 40 percent in Kansas, 35 percent in Colorado, 33 percent in Oklahoma, 30 percent in West Virginia, and over 20 percent in Illinois, Washington, and Ohio). Unfortunately, there is no accepted standard for how many at-will employees is enough, or what percentage would optimize the competing demands for responsiveness *and* expertise (accountability *and* professionalism). Although not necessarily mutually exclusive, these values represent the contemporary jargon that once dominated the *merit versus patronage* debate. In addition, it is also true that being an at-will employee need not imply that one's career prospects are doomed. Generations of unclassified civil servants have survived multiple gubernatorial administrations and served out their careers without catastrophic results.

Using the feedback from the respondents as a guide, however, the tone and direction of the HRM reforms that are now being advocated and implemented do not give much impetus for optimism. Several factors contribute to this conclusion. First, the newer generation of politicians is more likely than not to have a chip on its collective shoulder concerning the bureaucracy. Most of the new governors that were discussed previously came from the business sector and had very little experience in public service. [4] They are appointing like-minded agency directors, many of whom may lack confidence and trust in the senior public managers who have devoted their careers to programmatic or agency goals. Because most politicians want to make a quick mark due to the nature of the electoral clock and because this accomplishment requires change, career civil servants are caught in an uncomfortable squeeze. To the extent that they are subject to at-will removal, their prospects are often grim. One anecdotal account helps to solidify this point: of the 220 deputy directors who were in place at the time that South Carolina converted its positions to an at-will status, only 15 remained after five years.

Another factor that appears to be altering the face of classical notions of public HRM is the advent of term limits in some states. Several respondents made the insightful observation that term limits have helped to rupture long-standing alliances between legislators and public managers (notable examples are Arkansas and Oklahoma). The traditional bonds of mutual respect and understanding that form through long associations among career civil servants and veteran legislative leaders are weakened when the politicians' careers are restricted to six or eight years. This study did not contain sufficient cases (or data) to ascertain if there is a direct correlation between term limits and employee job security (short legislative careers lead to reduced job retention), but common sense would naturally lead us to that conclusion. To the extent that states adopt term limits—and that existing term limit provisions trigger continuing turnover among legislators—the trends that have been identified might well be magnified. The impact of term limits on the nature of career public employment is an issue that merits future research.

The vulnerability of civil servants is also affected by additional changes in HRM that are occurring as part of the reinvention movement. In addition to the effects of decentralization that were addressed earlier, broad banding and merit pay are making inroads in a significant number of states. Broadbanding refers to the reduction in narrow job classes with a corresponding increase in the breadth of pay grades (leading to greater flexibility), while merit pay is tauted as a solution to the traditional practice of rewarding civil servants mainly on the basis of longevity. More than half of the respondents indicated that some form of position classification and pay reform has either been implemented or is being planned. Although neither of these alterations in traditional HR practice is inherently problematic (indeed, the authors have argued *for* such reforms on many occasions), both translate into *expanded discretion* over large segments of the civil service. Political appointees and careerists who allocate duties and salary increases on the basis of legitimate performance criteria can unquestionably use these new tools to improve agency operations. Unfortunately, however, broad discretion over salaries and assignments can also be *misused*. The history of the federal Senior Executive Service provides ample evidence that political appointees cannot always be trusted to make good-faith decisions concerning their subordinates. Those who remember Edwin Meese's (Ronald Reagan's attorney general) instructions to his partisan brethren to "allocate performance ratings on the basis of political orthodoxy" might be justifiably alarmed by some of the HR reforms that are now occurring under the guise of accountability, responsiveness, and efficiency. This sentiment was echoed by one anonymous respondent in Rhode Island who described her state's pay-for-performance system as follows: "merit pay equals being rewarded for your political loyalty. Nothing else." Care and attention need to be devoted to ensuring that well-designed HR systems such as broad banding and merit pay are used appropriately and not as political whips to ensure public employees' partisan loyalty.

As at-will appointments penetrate deeper and deeper into public agencies, another serious consequence arises in the career ladder of civil servants. Ultimately, veteran managers reach a point at which their next promotion will push them into an unprotected position. If one has already qualified for retirement, this might not be such a treacherous decision. For those who are not yet prepared to accept the risk of possible termination, conversely, accepting a promotion is truly a roll of the professional dice. Several respondents commented that they had personally turned down promotions to avoid possible replacement during the next gubernatorial administration, and many complained that they cannot lure careerists into uncovered positions for the same reason. The phenomenon is so pronounced that those few who assume the risk by accepting promotions to unclassified positions are said to be engaging in *bungee cord management* (i.e., they feel like they're leaping out into space, taking a big chance, and hoping for the best). Anyone who is concerned about the quality of the public service—anyone who believes in the basic concept of a professional *career* in government—ought to be somewhat alarmed by the obvious implications.

This depressing litany would not be complete without a condensation of noteworthy quotes from some of the respondents. Each interviewee was asked to provide a subjective response to the question "Has the fundamental notion of job security in the public service changed over the past few years?" Respondents from 31 states (Table 1.1, column 5) responded in the affirmative. Some of the more poignant follow-up remarks are as follows:

> New workers aren't coming here for a career, but for a pit-stop. [Idaho]

> For people in high positions or with good pay, risk abounds. For underlings, job security is still fairly solid. But, in general, job security isn't what it used to be, and many old-timers are being forced out; the current administration is much more hard-line than ever before. [Michigan]

> Our perception of job security has changed drastically in the last five years. The politicians want us to "do more with less." Soon we'll be "doing everything with nothing." [Minnesota]

> There is no active move to increase the at-will workforce. Why bother? With layoffs, reorganizations, and reassignments, they can accomplish the same thing without attracting attention. [Missouri]

> The uncovering of positions is being done quietly. Old notions of job security are changing. We've seen more and more agency heads come in from the private sector bringing the private sector mentality. They're much more inclined to terminate workers. As the older generation of career employees retires, they're being replaced by outsiders with a different—almost anti-government—attitude. [Vermont]

> In this state, job security has changed drastically in the last few years. In addition to hundreds of layoffs, it's easy to reclassify workers and to RIF (reduction in force layoff) them with only two weeks notice. [Idaho]

> Politicians in this state continually argue that the merit system hinders performance and efficiency. It [the merit system] is probably doomed. [Nebraska]

> There is no longer any such thing as job security. "Just cause" dismissals are seriously threatened. [Rhode Island]

In addition to their obvious messages, these quotes provide insight into the fact that aggressive political administrations, or even career public managers, can force subordinates out of office whether or not they are technically at-will employees. Generally speaking, the only place in which this is *unlikely* to occur is in states that have strong collective bargaining laws and active union representation. Elsewhere, civil servants appear to be entering a new and disquieting phase of vulnerability. If this trend continues, then public agencies will have lost one or more of their most valuable recruitment assets, the ability to offer job candidates a secure career serving the public. The traditional three-legged stool—job security, decent benefits, and the personal satisfaction gained from devoting one's life to public service objectives—is losing one leg (if not the second, the benefits package) on which it has long relied to attract talent. Moreover, even the third leg—the notion of a *public service career*—is in serious jeopardy. Because these developments are occurring contemporaneously with the graying of the workforce, one might justifiably be very anxious about the quality and motives of the public employees who will replace those now retiring. Minimally, the essential nature of public service—and of the public managers who provide those services—is undergoing a metamorphosis before our eyes. The ultimate outcome of these changes will have a dramatic yet unpredictable impact upon our discipline for decades to come. Therefore, before much more time passes, we need to take a step back and reflect on or remember what was right with the civil service, and why employee protections were implemented in the first place. Although some facets of the civil service system may have evolved into bureaucratic dysfunctions or unnecessary red tape, many others are essential to a well-functioning public service and should not be unilaterally discarded. Reformers should take care; otherwise, continued unchecked, the current slate of reforms may swing the pendulum of HRM reform too far in a direction that could have lasting, disastrous consequences for the public service in state government in the United States.

REFERENCES

1. Bowman, J. S., Gertz, M. G., Gertz, S. C., and Williams, R. L., Civil service reform in Florida state government: Employee attitudes 1 year later, *Review of Public Personnel Administration*, 23, 286, 2003.
2. Coggburn, J., The effects of deregulation on state government personnel administration, *Review of Public Personnel Administration*, 20, 24, 2000.
3. Coggburn, J., Personnel deregulation: Exploring differences in the American states, *Journal of Public Administration Research and Theory*, 11, 223, 2001.
4. Goodsell, C., *The Case for Bureaucracy*, Chatham House, Chatham, NJ, 1994.
5. Gossett, C., Civil service reform: The case of Georgia, *Review of Public Personnel Administration*, 22, 94, 2002.
6. Hays, S. W., Employee discipline and removal: Coping with job security, in *Public Personnel Administration: Problems and Prospects*, Hays, S. W., and Kearney, R., eds., Prentice Hall, Englewood Cliffs, NJ, 1995, ch. 10.
7. Hood, C., A public management for all seasons, *Public Administration*, 69, 3, 1991.

8. Hou, Y., Ingraham, P. W., Bretschneider, S., and Selden, S. C., Decentralization of human resource management: Driving forces and implications, *Review of Public Personnel Administration*, 20, 9, 2000.
9. Kellough, J. E., and Nigro, L., Pay for performance in Georgia state government: Employee perspectives on GeorgiaGain after five years, *Review of Public Personnel Administration*, 22, 146, 2002.
10. Kellough, J. E., and Selden, S. C., The reinvention of public personnel administration: An analysis of the diffusion of personnel management reforms in the states, *Public Administration Review*, 63, 165, 2003.
11. Nigro, L., and Kellough, J. E., Civil service reform in Georgia: Going to the edge? *Review of Public Personnel Administration*, 20, 41, 2000.
12. Savas, E. S., and Ginsburg, S., The civil service: A meritless system, *The Public Interest*, 32, 70, 1973.
13. Shafritz, J., *Public Personnel Management: The Heritage of Civil Service*, Praeger, New York, 1975.
14. Staats, E., Personnel management: The starting place, *Public Personnel Management*, November–December, 434, 1976.

APPENDIX

HR Reform Interview Template

Reorganization

1. What, if any, types of administrative changes have occurred in your central HR office or personnel commission?
2. Has your governor's influence over HR policy increased, decreased, or stayed the same (please elaborate)?
3. Do you maintain a classic (centralized) "merit system"? If not, please explain.
4. Identify the HR functions that have been decentralized to line agencies. [Recruitment, Selection, Classification, Compensation, Performance Appraisal, Employee Relations, RIFs, Outsourcing, Other]
6. To what extent have labor-management relations—and the influence of employee unions—changed over recent years?

Management of the Civil Service

1. Has a senior executive service been created in your state? If so, how many employees are affected?
2. Has the governor's power of appointment expanded or contracted? Specify.
3. Please provide an estimate of the number of civil service employees who serve at will.
4. Has the definition of *exempt* or *unclassified* workers been altered? Explain.
5. Has the grievance process for employees been altered in any way? Explain.
6. Of the following, what issues are grievable under your state grievance law? [Reassignments, Reclassification, Compensation, Performance Appraisal, Transfers, Promotions, Terms of Employment, etc.]

Administrative Changes in HRM

1. To what extent has the number of position classifications been reduced? Specify.
2. Has your state broad banded?
3. What types, if any, of additional flexibility have line supervisors been given over the utilization of human resources? [Job Descriptions, Hiring, Classification, Salary, Duty Assignments, Performance Appraisal Protocol, Transfers, etc.]
4. Have you tried merit pay, and what has been the outcome?
5. Has the state altered its pension system in any way (please describe)?
6. To what extent has outsourcing been used in state government? Specify.
7. Has the conventional wisdom concerning the *job security* of civil servants changed in recent years? How so?
8. How has your state's HR turnover rate changed recently, and in what way?
9. What percentage of your labor force is "classified," "unclassified," "at-will," or "career protected"? Describe (estimate).
10. In your judgment, what does the future hold for your state's career civil service? Please specify likely directions of change.

2

FRAMING CIVIL SERVICE INNOVATIONS: ASSESSING STATE AND LOCAL GOVERNMENT REFORMS

R. Paul Battaglio, Jr.
University of Nevada, Las Vegas

Stephen E. Condrey
The University of Georgia

The past two decades have seen a renewed interest in reforming the structure and nature of civil service systems. In the United States, these reform efforts were spearheaded by the concepts of "reinventing government" and New Public Management (NPM). These efforts directly attack the long-standing model of specialized, hierarchical, and relatively closed bureaucracies that are governed by rules, paperwork, and official procedures.[1] As an alternative, the aforementioned concepts emphasize productivity, marketization, service orientation, decentralization, improved capacity to devise and track policy, and accountability for results.[2] This penchant to "let managers manage" has occasionally resulted in the diminution or outright demolition of job security in the public sector, replaced with at-will employment arrangements.

In the United States, federalism has exacerbated the problem of reforming civil service because it is not one "civil service," but a collection of separate systems. The result has been an assorted number of reform efforts at the federal, state, and local levels. The need for assessment of these reforms has been noted in the literature on public personnel.[3, 4, 5] Scholars and practitioners have called for increased quantitative and qualitative investigation on the subject, including analysis based on expert assessments, case studies, and descriptive and anecdotal or journalistic interpretations.[5] This chapter asserts that due to the splintered nature of public human resource management in the United States, civil service experimentation at lower levels of government, particularly the states, may be influencing personnel policy at the federal and local levels.

The discussion explores reform in four states (Georgia, Florida, New York, and Louisiana) and two local governments (Jefferson County [Birmingham], Alabama; and Chapel Hill, North Carolina). Four models of human resource management service delivery will be utilized as an organizing point for discussion. The chapter concludes with implications for the design and reform of civil service systems. Grasping the nature of these reforms is even more important given the fact that states may adopt policies without any formal understanding of their long-term impact on the system. The analysis provides practitioners and scholars with an organizing point for understanding the nature of these reforms. Conclusions illustrate the diffusion of policy from the state level to the federal level with respect to civil service reform.

FOUR MODELS OF HUMAN RESOURCE MANAGEMENT SERVICE DELIVERY

Table 2.1 identifies four methods for the delivery of human resource management services: the traditional model, the reform model, the strategic model, and the privatization/outsourcing model.[6] The fourth model is notable for its recent appearance in this country. Contracting out, load shedding, sale of state assets, vouchers, franchise agreements, deregulation, and other arrangements for transferring production of governmental goods and services are examples of the fourth method, a hallmark of New Public Management philosophy.[7]

The following six cases utilize the four models of human resource management service delivery as an organizing point for discussion and analysis. In explicating the cases, the authors draw on a variety of sources including personal interviews, survey research, review of pertinent administrative documents, and published scholarly research. In all instances, conclusions and implications are drawn from multiple sources.

Radical Reform: The Case of Georgia

In 1996, the reforms embodied in Georgia Act 1816 called for the removal of civil service protections for employees hired after July 1 of that year, the decentralization of authority for personnel policy and administration, and the establishment of a new performance management system built largely on performance-based pay.[4] This was accomplished not through restructuring and revising Georgia's personnel system but rather through the filling of vacant positions with "unclassified" titles, effectively abolishing state personnel board jurisdiction. Effective July 2, 1996, all new employees would be considered "at-will," unable to attain a property interest or tenure rights after serving the traditional one-year probationary period. The state has taken reform seriously, eliminating the merit system and opting for a private sector model. Consequently, changes have taken place in recruitment and hiring, pay raises and promotions, and downsizing and discipline.[8]

From the perspective of the line manager, reform has created an expectation of being able to hire immediately and with more flexibility than under the previous system. The legislation no longer requires that agencies confer with the central human resources department on matters of recruitment and selection. Agencies now have the authority to hire at any step within a given pay grade. The new selection process is designed to provide greater flexibility to agencies in their effort to recruit and compete for talented workers. At the same time, greater flexibility comes with a degree of responsibility for ensuring consistent and fair salary management practices for the agency's personnel office.[9]

Accordingly, at-will employment status is intended to give agencies greater flexibility in downsizing and discipline. The elimination of seniority means that new, at-will employees have no assurance of reassignment during downsizing and can be relocated without recourse. The length of process for discipline or termination has also been reduced dramatically. Classified personnel are disciplined according to a standard progressive method, beginning with an oral or written reprimand, then moving to suspension without pay or salary reduction, and finally to dismissal. Unclassified employees, being "at-will," have no appeal rights in disciplinary matters. These procedures will be the norm for disciplinary proceedings as the workforce increasingly becomes unclassified. It is too early to definitively discern the implications of these reforms, especially in light of the cronyism, favoritism, and unequal pay for equal work synonymous with spoils systems of the past.

Clearly, there are accountability concerns. The lack of uniformity among the various personnel systems in each of the agencies exacerbates this problem. Without a strong state office of personnel management to ensure uniformity in practice, how does one ensure fairness and

Table 2.1 A Comparison of Four Models of Public Human Resource Management

Function	*Traditional Model*	*Reform Model*	*Strategic Model*	*Privatization or Outsourcing Model*
Service delivery	Centralized	Decentralized	Collaborative	Contract
Goal orientation	Uniform enforcement of rules, policies, and procedures	Manager centered	Respectful of human resource management and organizational goals	Effective contract negotiator and administrator
Communication pattern	Top-down	Two-way	Multidirectional	Reports and contract monitoring
Feedback characteristics	Formal and informal complaints	Muted	Continuous	Muted
Value orientation	"Merit"	Immediate responsiveness to organizational mission and goals	Effective organizational functioning coupled with a respect for effective human resource management practices	Efficiency; private sector preference
Role of human resource manager	Enforcer of "merit"	Diminished authority and control	Organizational consultant	Contract negotiator and administrator

Perception of human resource management profession	Hindrance to effective organizational functioning	Adjunct collection of skills	Full managerial partner	Diminished
Role of education	Public personnel administration	Adjunct to managerial skills	Human resource management, general management, practical focus	Contract negotiation and administration skills

Source: Toward Strategic Human Resource Management, in *Handbook of Human Resource Management*, 2nd ed., Condrey, S. E., ed., Jossey-Bass, San Francisco, 2005. With permission.

performance? If there is no uniformity in practice, how does this affect personnel loyalty and commitment? Indeed, scholarship[4, 10] has demonstrated a great deal of employee pessimism with respect to the reforms of Act 1816. Discontent and frustration with the reform are not only present with rank-and-file employees. Recently, in conversations with one of the authors, several long-serving agency directors were aghast to learn that *Governing* magazine[11] had named Georgia's personnel system as the best in the country.

The state's reforms were brought about by a unique convergence of factors: a very powerful governor (Zell Miller, later a U.S. senator) with experience in human resource management and a distaste for the state's numerous and archaic personnel rules and regulations; an inbred central personnel management hierarchy unwilling (or, more likely, unable) to reform itself; well-placed, powerful bureaucratic actors who wanted more direct control over their agencies' personnel management systems; and weak employee unions.[3] This convergence, however, does not mean that it is alone in its significance, as the following case exemplifies. The systematic dismantling of the civil service system in Georgia serves as an example of the reform model illustrated in Table 2.1.

More Radical Reform: Florida and Service First

The State of Florida has undergone a dramatic overhaul of its civil service system over the past few years. Seeking the assistance of the private sector, Governor Jeb Bush aligned himself with the Florida Council of 100, an influential body of businesspeople. The result was a report asserting alleged government practices of mismanagement and abuse, the theme of which was hardly amicable to traditional civil service. Service First, the title given to the administration's personnel reforms, became law on May 14, 2001, ushering in a new public service for the state.

Opting not to phase in a new system over time, as Georgia had done with the move to "at-will" employees, Florida eliminated seniority immediately for all employees affected by Service First. This immediately gave managers the ability to target people or positions for downsizing as they saw fit. Those affected had little or no recourse for such actions, because they no longer possessed the right to appeal suspensions and dismissals under the new law. Suspensions and dismissals are now processed under a "reasonable cause" standard. In an effort to provide managers with an easier benchmark for dismissals with few strings attached, the term *reasonable cause* was broadly defined, excluding any discussion of the violator's intent.[8, 5] Consequently, the appeals process for "violators" has been altered. The Public Employee Relations Commission (PERC), which considers appeals for adverse actions, is no longer authorized to hear cases relevant to layoffs or transfers. Employees under the Career Service seeking disciplinary appeals are now subject to shortened timelines and reduced remedies. Capricious or prohibited actions can still be appealed to PERC, but it cannot alter penalties imposed by agencies and is incapable of considering "inequitable treatment of employees."[12, 5]

Additionally, recruitment of new employees emphasizes that candidates should meet minimum qualifications in an effort to simplify and expedite selection. Service First removed prior considerations that required that procedures be based on "adequate job analysis and valid/objective criteria."[12, 5] A memo circulated from the governor's office in the fall of 2003 mandated that at least two of three candidates for a new position be from outside the public sector and that before consideration was made for internal candidates, a comprehensive external search was to be completed.[12] Furthermore, pay raises and promotions are no longer based on formal pay tiers accumulated through seniority. Promotions are based on employee knowledge, skill, and abilities rather than formal testing, similar to methods emphasized in Georgia.

Furthermore, a large number of employees were shifted to "at-will" status. Due to the political difficulties of eliminating classified status for all employees, Governor Bush had to settle for a compromise of sorts with the legislature. The result was a shift, unlike Georgia's reforms, which only affected employees with a remotely managerial or supervisory title. This led to 16,000 positions being placed in the Selected Exempt Service (SES), leaving fewer than 120,000 employees in the personnel system as classified. Although recourse for these personnel has been reduced under Service First, they still enjoy the full protections afforded by grievance procedures and appeals for adverse job actions, unlike those in the SES.[8] Finally, the personnel system incurred major changes to classification and compensation. Service First dramatically simplified job titles and pay structures, a change intended to give managers greater flexibility in rewarding employees. Additionally, with the elimination of seniority, greater discretion has been granted to management on matters of pay raises and promotions.

Two reform issues distinguish Florida from the other case studies. First, a privatization initiative underway is aimed at outsourcing many of the human resource management functions. To make human resources a more market-like enterprise, the People First initiative contracted out many of the transaction or process functions to a private entity, Convergys (anonymous, personal communication, August 29, 2003).[12] Under the terms of the contract between the state and the service provider, Convergys is to support the state's workforce in the areas of human resources, benefits, payroll, and staffing administration.[12] Implementation proved problematic, and legislative hearings in 2005 revealed numerous problems. The arrangement with Convergys required electronic centralization of HR processes across all the state's departments. This doomed a smooth transition because, prior to the contract, there was no requirement that agencies employ similar software to collect, store, process, and retrieve HR data. As of this writing, although most of the initial implementation delays have been overcome, the word *Convergys* has become a lightning rod for complaints about delays in service, voice mail instead of live call takers, outsourcing functions to China and India, and errors in employee payroll and benefits. While the legislature holds hearings into managerial and employee dissatisfaction with the system, the governor's office defends the $350 million, nine-year contract, the largest privatization project of the Jeb Bush administration.[13]

The second issue that distinguishes Florida is the role that collective bargaining has played in the process. The American Federation of State, County, and Municipal Employees (AFSCME) filed a three-count lawsuit against the state and the Jeb Bush administration, alleging that Service First has "unconstitutionally waived and impaired collective bargaining rights protected by the Florida Constitution."[8] Lobbying efforts did obtain a partial victory through legislative revisions to the law limiting the extent of at-will status to employees in the SES. However, in 2002, the state Supreme Court ruled in favor of the governor's office, citing that the provisions of Service First did not represent issues that had to be collectively bargained. Although Florida is an "open shop" state, collective bargaining has seen renewed interest due to the at-will issue, accounting for significant increases in membership in the local AFSCME chapters.[8, 14]

Florida's reforms, like the preceding case, tend to fit the reform model, with the exception of outsourcing. The employment of Convergys places this case in the privatization/outsourcing model (as outlined in Table 2.1). However, the dilemma of balancing greater administrative flexibility at a cost to political accountability remains. One obvious concern is the fact that few were willing to make critical comments on the record for this chapter for fear of political retribution (anonymous, personal communication, August 29, 2003). Recent scholarly work[15] highlights this atmosphere of apprehension, particularly with respect to remuneration, reward issues, cutback pressures, training opportunities, and administrative layering. Polling state employees, the researchers found serious reservations concerning Service First, especially in its ability to enhance productivity. Employees expect at-will employment to be extended, reject the idea that pay will be enhanced, see reform as a distraction from real issues, and claim that citizen suspicion of government derives largely from activities in the political arena, not from citizen displeasure with services.

Changes in hiring, suspension, and dismissal procedures comprise a particularly alarming threat to political neutrality in Florida's civil service.

These changes, like those in Georgia, represent a dramatic shift in the application of personnel services in the public sector. Furthermore, the trend toward privatization in the delivery of government services, underscored in the case of Convergys, has placed traditional merit systems in conflict with the private sector. Florida's reforms, then, exhibit features of both the reform model and the privatization model as illustrated in Table 2.1.

A Collaborative Approach: Modernizing the New York Civil Service

In September 1995, New York Governor George Pataki instructed Civil Service Commissioner George Sinnott to head a task force that included the directors of state operations, the Governor's Office of Employee Relations, and the Governor's Office of the Budget, along with input from the public employee unions, to carry out a comprehensive overview of the civil service system.[16] The result of this initiative was the emergence of what has become New York's *New* Civil Service. Past reform efforts failed as a result of insurmountable political, legal, organizational, and procedural obstacles,[17] including the competing concerns of a constitutionally based merit system, highly codified civil service laws, 70-plus state agencies, seven employee organizations, the legislature, the budget, and the courts.

However, the New Civil Service was implemented by way of "incremental change through administrative reform." A collaborative approach involving the administration and the employee unions enabled the state to move forward with the New Civil Service.[18] Commissioner Sinnott involved the unions in the process, successfully putting an end to reform concerns. This compromise was solidified by sunset legislation; if there were any abuses, the legislation could be terminated. The partnership successfully lobbied a joint legislative committee for passage of transfer legislation, which has been renewed ever since. This multiconstituent approach was sustained through most of the reform process. The changes to the civil service included transfer legislation, improvements to testing and test-reporting procedures, enhanced applicant lists, a public management internship program, a reduction in and consolidation of state titles, technological improvements, and communication improvements between the state and local agencies.[19, 20, 17, 21] These initiatives were a dramatic shift to a civil service system rooted in tradition and mired in gridlock.

The transfer legislation drafted by the taskforce and adopted by the legislature on March 29, 1996, permitted the state to act as a single employer, allowing the Department of Civil Service to transfer employees between agencies instead of dismissing them during reductions in force. In addition, a strict hiring freeze and a newly developed early retirement incentive with multiple windows resulted in a reduction in the state workforce by 6,000 positions in fiscal year 1996. In so doing, the number of involuntary separations was limited to 235 employees, in contrast to the thousands of layoffs under the earlier retirement system.[19, 16]

Improved testing, another feature of these reforms, is intended to provide employees with the opportunity to compete for permanent status as required by law. Improvements in testing for promotion eliminated a backlog of over 600 titles for which no promotion tests had been scheduled. Relying entirely on internal resources, the Department of Civil Service developed and administered promotion test batteries using rigorous state-of-the-art selection methodologies. This new approach has benefited both employees and managers by providing them with a more timely and efficient method of promotion.[19, 16]

Additionally, the Department of Civil Service touts several technological improvements: the establishment of a Civil Service Web site that posts exam announcements, providing candidates with prompt results; "employee test profiles," which provide candidates with a summary indicating their performance in each subject area of the exam; timely lists of candidates eligible for appointment; and the capacity for applicants to register via telephone and pay exam fees via credit card. Accordingly, while emphasizing the need for efficiency, fundamental principles and best practices of civil service, such as hiring and promotion based on merit, are retained.[19, 16]

The state civil service authority not only extends to all state employees but also subjects local counties and municipalities to state rules and laws, particularly through routine audits. The director of human resources for Onondaga County (Syracuse), New York, Elaine Walter, provided insight into the impact of the New Civil Service reforms, reporting that several of the reforms mentioned above have had a significant impact on human resource directors at the local level, specifically comprehensive reforms in testing and scoring as well as technological improvements (E. Walter, personal communication, September 5, 2003). These reforms have streamlined the hiring process, making for more timely and predictable notice to potential new hires. The process has eliminated many of the provisional hires not only at the state level but at the local level as well. Rather than keeping these employees waiting on testing results for nine months, the more efficient process has allowed for results to be posted in as little as two. Moreover, efficient testing has affected recruitment at the local level, where human resource directors are now able to administer these tests on demand and provide potential employees with timely results. This has been particularly helpful for local authorities in the competitive recruitment market for information technology jobs. Additionally, the use of broad banding in the application and recruitment process has given local authorities a great deal of flexibility. Consideration is not based solely on numerical test scores, so the broad banding of test scores has provided a larger pool from which to recruit. Local authorities have also seen a significant impact from improved outreach services from the state civil service system. Commissioner Sinnott, once a director at the local level, has made considerable use of employees at the state level who serve as local liaisons, supplying them with training and other needs. This outreach has been helpful for increasing the lines of communication between local and state authorities, particularly in communicating the positive outcomes of reforms.

Unions have played a particularly significant role. At the local level, this has made the work of human resource directors somewhat complex. When dealing with dismissal, discipline, or even hiring and salaries, local officials have additional procedures to consider because of union involvement. Although some counties have established cooperative relationships with their respective unions, allowing for a smooth reform transition, others have not. The unions' involvement in New York politics makes additional reforms incremental at best. Reforms such as those in Georgia and Florida would be impossible to undertake given the lobbying power of state unions.

These reforms, unlike those of the two previous case studies, seem to best fit the strategic model as depicted in Table 2.1. New York's reforms exhibit features of the strategic model, particularly with respect to their impact on local governments. The New York case balances the competing demands of the traditional and strategic models, recognizing the benefits of some form of centralization but also realizing that human resource management takes place throughout an organization and should support, not hamper, the organization's overall goals. A common theme in this case and in other reform efforts is the effectiveness of popular leaders such as George Sinnott. Sinnott's ability to influence supporters and opponents added to the state's efforts to reform an archaic system through incremental statutory reform initiatives. This decentralizing trend is evident in the impact of reform on local authorities, such as those of Onondaga County. Reform efforts in New York, however rudimentary, have brought it to parity with other state civil service systems. This is a considerable achievement given the long history of impediments to reform in the state.[20] This case stands in stark contrast to the antimerit values emphasized in the radical reforms in the preceding cases. Additionally, scholarship[22] suggests that local human resource managers in New York have realized the efforts of the New Civil Service by paring down excessive rules and regulations. This has enabled local managers to function more efficiently and to focus on achieving their organizational mission within a competitive environment.

The Executive as Initiator of Strategic Reform: The Case of Louisiana

In the fall of 2000, an initiative to privatize the Louisiana Department of Economic Development (LDED) was placed on the ballot. The proposal, dubbed "Louisiana, Inc.," was part of a larger initiative by then-Governor M. J. "Mike" Foster, Jr. to diversify the economy through institutional reform known as Vision 2020. Legislation created in the spring of 2000 proposed replacing the LDED with Louisiana, Inc., a private enterprise. A factor in the legislation was the status of state employees in the new department. If the legislation passed, they would be exempt from the merit system but subject to administrative approval; that is, "at-will." Louisiana, Inc., was to operate outside of government, but would be accountable to state open-meeting laws, state public records laws, and the state ethics code.[23] Operating outside the scope of government, the intent was to eliminate red tape that typically slowed down the personnel process, giving the institution the potential to hire private sector professionals for equivalent pay.

The shadow of past executive abuses still preoccupies the Louisiana electorate;[a] consequently, this measure failed at the polls. Yet even as the governor had traveled across the state attempting to drum up support for the privatization effort, policy analysts, aware that the proposal's odds of being approved were slim, were hard at work on a contingency plan in the event of voter disapproval. The plan was put into place in the spring of 2001 through an executive order calling for the creation of a departmental reorganization task force aided by private sector consultants. It agreed to a "streamlining" process, compacting seven departmental offices into three: the Office of the Secretary, the Office of Management & Finance, and the Office of Business Development. The new Office of Business Development would include "cluster-based" economic development, comprising nine cluster professionals and staff as well as five service groups. The directorships of these cluster and service groups would be unclassified positions. These exempt status posts would be appointed by the governor's office and would serve at the governor's pleasure.

Reform at the LDED was part of a larger trend in decentralizing and reorganizing Louisiana government under ASCEND 2020 (Advancing Service, Creating Excellence, Nurturing Distinction), a component of the governor's Vision 2020. But the state government was too large and too diverse for a one-size-fits-all policy. Complying with Vision 2020, ASCEND 2020 sought to delegate authority and local discretion to the human resource directors of each agency. The role of the Louisiana Department of State Civil Service (LDSCS) was to focus on general policy development, skill development, communication, assistance, and assessment. The four major components of ASCEND 2020 included a decentralized personnel transaction process, the reorganization of the Department of State Civil

Service from a functional orientation to an agency service center design, the establishment of an Internet vacancy-posting site, and the conversion of personnel records from paper to computer imaging.[24] In compliance with ASCEND 2020, the LDSCS has discarded its role of enforcer/processor and has reestablished itself in a new dual role of consultant/advisor and objective evaluator.

To administer substantial changes to the Louisiana civil service, authority was delegated to state agencies to approve all personnel transactions.[24] Accordingly, the LDSCS established two new divisions: the Human Resource Program Assistance Division and the Human Resource Accountability Division. The Assistance Division, created to provide agencies with a single point of contact, is responsible for general knowledge of civil service practices and serves as an advocate for agencies in expediting solutions to human resource problems. The Accountability Division, established to address performance and accountability concerns, is responsible for assessing approximately 50 state agencies each year. Additionally, the Assistance and Accountability Divisions are responsible for identifying training needs and subsequently developing and delivering necessary training.[24] Beginning in July 2002, agency managers, supervisors, and human resource directors were required to take courses designed to augment managerial knowledge and skills.

Furthermore, departments are now equipped with better access to information about all employees and have access to a Civil Service Internet vacancy-posting site established to eliminate availability problems by requiring interested candidates to respond directly to the agency where the vacancy occurs. The network has reduced the time needed to fill special announcement vacancies because they can now be posted immediately on the Internet.

Louisiana is an example of a government that has attempted reform through strategic management. In an interview, Governor Foster explained that coordinating reform within the political climate of Louisiana necessitated recruiting a board that was willing and able to look past the political ramifications of these reforms.

> I spent a lot of time being involved and knowing who was being appointed [to the Civil Service Board]. We ended up with a very good board and a very good executive director. You can take an interest and get a board that's a good board. Again, it all goes back to who sits in this chair. If you get somebody who accepts that everything is political, everything is a political payoff, it's going to fail. If you can get somebody in this job that tries to do things not on a political basis, it will work well, and it has. (M. J. Foster, Jr., personal communication, August 6, 2003)

The administration was able to create a more flexible system while including rules and procedures that allowed for merit considerations such as seniority in hiring and promotions. Thus, Louisiana's civil service reforms can be characterized by incremental reform through the careful use of power in the executive office—features of the strategic model. The reform efforts have dispersed personnel authority throughout the human resource units, giving them the ability to make crucial decisions concerning employee recruitment, selection, classification, and remuneration.[6] In contrast to the aforementioned cases, Louisiana's reforms have been implemented prudently and cautiously over the eight years of the Foster administration. Reform models typically emphasize responsiveness to the immediate needs of the organization; however, this promptness is often accompanied by a lack of central organizing focus, and problems of equity and fairness among organizational units often ensue.[6] These pitfalls have been avoided in Louisiana due to the administration's careful attention to detail and its goal of creating a more efficient administrative structure not solely influenced by partisan politics or political ideology. It remains to be seen if this progress will be sustainable with a new governor and the recent catastrophic events associated with Hurricane Katrina.

The Courts as an Initiator of Reform: The Unique Case of the Personnel Board of Jefferson County, Alabama

The Personnel Board of Jefferson County, Alabama, illustrates a unique chapter in the history of civil service reform in the United States. The federal court–ordered reforms imposed on the board are the only such instance of its kind that could be documented by the authors. The board is responsible for hiring and promotion in Jefferson County and most county municipalities, including the City of Birmingham. The NAACP initiated litigation against the county Personnel Board in 1974, alleging discriminatory practices in job selection, tests, and hiring. In 1981, a federal consent decree was reached to develop "non-discriminatory tests" and to establish "fair job selection procedures and hiring tests."[25]

In July 2002, a federal court found the Personnel Board in contempt for violating the terms of a December 1995 order that extended and modified the 1981 Consent Decree to rectify discriminatory practices. The federal judge appointed a "receiver" to function as the "sole board member" in orchestrating court-ordered changes to the discriminatory practices. According to the ruling, the receiver was to "take over all powers state law assigns to the three member board, its executive director and the Citizen Supervisory Commission."[25] Dr. Ronald R. Sims, senior professor in the Graduate School of Business at the College of William and Mary, was ordered to serve as the receiver at the pleasure of the federal district court. The court-appointed receiver was ordered by the federal judge to "manage and control property and employees, and perform contractual, financial, legal, and personnel duties" of the Personnel Board.[25]

To meet the court-imposed duties, Sims began a full reorganization of the board. Sims's reorganization effort included the following:

- Conducting a five-year survey of all job classifications and pay of civil servants
- Assessing the basic skills and abilities of employees and creating appropriate job training/professional development programs to build more in-house competency
- Recruiting a qualified consultant to quickly develop new selection procedures for police and sheriff's deputies, and to develop similar procedures for 19 of the 33 job classifications remaining in the consent decree
- Developing plans for buying equipment and hardware to build a technology infrastructure that will modernize and streamline job selection and promotion procedures
- Rewriting the rules and regulations for greater clarity, uniformity, and compliance with state and federal requirements[26, 27]

The first year of reorganization efforts failed to provide an interim job-selection mechanism, which was particularly problematic for personnel in public safety. Initial findings by Sims indicated that many employees were not qualified to do their jobs, that some ignored rules and regulations or made them up as they went along, and that the county's computer system could not handle thousands of civil servant files.[26, 27] Sims's initial agenda addressed these concerns, attempting to improve the board's operations in hiring competent managers and other staff, establishing professional development training for staff, and formulating new rules and regulations.

The court order gave Sims the power to incur expenses in a "cost-effective" manner while carrying out the duties of the consent decree.[25] $8.5 million was budgeted, yet after deliberation with staff and personnel at the Personnel Board, Sims requested an additional $7 million "for staff development, professional services, legal fees and computer equipment."[26] State law required that this additional revenue come from both city and county sources. Participating governments in Jefferson County were required to pay a percentage of the board's operating costs based on their number of employees. Sims's efforts to build a highly qualified testing division led to the addition of 16 new testing professionals. Additionally, Sims created three teams related to recruitment, training, and performance within the Personnel Board.[28] He asserts that new technologies have enabled the board to enhance its five-year classification and compensation survey. The board was released from receivership in July 2005.

Although the efforts of the receiver attest to increased professionalization of board activities and functions, the Jefferson County Personnel Board still clearly operates as a traditional civil service model as depicted in Table 2.1, with tight centralization of human resource functions and a heavy reliance on "objective tests." This reliance led to the dismissal of the African American provisional police chief of Bessemer, Alabama, based on the fact that his score on a written examination was not among the top ten.[29] This action was taken despite his 32 years of law enforcement experience and his having served previously as police chief for the City of Birmingham, a much larger jurisdiction.

HRM in Chapel Hill, North Carolina: A Case for Best Practices

Drawing upon methodology and consulting experience, the authors identify Chapel Hill as an exemplar of best practices in human resource management.[30] An essential element is its human resource management relations committee, which meets on a monthly basis to receive information concerning policies and practices as well as to voice concerns that committee members or other employees may have. The committee consists of representatives from every department and from all levels of the town's organizational structure. This two-way communication between administrators and employees functions as an effective tool for demonstrating meaningful involvement in the process.

The Town of Chapel Hill has also constructed a remarkably competitive compensation and benefits system, enabling it to compete effectively in recruitment. A broad pay range allows for rapid movement to the midpoint of the range and then slower salary growth toward career end. A respectable benefits package is also available. Additionally, Chapel Hill has established a responsive classification system based on point-factor methodology adjusted by labor-market data on an annual basis. Regular position audits are conducted; a comprehensive review of the classification structure is conducted every four to seven years.

It should be clear from the case studies that the political environment must be one that is conducive to change. Chapel Hill's town council is open to change and collaboration with town administrators. The two work together to recognize and promote the importance of a strategic human resource system. This cooperation is limited to the policy level, giving administrators freedom to coordinate things at the operational level. Moreover, the human resource system is an integral part of the overall management infrastructure.[31, 6, 32] The human resource director and staff function as integral partners in making management decisions that affect town operations and support services. This integrated approach enhances effective management through the decision-making process.

Furthermore, the town has made a determined effort to build a professional human resource staff to effectively manage large-scale projects and classification studies in coordination with consultants. This staff consists of specialists in compensation, benefits, risk management, safety, and recruitment and selection. Moreover, Chapel Hill has instituted aggressive recruitment and professional-selection techniques. Human resource staff participate in career fairs at colleges and universities, searching nationally for department head–level positions and providing extensive and detailed information to prospective employees concerning the town. In addition, the town makes extensive use of nonmonetary rewards related to service and performance to maintain an organizational climate conducive to employee involvement, retention, and loyalty.

The case of Chapel Hill represents a strategic and modernized approach to human resource management. Taken individually, each of the items discussed above will not result in an outstanding human resource management department or function. Collectively, however, they signal a department in tune with the needs of the organization's employees, its management purpose, and the citizens it serves. The Chapel Hill model is characterized by a collaborative system of service delivery; goal orientation that is respectful of human resource management and organizational goals; a multidirectional communication pattern involving administrators, employees, town council members, and citizens; a role for the human resource director as an integral organizational manager and consultant; and an emphasis on the role of education in building a professional human resource staff that focuses not just on human resource management practices but also on general and practical management applications.

CONCLUSIONS AND IMPLICATIONS

Building an effective human resource management system cannot be accomplished overnight; it requires internal competence and external support. As such, it is necessarily an incremental process whereby major actors in the organization (political leaders, management, employees, and citizens) gain confidence and respect in the human resource department and its ability to facilitate an effective and responsive system of personnel management. Those seeking an effective human resource system should not look to the latest management fad or "quick fix" but rather should concentrate on the proper resources (both monetary and human) and buy-in of the organization's major stakeholders.

The cases illustrate a variety of efforts to reform and administer human resource systems. Table 2.2 summarizes the cases and depicts which

Table 2.2 A Comparison of the Six Case Studies Using the Four Models of Public Human Resource Management

Case	*Traditional Model*	*Reform Model*	*Strategic Model*	*Privatization/ Outsourcing Model*
Georgia		X		
Florida		X		X
New York	X		X	
Louisiana	X	X	X	
Jefferson County, Alabama	X			
Chapel Hill, North Carolina			X	

model(s) of public human resource management each embodies. A review of Table 2.2 along with Table 2.1 suggests several lessons. First, incremental, administratively oriented reform appears to have met with moderate to high levels of success (Louisiana, New York, and Chapel Hill). These cases illustrate the importance of not squandering political capital. Through incremental change supported by key constituencies regardless of political affiliation, strategic reform is possible. This reform emphasizes a central organizing approach to reform policy while supporting a decentralized approach to its implementation. In contrast, politically motivated reforms are met with resistance, skepticism, and fear (e.g., Georgia and Florida). These radical reforms may lead many to leave government service[15, 3, 33, 4] and may not enable these governments to attract the best and the brightest. Finally, the findings suggest that even extensive professionalization of human resource management under a traditional model of service delivery will not serve the managerial needs of client agencies. The case of the Personnel Board of Jefferson County, Alabama, demonstrates that even a large influx of new spending aimed at professionalizing a highly centralized, recalcitrant system may not be money well spent. As a whole, these cases should illustrate that it is one thing to attempt to strategically modernize civil service systems and quite another to attempt to radically reform such systems.

As the "human capital" crisis intensifies, it is prudent to continue to monitor reforms in civil service systems, especially current efforts at the federal level. At this time, it appears that unlike the original evolution in government bureaucracy—reform spurred by addressing failures at the federal level, then trickling down through the states—there appears to be an inverse policy diffusion, where reforms in the cases above and elsewhere act as the driving forces for changes at the federal level. Nowhere is this more evident than in federal reforms in the wake of 9/11.[34]

The cases presented are meant to be illustrative of various reform efforts, not a definitive treatise. It is hoped that this chapter will add to the growing body of knowledge related to civil service reform and toward an effort to begin to systematically analyze these and other civil service systems. Unlike prior human resource reforms such as the Civil Service Reform Act of 1978, state and local governments are not taking their cues directly from the federal government, but rather from a variety of governments at the state and local levels. This trend emphasizes the importance of studying these reform efforts to draw lessons from their outcomes for policy modeling and effective practice.

Note

a. Former governor Edwin Edwards is presently serving an eight-year prison term for federal racketeering charges. Two other state officials, the commissioners of insurance and elections, were released from prison in 2005 after serving time for similar charges.

ACKNOWLEDGMENTS

The authors would like to thank Jason Fleury, Christine Kolaya, and Christine Ledienka of the Carl Vinson Institute of Government for their assistance in preparing this chapter. The authors are also grateful to those who gave of their time for interviews and to provide information related to writing this chapter. The authors are also appreciative of the helpful suggestions of anonymous reviewers.

REFERENCES

1. Maranto, R., and Condrey, S. E., Why radical reform? The rise of government by business, in *Radical Reform of the Civil Service*, Condrey, S. E., and Maranto, R., eds., Lexington Books, Lanham, MD, 2001, 1.
2. Kettl, D. F., *The Global Public Management Revolution: A Report on the Transformation of Governance*, Brookings Institution, Washington, DC, 2000.
3. Condrey, S. E., Reinventing state civil service systems: The Georgia experience, *Review of Public Personnel Administration*, 22(2), 114, 2002.
4. Kellough, J. E., and Nigro, L. G., Pay for performance in Georgia state government, *Review of Public Personnel Administration*, 22(2), 146, 2002.
5. West, J. P., Georgia on the mind of radical civil service reformers, *Review of Public Personnel Administration*, 22(2), 79, 2002.
6. Condrey, S. E., Toward strategic human resource management, in *Handbook of Human Resource Management*, 2nd ed., Condrey, S. E., ed., Jossey-Bass, San Francisco, 2005, 1.

7. Fernandez, S., Lowman, C. E., and Rainey, H. G., Privatization and human resource management, in *Public Personnel Management: Current Concerns, Future Challenges*, 3rd ed., Ban, C., and Riccucci, N. M., eds., Longman, New York, 2002, 225.
8. Walters, J., Life after civil service reform: The Texas, Georgia, and Florida experiences, IBM Endowment for the Business of Government, Armonk, NY, October 2002.
9. Lasseter, R. W., Georgia's merit system reform 1996–2001: An operating agency's perspective, *Review of Public Personnel Administration*, 22(2), 125, 2002.
10. Kellough, J. E., and Nigro, L. G., Civil service reform in Georgia: A view from the trenches, in *Civil Service Reform in the States: Personnel Policies and Politics at the Subnational Level*, Kellough, J. E., and Nigro, L. G., eds., State University of New York Press, Albany, 2006, 161.
11. Barrett, K., et al., Grading the states '05: The year of living dangerously, *Governing*, February 2005, retrieved January 11, 2006, from http://governing.com/gpp/2005/intro.htm.
12. Guy, M. E., Civil service reform: A comparative perspective, presented at the University of Georgia, Athens, April 2004.
13. Cotterell, B., Crist urged to warn workers personnel data may have gone overseas, *Tallahassee Democrat*, January 18, 2006, retrieved January 18, 2006, from http://www.tallahassee.com.
14. Walters, J., Civil service tsunami: Florida's radical overhaul of its personnel system is making big political waves, *Governing*, May, 34, 2003.
15. Bowman, J. S., et al., Civil service reform in Florida state government: Employee attitudes 1 year later, *Review of Public Personnel Administration*, 23(4), 286, 2003.
16. Sinnott, G. C., Civil service—bully, bully: New York State Department of Civil Service, 1998, retrieved July 21, 2003, from http://www.cs.state.ny.us/pio/bully.htm.
17. Vonnegut, M., New York state's new civil service, prepared for nomination for the Eugene H. Rooney, Jr. Innovative State Human Resource Management Award, National Association of State Personnel Executives, Lexington, KY, 1999.
18. Thompson, F., and Malbin, M. J., Reforming personnel systems in New York State: Interview with George C. Sinnott, *Rockefeller Institute Bulletin*, 1999, retrieved July 21, 2003, from http://www.cs.state.ny.us/pio/rockefellerbulletin.htm.
19. New York Department of Civil Service, *Quality Standards/Innovative Applications: Award Winning Performance from New York State's* New *Civil Service*, State of New York, Department of Civil Service, Albany, 1998.
20. Riccucci, N. M., Civil service reforming in New York: A quiet revolution, in *Civil Service Reform in the States: Personnel Policies and Politics at the Subnational Level*, Kellough, J. E., and Nigro, L. G., State University of New York Press, Albany, 2005, 405.
21. Walters, J., Untangling Albany, *Governing*, 12(3), 18, 1998.
22. Mesch, D. J., Perry, J. L., and Wise, L. R., Bureaucratic and strategic human resource management: An empirical comparison in the federal government, *Journal of Public Administration Research and Theory*, 5(4), 247, 1995.
23. Louisiana Economic Development Council, *Louisiana: Vision 2020. State of Louisiana Master Plan for Economic Development*, Office of the Governor, Baton Rouge, 1999.

24. Soileau, A. S., Advancing service creating excellence nurturing distinction: ASCEND 2020, prepared for nomination for the Eugene H. Rooney, Jr. Innovative State Human Resource Management Award, National Association of State Personnel Executives, Lexington, KY, 2002.
25. *United States of America v. Jefferson County, Alabama, et al.*, Civil Action No. CV-75-S-666-S (2002).
26. Howell, V., Repairer talks to mayors about costs, *Birmingham News*, January 17, 2003, 1A.
27. Sims, R. D., Fixing Jefferson County Personnel Board under way, *Birmingham News*, February 2, 2003, 6C.
28. Sims, R. D., Personnel Board can't take a break at halfway point, *Birmingham News*, July 6, 2003, 5C.
29. Gordon, R. K., Bessemer names new acting chief, *Birmingham News*, September 23, 2003, 1B.
30. Condrey, S. E., and Slava, S., Human resource management best practices: The case of Chapel Hill, North Carolina, presented at the Conference on Best Practices in Local Governance and Development, Uzhhorod National University, Ukraine, August 2001.
31. Ban, C., The changing role of the personnel office, in *Handbook of Human Resource Management*, Condrey, S. E., ed., Jossey-Bass, San Francisco, 1998, 19.
32. Perry, J. L., and Mesch, D. J., Strategic human resource management, in *Public Personnel Management: Current Concerns, Future Challenges*, 2nd ed., Ban, C., and Riccucci, N. M., eds., Longman, New York, 1997, 21.
33. Facer R. L., II, Reinventing public administration: Reform in the Georgia civil service, *Public Administration Quarterly*, 22(1), 58, 1998.
34. Naff, K. C., and Newman, M. A., Federal civil service reform: Another legacy of 9/11? *Symposium on the Management of HR in the 21st Century: The Federal Government Experience, Review of Public Personnel Administration*, 24(3), 191, 2004.

3

AT-WILL EMPLOYMENT: ORIGINS, APPLICATIONS, EXCEPTIONS, AND EXPANSIONS IN PUBLIC SERVICE

Sally C. Gertz
Florida State University College of Law

INTRODUCTION

The president of Florida State University once told his labor attorney to negotiate an employment contract with Bobby Bowden, the "winningest" coach in Division One college football, "for as long as he wants."(1) And during the term of his contract, of course, Bowden could only be dismissed "for cause." By contrast, most American workers have no hope of obtaining an employment contract for a guaranteed term. Their contracts are silent regarding the length of employment, which means they are "at-will" employees—terminable at the will of the employer for good reason, no reason, or bad reason. Despite its prevalence, there has been ongoing, sharp debate among American legal scholars for at least the last 30 years about the continued use of the employment-at-will doctrine. Appalled by the reprehensible employer behavior that "employment at will" countenances, legislators and courts have created exceptions aimed at curbing particular abuses (most notably, the antidiscrimination statutes), but the core employment-at-will doctrine remains intact.

Increasingly, the government workforce is part of the employment-at-will debate. In recent years, Georgia removed "just cause" protections for all new state employees and made them "at-will," and Florida moved approximately 16,300 state employees from "Career Service" to "Selected Exempt Service," making them at-will. State employees in Florida challenged the "take back" of their "just cause" protection in courts, but judges have been loath to intervene in what they see as legitimate policy debates. As more public employees become at-will, it is apparent that problems identified in the private sector likewise are present when the doctrine is utilized to define the employment relationship in the public sector. And some problems—like the lack of transparency the doctrine foments—are even more troubling when they occur in government workplaces.

This chapter describes the development of the employment-at-will doctrine in American jurisprudence and the development of the legislative and judicial exceptions. Next, legal scholarship criticizing and defending the doctrine is summarized, and reform initiatives are reviewed. Finally, two issues related to the expansion of employment at will in the public sector are discussed: the constitutionality of "taking back" job security from public employees, and the impact that eliminating due process hearings will have on the transparency of government.

THE ORIGIN OF EMPLOYMENT AT WILL

What is the duration of employment if an employer and employee fail to specify a term? This question is seminal to the development of the employment-at-will doctrine. According to Blackstone's commentary on English common law, the employment relationship in England was viewed as a contractual one, with the terms of the contract either expressly or implicitly agreed upon. If no length of term for the employment relationship was expressly agreed upon (either orally or in writing), then a term of one year from hiring was presumed, but either party could rebut this presumption with facts showing a different intent. Custom in the industry and the length of the pay period were two facts used to show what the parties implicitly intended when there was no express agreement.[(2)]

Early court decisions in the United States largely followed the English common law in this area, but they did not adopt a presumption of annual hiring. When the contract was silent, some courts presumed employment was for the period of payment. Others approached the question with no presumption. They scrutinized the facts surrounding the formation of each employment contract and attempted to discern the parties' intent. Not surprisingly, given these contrasting approaches, the law had become muddled by 1877, when treatise writer Horace Wood weighed in and declared, "With us, the rule is inflexible . . . a general or indefinite hiring is . . . a hiring at will."[3, 4]

Wood's pronouncement had little immediately apparent impact, but in 1895 the prestigious New York Court of Appeals reversed its course (this court previously had applied a presumption that employment was for the period of payment) and quoted Wood as authority for holding that an employee who had been hired for a stated annual salary could be dismissed midyear without cause.[5] By 1930, employment at will was the governing American principle, and its basic tenets remain undisturbed today. If no duration of employment is specified in an employment contract—and only upper-level managers and some professional employees receive contracts with a specified duration—then the default rule is that the employment is terminable at will, by either party without notice. And, courts concluded, a necessary corollary follows: because an indefinite employment contract can be lawfully terminated at any time, it can be terminated for any reason. If employees have no *right* to continued employment, then from the law's perspective it does not matter *why* their employment is terminated. The Tennessee Supreme Court famously summed up this blind-eye approach as follows: "men must be left, without interference . . . to discharge or retain employees at will for good cause or for no cause, or even for bad cause without thereby being guilty of an unlawful act per se."[6]

Why did American law diverge from English common law and develop this way? Some commentators see this trailblazing as a logical extension of contemporary courts' expansive views on employers' right to control their property and on individuals' right to freely enter into contracts. On other levels, it has been explained as the outgrowth of laissez-faire capitalism, as a way for capitalists to deflect the advances of managers and white-collar employees, and as a reflection of the dominant pattern of short-term employment at the time.[7] Whatever its roots, the doctrine of employment at will flourished in the United States, with predictably harsh results.

Unfettered freedom of contract permitted employers to refuse to hire disfavored groups, to engage in opportunistic firings (for example, to avoid paying pensions), and to punish employees for behaving in socially desirable ways (for instance, by giving truthful testimony to courts). Eventually lawmakers and courts became convinced that the at-will doctrine was inadequate and began carving out legislative and judicial "exceptions." The result is a doctrine dotted with holes—some gaping and others miniscule. Employment at will remains the avowed rule that underlies and informs all discharge law, but the contemporary version contains a looming qualifier: employers can discharge employees for good reason or for no reason, or even for bad reason, *but not for some particular bad reasons condemned by law.*[8]

EXCEPTIONS TO EMPLOYMENT AT WILL

From the 1930s to the 1950s, collective bargaining was seen as the best method for voluntarily and creatively setting the terms and conditions of employment at workplaces. From 1960 to the present, the trend has been toward more direct government intervention—federal and state, legislative and judicial—into employees' individual relationships with employers. This growth in direct government regulation probably resulted, at least in part, from the decline of unions and a need to fill the void left by their waning influence. According to the Department of Labor, in just the last 20 years the rate of organization has decreased from 20.1 percent in 1983 to 12.9 percent in 2003. During this period, public sector membership remained steady at around 37 percent, which means that private sector membership nose-dived from approximately 16 percent in 1983 to 8.2 percent in 2003, a loss rate of almost 50 percent in 20 years.[9]

One primary goal of direct government intervention has been to curtail the shocking "bad reasons" for which employers can lawfully discharge at-will employees. In general, legislators and courts stepped in with two types of prohibitions: antidiscrimination prohibitions that prevent employers from discharging employees based on particular characteristics (such as race, sex, disability, and age) and antiretaliation prohibitions that prevent employers from discharging employees for exercising various legal rights and duties (such as union organizing, whistle-blowing, and attending jury duty). Despite the limits they place on employers' discretion, these antidiscrimination and antiretaliation doctrines enjoy wide consensus, primarily because they promote the interests of the public, for example, by promoting racial and sexual equality and supporting the needs of law enforcement, rather than solely the interests of individual employees. Many commentators have noted that these "public goods" and "third party effects" make government intervention in the workplace more palatable to legislators and courts.[8, 10, 11] Heated debate still occurs over particular extensions and applications of the antiretaliation and antidiscrimination doctrines, but these core "bad motive" exceptions have been widely accepted; virtually no one is clamoring for their repeal. In addition to the bad motive exceptions, courts have carved out several exceptions based on contract law. And occasionally, other legal theories, such as defamation, intentional infliction of emotional distress, and violation of privacy rights, provide remedies when employers act outrageously in the course of dismissing employees.

Statutory Exceptions

Antiretaliation Statutes

The National Labor Relations Act (NLRA) of 1935 was the first important statutory exception to employment at will. In the 1930s, collective bargaining was seen as a socially desirable activity, so first in the railroad industry, and then in the entire private sector, the act prohibited the discharge of employees engaged in union activities. Drafters of the law realized that enforcement of the act depended on employees being willing to bring charges and provide testimony, so they also prohibited retaliation against employees who brought or participated in enforcement proceedings.[12] The NLRA became a template for other antiretaliation statutes protecting voluntary, socially valued conduct. Some regulate working conditions (such as the Fair Labor Standards Act of 1938, which bars retaliation against employees who file complaints or participate in proceedings),[13] whereas others regulate non-work-related activity that could harm the public (such as the Clean Air Act of 1963, which protects employees who report violations of clean air standards).[14] In addition to the antiretaliation provisions contained in discrete federal and state regulations, there are broader federal and state "whistle-blower protection" statutes that provide remedies for employees who are retaliated against for reporting any unlawful employer conduct.

Antidiscrimination Statutes

Title VII of the Civil Rights Act of 1964 prohibits employers from discriminating on the basis of race, color, religion, sex, or national origin.[15] Title VII and its progeny prohibit adverse employment actions (including discharges) based on traits that have unfairly been the basis for a group's disadvantage. The Age Discrimination in Employment Act,[16] the Pregnancy Discrimination Act,[17] the employment provisions of the Americans with Disabilities Act,[18] and the Immigration Reform and Control Act[19] (prohibiting discrimination on the basis of citizenship status) added additional traits to this list. Not satisfied, states, too, added traits they deemed worthy of protection from employers' vicissitudes—marital status, ancestry, medical condition, sexual orientation, and veteran status, to name a few.

Judicial Exceptions

Legislators were the first to carve out exceptions to the employment-at-will doctrine, but judges' hole poking gained more notoriety. In general, judicially created exceptions fall into three categories: exceptions based on public policy, exceptions based on implied contracts, and exceptions based on an implied covenant of good faith and fair dealing. The public policy exception is a tort theory; the other two are contract theories. Only Florida, Georgia, Louisiana, and Rhode Island appear to have failed to embrace at least one of these judicial exceptions.[20, 21]

Public Policy Exception

Most cases declaring a discharge unlawful because it offends public policy fit neatly into the antiretaliation model developed by federal and state legislation. These cases afford a legal remedy to individuals who have been discharged for voluntary conduct that society values and seeks to encourage. The conduct courts protect generally involves employees' exercise of a clear legal right (e.g., filing a workers' compensation claim), performance of a clear public duty (e.g., attending jury duty), and refusal to violate the law (e.g., by committing perjury), and may extend to blowing the whistle on employers' illegal conduct even though there is no clear legal duty to report it (e.g., reporting a nursing home's violation of patients' rights). The common denominator is that the public policy in question must enjoy a clear mandate, which usually means that it has been expressed legislatively in an administrative rule, statute, or constitution. Estimates vary slightly, but approximately 44 states recognize the common law claim of violation of public policy as an exception to the rule of employment at will.[20, 21] In practice, this exception is seldom useful to an arbitrarily discharged employee because well-trained employers rarely commit the kind of flagrant acts that violate public policy.[22]

Together, the antidiscrimination statutes, antiretaliation statutes, and judicial public policy exception make up the law of wrongful discharge. In each, if an employee can prove a particular bad motive by the employer, the employee can recover damages—and the damages may be hefty. Depending upon the claims raised and injuries proven, in addition to lost wages (front pay and back pay) and benefits, employees may be able to recover damages for emotional distress, pain and suffering, punitive damages, and attorneys' fees—the large damage awards that attract plaintiffs' attorneys and frighten employers.

Implied Contract Exception

Courts also recognize an exception to the rule that an employer can discharge at-will employees at any time, for any reason, when they find that employers have made contrary promises. If an employer distributes a handbook or other written policies that list the offenses that generate discipline, assures employees they will only be disciplined "for cause," or details procedures that will be followed by the employer when discipline is taken, then any discharge that does not follow the guidelines is a breach of contract. Likewise, if an employer made oral promises to an employee, the employer may be required to abide by them. As the New Jersey Supreme Court blithely observed, "If such a commitment is indeed made, obviously an employer should be required to honor it."[23]

Although accepted in approximately 44 states, this exception also has had little impact on employees' rights.[20, 21] A written disclaimer is all that is necessary for an employer to evade promises it made elsewhere in writing. And an employer who provided a handbook full of promises to employees when they were hired can revoke those promises simply by issuing a new handbook. To be binding, oral commitments must result from specific bargaining over job security, which means they usually only benefit people in high-level jobs. General oral assurances that employees will be retained during good service are not binding.[22, 24]

Implied Covenant of Good Faith and Fair Dealing Exception

In American law, there is an implied obligation to act in good faith that attaches to every contract. But should this obligation attach to an at-will employment contract? Isn't a "good faith" obligation incompatible with an at-will employer's right to discharge an employee for no reason or one of the still unprohibited bad reasons? In a word—yes. Most courts have rejected plaintiffs' invitations to apply the doctrine to at-will employment contracts on the grounds that the doctrine is amorphous, is too broad, and might destructively limit employers' prerogatives. Courts have refused to use this implied obligation to impose a just cause requirement in an employment relationship that is, in fact, at will. Only approximately 12 states permit use of the doctrine to challenge at-will discharges.[20, 21, 25]

Early indications were that this doctrine might be a vehicle to insert a basic fairness requirement into American discharge law. For example, when a foreman discharged a married woman for refusing to date him, the New Hampshire Supreme Court invoked the covenant of good faith and declared that termination of an at-will contract of employment "which is motivated by bad faith . . . constitutes a breach of the employment contract."[26] The California Court of Appeals relied upon the implied covenant of good faith to grant protection to an employee with 18 years of service who was discharged without cause. The court held that "termination of employment without legal cause after such a period of time offends the implied-in-law covenant of good faith and fair dealing contained in all contracts, including employment contracts."[27] Later, another California court used the covenant to grant protection to an employee with only seven years of service.[28] These decisions were widely understood to hold that the implied covenant of good faith granted protection from arbitrary discharge to all long-term, at-will employees. And in the California cases, violation of the covenant was a tort, with its potentially large damages.

But cases like these were rare, and later cases circumscribed them. For the most part, courts recognizing the theory have used it to force employers to pay employees money that is owed. For instance, in *Fortune v. Nat'l Cash Register Co.* (1977), the Massachusetts Supreme Court used the covenant to award damages to an at-will salesman who was fired one day after he obtained a $5,000,000 order from a customer; the court found the company discharged him to avoid paying a commission.[29] And most courts calculate the remedy using contract law principles (generally, the amount due under the contract) rather than tort law principles (designed to punish offenders).

APPLICATIONS OF CONTEMPORARY EMPLOYMENT AT WILL: CRITICISMS, DEFENSES, REFORMS

Criticisms

Critics of contemporary employment at will decry its failure to provide human beings with basic fairness and simple justice. To an employee, the economic and emotional consequences of arbitrary or wrongful discharge can be tragic: deteriorations in physical and psychological health, and losses in wages, seniority, status, pension, health insurance, and employability, are likely. These consequences impact not only the employee and her family, but also society at large because unemployment has close ties to poverty and crime. Employees are human beings, critics remonstrate, and certain minimal components of workplace fairness (safety, nondiscrimination, and merit) are necessary to human dignity.[24, 30–34] Every other major industrialized democracy (and many developing countries) have adopted a general legal protection against unjust discharge as an essential aspect of social justice. Critics urge that we join this community of enlightened nations and meld compassion with efficiency in discharge law because, as the European Union proposal states, "labor is not a commodity . . . everyone has the right to lead a life in accordance with human dignity and adequate social protection."[35]

Employers' representatives often claim that judges and lawmakers already have decimated employment at will and forced employers to apply a de facto just cause standard to all discharges. The truth is that most at-will employees have few realistic avenues to challenge arbitrary discharges. The antidiscrimination doctrines offer inadequate protection to those covered (and virtually no protection to middle-aged white males), and few employees have engaged in conduct protected by the antiretaliation doctrines. Employers easily evade contract exceptions. With a bit of care, an employer can arbitrarily discharge an employee, for example to hire a crony, without violating any legal rights.

According to critics, the modern employment-at-will doctrine—with its hodgepodge of legislative and judicial exceptions—does not even adequately limit the egregious, socially harmful discharges that everyone agrees should be eliminated (discriminatory and retaliatory discharges) because employment at will undermines legislative and judicial remedial schemes. Whereas in a just cause system *an employer* must prove *any legitimate reason* for discharge, in a wrongful discharge model, *an employee* must prove *one bad motive* by an employer. The employee shoulders this burden even though the employer controls all the documents and witnesses and has been trained to be cautious in its statements and diligent in documenting employees' shortcomings. (Employees with blemished records face even greater obstacles of proof than perfect ones.) For employees, obtaining a remedy usually requires filing an action in court or with an agency, but low- and middle-income plaintiffs will find it difficult to engage a lawyer; they cannot pay up front, and their potential recovery is not large enough to generate a worthwhile contingency fee. Experienced plaintiffs' attorneys estimate that only 5 percent of individuals with an employment claim are able to obtain counsel. For those who manage to file claims, success rates and awards are modest.(36) The wrongful discharge model forces an employee to overcome fearsome delays, costs, and difficulties in proof—while out of a job and without relief. It should be expected that many employees with legitimate claims would fail to overcome these burdens or opt out of trying.(8)

The wrongful discharge model not only fails to remedy discrimination in the workplace; perversely, it also creates problems of its own. Employers may be more cautious in disciplining those with protected traits (e.g., women and minorities) than those without them, leading to divisive tensions and polarization. This dynamic may also increase employers' incentive to discriminate in hiring. Finally, the current regime encourages employees to allege discrimination (if they possess a protected trait) to secure impartial review of a discharge when, in fact, the decision may simply have been unfair, not discriminatory.(8, 37)

The employment-at-will doctrine also seriously impedes workers' willingness to engage in "speech" that total quality management systems and antiretaliation doctrines seek to encourage. Employees who are subject to summary discharge (with unreliable recourse) will be less likely than those with job security to participate in workplace decisions (by criticizing supervisors, questioning workplace conditions or methods of production, or seeking better mechanisms). And they will be less likely to disclose or refuse to engage in illegal, or possibly illegal, conduct. In an employment-at-will regime, it is the rare heroic (or foolhardy) employee who will speak out and take such risks. Silence or complicity is much safer.[38]

A secure workforce is a better workforce according to critics. They point to studies showing that employees with job security are more likely to be productive and have quality output,[39, 40] more loyal and cooperative, more likely to achieve technical progress and innovation, and less likely to sue employers.[41, 42] They also cite studies showing that it is easier to recruit employees if job security is offered, and harder to recruit employees if employment at will is the stated policy.[22, 30, 41, 43, 44]

Employment-at-will detractors contend its prevalence (approximately 85 percent of private employers use employment at will)[45] reflects the limited bargaining power of most working people—not their free choice to contract for terms they want—as demonstrated by the fact that when employees aggregate their power in unions, they demand job security. Employers are repeat players with many advantages. One frequently noted asymmetry is the lack of information employees possess compared to employers. Employees have little information about employer practices regarding discipline and discharge, and they lack accurate information about their legal rights. Studies have shown that workers greatly overestimate the legal protections available to at-will workers.[46–49]

Critics also note that, compared to employers, employees have few options. They invest heavily in gaining firm-specific skills and establishing ties to their communities, which limit their mobility. Behavioral economists have noted an "endowment effect" that further disadvantages employees: that is, employees are more likely to value what they have over what they might obtain in the open market. Employees may not realize it when they take a job (and may not negotiate accordingly), but they are likely to develop a strong attachment to a long-term employment relationship and community and to experience a deep sense of loss if it is disrupted.[31, 50]

According to critics, the cost of converting at-will workplaces to just cause workplaces would not be high because employers already maintain systems to justify discharges in case their lottery number comes up and they are one of the unlucky few forced to defend a discharge claim in court. Although few face judgments, none are immune from the possibility. Indeed, prompted by self-interested human resource professionals, employers significantly overestimate the potential legal liabilities they face when they lay off and terminate employees and respond by overinvesting in defensive personnel practices.[51] Unfortunately, the gains to employees are not equal to the costs incurred by employers. Why not redistribute this waste and invest in a just cause system that would provide fairness and limit damage awards?[52]

Critics of employment at will concede that a just cause requirement would somewhat reduce employers' flexibility, but they claim the imposition would be minimal. Other industrial democracies have not found it to be a huge burden on productivity. Why would employers need to discharge good employees to be efficient (unless for economic reasons and all of the just cause regimes being recommended permit discharges for business reasons)? After all, the merit system in government was created to make it more efficient. The popular view that long-term employment is less common in the modern global market economy seeems to be true for some segments of the workforce—for example, men—but not for others, like women. Notably, for government employees, job tenure increased from 1983 to 1996.[53, 54]

Defenses

Employment at will is defended primarily on the basis of market economy theories. Economically oriented writers argue that both parties have sufficient incentives to make the relationship work without the need for outside intervention. The employer has invested in recruiting and training and has a self-interest (profit) in keeping productive employees and not obtaining a reputation for treating employees unfairly. For these reasons, most employers create a norm of not firing workers without cause; they hesitate even to fire mediocre workers. Arbitrary discharges are costly and therefore rare. If lower-level supervisors discharge employees arbitrarily, management eventually will discover these abuses and correct them and management will be better at catching and correcting these abuses than outside decision makers would be.[55, 56]

Defenders of employment at will argue that most employees prefer higher wages to job security (which would increase employers' costs and reduce wages), and that is why employment at will dominates. Some groups, such as the young, prefer higher wages even more strongly. Given the rarity of arbitrary firings, at-will proponents believe employees make rational market choices when they opt for higher pay rather than just cause protection. Freed and Polsby found that an employee's chance of being arbitrarily fired was only 0.5769 percent.[57] Because there is no harm to the public from allowing this freedom of contract, defenders of at-will employment oppose paternalistic regulations, such as a just cause requirement, that would make both employers and employees worse off.[51, 58]

According to at-will supporters, the cost of providing a questionable "tenure good" to all employees would be extraordinarily high. In addition to the obvious direct administrative costs—the public's cost for courts, employees' costs for attorneys and arbitrators, and employers' costs for attorneys, arbitrators, and damage judgments—there are less obvious indirect costs: not terminating bad workers, giving severance pay to terminated workers to avoid lawsuits, and adding management layers to centralize and monitor hiring and firing decisions and keep records. Dertouzos and his colleagues estimated the direct and indirect costs of adopting the wrongful discharge exceptions in California. They found the direct costs were, at most, $200 per worker per year, but the indirect costs were 100 times greater.[59, 60] These costs may lead not only to lower wages, but also to higher unemployment because employers may be less willing to hire employees if there are restrictions on firing them.[59, 61]

Maintaining employers' flexibility to handle the "shirking problem" is often cited as a reason to keep employment at will. Employees, especially midcareer employees, have an incentive to shirk because they know an employer cannot easily replace them due to training and recruiting costs; they only have to perform better than a rookie to keep their jobs. Shirking is hard to detect and monitor, and some decisions are necessarily subjective. Employers need to be able to make these judgments without being second-guessed. A "just cause" or "good faith" requirement would intrude too deeply on employer discretion in this area.[32]

According to at-will supporters, just because critics can identify problems with the market, does not mean policy makers can reach normative conclusions about how the law should respond to them. For example, employees may misperceive their legal protections and make bad bargains when they agree to employment at will, but that does not mean a just cause rule should be imposed. Why not mandate a posted notice informing employees of their legal rights like workers' compensation law requires? And employees may misperceive how attached they will become to their jobs (the endowment effect) and fail to negotiate for job security, but that does not necessarily mean it is in society's best interest to give additional legal protection to job security. Job losses may have societal benefits, such as redirecting employees to emerging industries, as well as detrimental effects.[31]

Proponents of employment at will stress our need to be competitive in the new global market economy and to keep pace with technological change. To do this, they believe employers must be able to hire and fire employees quickly, without protracted legal battles. They blame Europe's stagnant economy in the 1980s and 1990s, at least in part, on its overprotective employment regulations and point out that many European countries have withdrawn worker protections in recent years to become more productive.[35, 62]

Reforms

In 1987, Montana became the first, and to date the only, state to enact a comprehensive law protecting at-will employees from arbitrary discharge. Under the act, an employer may not discharge a nonprobationary employee without good cause, which is defined as "reasonable, job-related grounds for dismissal based on a failure to satisfactorily perform job duties, disruption of the employers' operation, or other legitimate business reason." Employees must exhaust written internal procedures before filing suit, and must file suit within a year of discharge. In lieu of going to court, the parties may agree to binding arbitration. A wrongfully discharged employee can recover a maximum of four years' lost wages and fringe benefits, but must seek other employment to mitigate damages. Punitive damages are possible only if the employer engaged in "actual fraud or actual malice." No other damages are allowed.[63, 64]

Puerto Rico and the Virgin Islands, unincorporated territories of the United States, also provide statutory protection from arbitrary discharge. Enacted in 1976, Puerto Rico's statute provides that employees dismissed without just cause are entitled to severance pay based on length of service: one month's salary for 0–5 years, two months' salary for 5–15 years, three months' salary for 15 years, and an additional week for each additional year of service. The statute does not allow any other civil liability.[65] The Virgin Islands statute, adopted in 1986, allows wrongfully discharged employees to file an administrative complaint seeking reinstatement and back pay, or to file a lawsuit for compensatory and punitive damages.[66]

In 1991, the Uniform Law Commissioners passed the Model Employment Termination Act (META) by a vote of 39 to 11 of the state delegations. This quasi-governmental body, made up of lawyers, state judges, and legislators appointed by their state political processes, seeks to have state legislatures adopt uniform statutes in areas deemed desirable; the most famous example is the Uniform Commercial Code. META states, "An employer may not terminate the employment of an employee without good cause." "Good cause" may be based upon either employee conduct or business needs. Employers must provide terminated employees with a written statement of reasons for termination; then employees are given 180 days to demand arbitration. At arbitration, *the employee* must show *absence of good cause* for termination. A prevailing employee may be awarded reinstatement, or a scheduled severance pay (not to exceed 36 months of pay, reduced by likely earnings) plus attorney's fees and costs.[67] To date, no state has adopted META. Undaunted, one prominent scholar supporting the act encourages a long-term view: he notes that it took us 50 years longer than Germany to enact Social Security and predicts that by the year 2032 the vast majority of states, or preferably the U.S. Congress, will have seen the light.[22] Most observers see little chance for more timely change. As Professor Peter Cappelli of the Wharton School observed, "Issues like unions and protections for employees have become so politicized that it is almost impossible to have serious policy discussions about them . . . Unions and employers have each other in a political standoff on almost every issue associated with labor policy."[68]

Meanwhile, arbitration has provided some additional opportunities for nonunionized, private employees to challenge discharges. A number of employers have begun to require employees to arbitrate certain workplace disputes (and waive the right to litigate them) as a condition of employment. In 1991, in *Gilmer v. Interstate/Johnson Lane Corp.* (1991), the Supreme Court approved this practice; a stockbroker who signed an employment contract containing a mandatory arbitration clause was precluded from filing an age discrimination claim in court.[69] If the workplace is unionized, the union may be able to force employees to arbitrate discharge disputes (instead of litigating them in courts) by including such a requirement in a collective bargaining agreement (the lawfulness of this is less clear).[70] Of course, the arbitrator can only enforce the contract. Most agreements only require arbitration of "legal rights." In an at-will employment workplace, inevitably that means unlawful discrimination claims because there are few other "legal rights." Still, for claims that are covered, arbitration is cheaper, simpler, and faster; can be accomplished without an attorney if necessary; and may yield better results for employees.[22, 71] In 1995, the Task Force on Alternative Dispute Resolution in Employment issued *A Due Process Protocol for Mediation and Arbitration of Statutory Disputes Arising out of the Employment Relationship* in an attempt to ensure that arbitration procedures being imposed on employees were fair.[86]

Mediation of employment disputes also has increased in the past decade, prompted in part by the federal government passing laws directing or encouraging mediation in federal agencies. A 1995 Government Accounting Office study reported that 52 percent of large private employers have alternative dispute resolution programs for nonunion personnel. As with arbitration, mediation is usually restricted to alleged violations of legal rights—or, in other words, unlawful discrimination—although some major employers do offer mediation of an extensive jurisdictional scope (e.g., Paine Webber, Credit Suisse First Boston, and McGraw-Hill).[37]

Finally, many firms tout their adoption of in-house "due process" models. One study showed that internal disciplinary procedures for nonunion employees in private firms rose from about 5 percent in 1960–1965 to 45 percent in 1985.[72] Most companies' procedures consist of either an informal or formal "open-door" policy allowing aggrieved employees to approach anyone in management about their complaint. Few offer substantive guarantees. On the contrary, to avoid the judicially created "implied contract" exception, the trend has been for employers to remove promises of fair treatment from their written policies. Corporate "due process" mechanisms have proliferated, but they fail to live up to their promise in two crucial ways: they do not allow external, impartial resolution of grievances or provide substantive guarantees that discipline will be for just reasons.[37]

EXPANDING EMPLOYMENT AT WILL TO CLASSIFIED CIVIL SERVANTS: THE CONSTITUTIONAL ISSUES

Seeking greater flexibility in personnel management, government leaders at all levels in recent years have sought to expand the use of at-will employment in the public sector. These efforts have met with varying degrees of political and legal resistance. In Georgia, there was little opposition to the governor's plan to make all newly hired state employees at-will, but in Florida state employees and their union waged a fierce battle against removal of just cause protections from 16,300 state employees. In the courts, Florida state employees primarily sought refuge in constitutional protections. They challenged the state's "take back" of job security on constitutional grounds in three cases: *Croslin v. Bush* (2002),[73] *Florida Public Employees Council 79, A.F.S.C.M.E. v. Bush* (2002),[74] and *Muldrow v. Bush* (2002).[75] Not surprisingly, none of the plaintiffs prevailed on their constitutional claims. Courts around the nation have reviewed similar legislation and have almost always found it lawful.

Procedural Due Process and Taking Claims

Numerous courts have addressed whether removal of public employees' job security constitutes a taking of property without due process of law in violation of the Fifth and Fourteenth Amendments to the U.S. Constitution and similar provisions in state constitutions (see Table 3.1). Courts apply a two-part analysis to these procedural due process claims: first they ask whether plaintiffs have a legitimate property interest; if the answer to the first question is yes, then they ask whether plaintiffs received all the process that was due to them.

Almost all courts confronting the question have concluded that classified employees have a property interest in their continued employment that is implicated when just cause protection is removed through reclassification. Five federal courts and two state appellate courts have reported decisions with this holding (see Table 3.1). The exception to this trend appears to be Florida. In *Department of Corrections v. Florida Nurses Ass'n.* (1987), the Florida Supreme Court stated that a classified employee's "right to continued employment during good behavior" is different from a classified employee's right to expect "that career service, or any particular position therein, will exist for infinity." According to the court, the latter is not a "right" but "a mere hope" that policy makers will continue to bestow career service benefits on a position.(76) At least three trial courts in Florida have construed this language to mean that classified employees who are moved to unclassified status are not being deprived of a property interest.(77)

If, as most courts conclude, classified employees have a property interest that is implicated by reclassification, what process is due before it can be taken away? When an *individual* is deprived of a property interest, procedural due process requires individual notice and an opportunity to be heard. In *Gattis v. Gravett* (1986), the Eighth Circuit federal court handed down the rule that when *a legislature* extinguishes a property interest via legislation that affects *a general class of people*, "the legislative determination provides all the process that is due."(78) The rule announced in *Gattis* has been uniformly followed in subsequent cases (see Table 3.1).

At least since *Gattis*, it has been clear that legislatures can lawfully alter civil service statutes and remove employees' classified status. But do legislatures have to compensate employees for this deprivation of property under the "Takings Clause" of the Fifth Amendment to the U.S. Constitution? In *Wilkinson v. State Crime Laboratory Commission* (2002), the Rhode Island Supreme Court said, "Yes." The Rhode Island civil service statutes provided two tiers of protection for permanent civil servants: classified status and full status, which conferred even greater job protection. Removal of mere classified status might not have required compensation, but removal of full status did. The court held that "achieving full status under the merit system provides state-government employees with a property right *in the position and classification that they hold at the time they achieve full status*, entitling such employees to due-process and just-compensation protections against any attempted elimination or alteration of their property rights"(79) (emphasis added). To date, no other reported case appears to have addressed the issue of compensation (see Table 3.1).

Impairment of Contract

Article I Section 10 of the U.S. Constitution, and similar provisions in state constitutions, forbid the enactment of laws that impair the obligations of contracts. Several courts have addressed whether legislation removing employees' classified status violates these provisions. (See Table 3.1.) Two Georgia appellate courts found that civil service provisions did, indeed, create contracts between employees and the government; they focused on defining the terms of the contracts. In *Clark and Stephenson v. State Personnel Board* (1984), the Georgia Supreme Court found that the contract (statute) required the state to afford employees the rights in existence at the time they became classified. When plaintiffs became classified, the statute required notice of charges before demotion, so the state breached the contract when it demoted plaintiffs without notice.[80] In *DeClue v. City of Clayton* (2000), the Georgia Appellate Court found that the contract (personnel policies) explicitly did not create an "expectation of continued employment" and was subject to change, so there was no contract violation when the city adopted new policies.[81]

Substantive Due Process, Equal Protection Clause

The Fourteenth Amendment to the U.S. Constitution protects citizens from state action that is arbitrary and irrational or motivated by bad faith, and the Equal Protection Clause of this amendment prohibits states from treating classes of persons differently for arbitrary reasons. Legislation removing employees' classified status has been attacked for each of these reasons, never with success. Unless a fundamental right or a suspect class is involved, and so far they have not been, then the legislation only needs a rational basis to be upheld. Bad faith might be found if plaintiffs could prove legislation was targeted at them individually rather than at a class of employees, but even when the legislation affected only four individuals this claim failed. (See *Conway v. Searles* [1997], Table 3.1.)

EXPANDING EMPLOYMENT AT WILL TO CLASSIFIED CIVIL SERVANTS: REDUCING THE TRANSPARENCY OF GOVERNMENT BY ELIMINATING DUE PROCESS

Courts are unlikely to stop government employers from removing classified employees' job security. This battle will be fought in the policy arena. One issue that should be part of the conversation is the impact that removing job security will have on the transparency and, as a result, the accountability of government. At-will employment will significantly reduce the amount of information available to members of society about the operation of their government. Based on experience in the private sector, it should be expected that at-will public employees will be less likely to question workplace decisions, to disclose workplace conduct that appears to violate the public trust, or even to talk to outsiders. Although at-will public employees enjoy some protections for their speech that at-will private employees do not, for example the First Amendment and public employee whistle-blower statutes, these protections suffer from the same infirmities as the antiretaliation provisions that purport to safeguard at-will employees' speech in the private sector. The doctrines are quite narrow (the First Amendment protects speech of "public concern" that is not "disruptive"; Florida's public employee whistle-blower statue protects signed, written reports of misfeasance or malfeasance sent to the inspector general). And they require employees to access attorneys, file court actions, endure long delays, and meet difficult proof requirements while they are out of work. The doctrines of sovereign immunity, qualified immunity, and exhaustion of administrative remedies may further limit government employees' remedies. In sum, these inaccessible and unreliable remedies will not make at-will government employees confident they can speak out about questionable agency conduct and keep their jobs.

Removing job security will diminish the information available about the performance of governmental agencies in another way—by eliminating due process hearings. Hearings provide occasional opportunities for lawmakers, agency heads, and citizens (usually via newspapers) to peek inside agency workplaces and see how the government's work is being accomplished. For example, in *Declet v. Department of Children and Family Services* (2000), a child abuse investigator appealed his discharge for lying (he was dismissed, along with others, after an abused child receiving protective services died). His discharge was upheld, but evidence adduced at the hearing revealed these "facts": Declet's caseload was unmanageably high, he never received essential training, he did not have a computer that functioned, and he frequently had to babysit abused children in his office while he worked because there were no facilities for them.[82] Declet did not alert the *Miami Herald* or the inspector general to these serious problems, but he did disclose them to the administrative law judge at his due process hearing. And judicial facts enjoy high credibility, so when they reveal operational problems like these, they are often relied upon—by agency heads seeking to hold managers and supervisors accountable, and by citizens seeking to hold government leaders accountable.

Already in Florida there are fewer Career Service "due process" hearings. From 1999 to 2004, the number of Career Service appeals adjudicated (not including withdrawals, dismissals, and settlements) declined as follows: 226, 142, 145, 98, 107, 106.[83] This downward slope likely reflects, at least in part, the diminished population of Career Service employees due to the governor's initiatives to downsize, privatize, outsource, and reclassify. In December 1999 there were 110,952 Career Service employees; in December 2004 there were 85,809.[84, 85]

Finally, removing just cause protection from public employees reduces access to information about government's managerial behavior in ways Kafka readers would admire. On January 6, 2005, the *Tallahassee Democrat* reported that the governor fired the secretary of the Department of Elder Affairs, an at-will employee, after a "quick, secretive investigation into allegations of sexual harassment." Without warning, the secretary was ordered not to return to his office, to turn in his keys, and not to talk to anyone. He was informed that others would pack up his personal belongings. He was not told what the allegations were or who made them. No investigative report or witness statements were furnished to him (or to the reporter who requested them) because "*nothing in the investigation was written down*."[87] Career service employees receive notice of the allegations against them and an opportunity to refute them, but at-will employees receive only a one- or two-sentence letter stating, "Your services are no longer needed." Undoubtedly, many employees are guilty and know exactly what they did, but some are innocent (experience proves that mistakes happen) and some are not as guilty as it seems (e.g., supervisors allowed other employees to do the same thing without punishing them). These unfortunate employees have nothing but smoke and fog to challenge. And in the public eye, as stories like these become more common, state government is gaining a reputation for being a secretive, unfair, and unkind employer.

CONCLUSION

In both the public and private sectors, the need to ensure fairness to individual employees has not been seen as persuasive enough reason to grant American employees just cause protection. Job security has been granted only when other "public goods" have been furthered. Eradicating patronage was the reason used to justify merit principles in the public sector, but policy makers may no longer see this as necessary or sufficient to outweigh other objectives (concerns about the return of patronage were peremptorily dismissed by lawmakers in Florida). One issue that commentators should address is the detrimental effect that removing public employees' job security will have on government's transparency. Many Americans already distrust their government; allowing agency heads to fire civil servants with obscurely worded pink slips instead of open, fair hearings will only make this worse.

Table 3.1 Reported Federal and State Court Decisions Addressing the Constitutionality of Removing Civil Service Protections

Case Name and Facts	*Can Classified Status Be Removed?*	*Legal Issues and Court's Rationale*
Rea v. Matteucii, 121 F.3d 483 (9th Cir. 1997) Nevada legislature moved the hearing officer position from classified to unclassified service. A month later, plaintiff was fired without cause.	Yes	*Procedural Due Process Claim*. Plaintiff had a property interest in her continued employment as a hearing officer. The state deprived her of a property interest when it reclassified her position, but the legislative process provided all the process that was due.
McMurtray v. Holladay, 11 F.3d 499 (5th Cir. 1993) Mississippi legislature exempted all personnel actions in one department from state personnel procedures for a year. It also eliminated all existing department positions and created new ones. Twenty-nine classified employees were not rehired in the new positions.	Yes	*Procedural Due Process Claim*. Plaintiffs had a property interest that was extinguished by the act, but the legislative process provided all the process that was due. If the act was a "taking" pursuant to the Fifth Amendment, plaintiffs' claim for just compensation would be barred by the Eleventh Amendment (a citizen may not sue his own state in federal court).
Gattis v. Gravett, 806 F.2d 778 (8th Cir. 1986) Arkansas legislature passed an act moving majors from classified to unclassified service. The sheriff fired the plaintiffs six weeks later without notice or a hearing.	Yes	*Procedural Due Process Claim*. Plaintiffs had a property interest in continued employment in their positions. The legislature deprived plaintiffs of a property interest by removing them from classified service, but the legislative process provided all the process that was due.

Conway v. Searles, 954 F.Supp. 756 (D. Vt. 1997) Vermont legislature passed an act transferring four high-level managers from classified to exempt status.	Yes	*Procedural Due Process Claim*. Plaintiffs had a property interest in their right to just cause employment, but the legislative process provided all the process that was due. *Substantive Due Process Claim*. The legislature had a rational reason for enacting the statute. The statute was not arbitrary or irrational.
Corrections Officers Local 419, AFSCME v. Weld, 768 F.Supp. 397 (D. Mass. 1991) The Massachusetts state budget transferred control of 300 correctional officers who were civil service employees to the sheriff of Suffolk County and removed them from coverage of the civil service law. About 150 employees had permanent status.	Yes	*Procedural Due Process Claim*. The plaintiffs had a property interest, but the legislative process provided all the process that was due. *Substantive Due Process Claim*. The legislation had a rational basis and was not arbitrary or irrational.
Wilkinson v. State Crime Laboratory Commission, 788 A.2d 1129 (R.I. 2002) R.I. had a two-tier civil service system: classified status, and full-status (after 20 years service) that gave even greater job protection. The plaintiff had full-status when a state law moved his position to unclassified service and he was terminated.	No	*Procedural Due Process and Taking Claim*. Full-status gave plaintiff a property interest in his continued employment. He could not be moved to an unclassified position unless the state provided just compensation for the taking of his property interest. *Statutory Interpretation*. The statute did not clearly and explicitly say it was retroactive, so it operated prospectively and only affected employees who had not obtained full-status before the law was passed.

--*continued*

Table 2.1 ***(continued)***
Reported Federal and State Court Decisions Addressing the Constitutionality of Removing Civil Service Protections

Case Name and Facts	*Can Classified Status Be Removed?*	*Legal Issues and Court's Rationale*
Department of Corrections v. Florida. Nurses Ass'n., 508 So.2d 317 (Fla. 1987) Florida legislature passed a law removing state-employed physicians, nurses and attorneys from the career service system and placing them in an exempt category. The law applied to employees who had achieved permanent status in the career service system and to those who had not.	Yes	*Procedural Due Process Claim.* Plaintiffs did not claim violation of procedural due process rights, but the court said "any expectation that career service, or any particular position therein, will exist for infinity is at most a mere hope" implying there was no property interest in remaining a classified employee. *Substantive Due Process and Equal Protection Claims.* The legislature had a rational basis for the legislation. It was not arbitrary or capricious. There was no suggestion that the statute was a bad-faith subterfuge to discharge or deny rights to an employee or group of employees. No fundamental right or suspect class was involved.
Clark and Stephenson v. State Personnel Board, 314 S.E.2d 658 (Ga. 1984) Georgia legislature passed an Act removing majors from classified service. Two majors were demoted to captain, a position still in the classified service.	No	*Impairment of Contract Claim.* The Merit System Act created a constitutionally protected contract between classified employees and the state. The legislature can move classified positions to unclassified, but parties to the contract keep the rights they had under the Act at the time they became classified. The Act governing plaintiffs required prior written notice before a demotion. Because plaintiffs did not receive prior written notice, the demotions were invalid.

DeClue v. City of Clayton, 540 S.E.2d 675 (Ga. Ct. App. 2000) The city's employment manual said employees did not have a property interest and were at-will. However, it also listed grounds for disciplinary action (implying discharge would be for cause), required notice of charges and progressive discipline, and set forth appeal rights. The city removed the latter provisions from the manual. Plaintiff was fired without notice or a hearing.	Yes	*Procedural Due Process Claim*. If plaintiff had a property interest in continued employment with the city, he received all the process that was due because he had notice of the changes and the opportunity to voice his opinion about them. *Impairment of Contract Claim*. The city created a contract with DeClue when it adopted personnel policies providing discharge only for cause, but the policies said they were subject to change so no vested right in their retention was created.

ACKNOWLEDGMENTS

The author would like to thank Paolo Annino, Jim Bowman, and Charlene Luke for their helpful editorial comments, and Ana Eliza Friere and Mary McCormick for their skillful research assistance.

ENDNOTES

1. Ruberg, Charles, personal communication April 23, 1984.
2. Blackstone, William, 1 *Commentaries* 4130.
3. Wood, Horace G., *Master and Servant,* 2nd ed., § 136 (1877).
4. Feinman, J. M., The development of the employment at will rule, *American Journal of Legal History*, 1, 20, 118, 1976.
5. *Martin v. New York Life Ins. Co.*, 42 N.E. 416, 417 (N.Y. 1895).
6. *Payne v. Western & All. R.R.*, 81 Tenn. 507, 518 (1884).
7. Morris, A. P., Exploding myths: An empirical and economic reassessment of the rise of employment at-will, *Missouri Law Review*, 59, 679, 1994.
8. Estlund, C. L., Wrongful discharge protections in an at-will world, *Texas Law Review*, 74, 1655, 1996.
9. *News: Bureau of Labor Statistics*, U.S. Department of Labor Bureau of Statistics, Washington, DC, 2004, 1–11, retrieved January 31, 2006, from http://www.bls.gov/news.release/archives/union2_01212004.pdf.
10. Schwab, S. J., Wrongful discharge law and the search for third-party effects, *Texas Law Review*, 74, 1943, 1996.
11. Protecting employees at will against wrongful discharge: The public policy exception, *Harvard Law Review*, 96 (June), 1931, 1983.
12. National Labor Relations Act, 29 U.S.C. §§ 141-169 (2000).
13. Fair Labor Standards Act of 1938, 29 U.S.C. § 215(a)(3)(2000).
14. Clean Air Act of 1963, 42 U.S.C. § 7622(a)(2000).
15. Title VII of the Civil Rights Act of 1964, 42 U.S.C. § 2000e-2(a)(2000).
16. Age Discrimination in Employment Act of 1967, 92 U.S.C. § 623(d)(2000).
17. Pregnancy Discrimination Act, 42 U.S.C. § 2000e (k)(2000).
18. Americans with Disabilities Act, 42 U.S.C. §§ 12101-12213(2000).
19. Immigration Reform and Control Act, 8 U.S.C. (2000).
20. 9A *Labor Relations Reporter* (BNA) 505:51 (2004).
21. Schanzenbach, M., Exceptions to employment at will: Raising firing costs or enforcing life-cycle contracts? *American Law & Economics Review*, 5 (Fall), 470, 2003.
22. St. Antoine, T. J., Labor and employment law in two transitional decades, *Brandeis Law Journal*, 5 (Spring), 495, 2004.
23. *Wooley v. Hoffman-La Roche, Inc.*, 491 A.2d 1257, 1264 (N.J., 1985).
24. Summers, C. W., Employment at will in the United States: The divine right of employers, *University of Pennsylvania Journal of Labor and Employment Law*, 3, 65, 2000.
25. Lillard, M. C., Fifty jurisdictions in search of a standard: The covenant of good faith and fair dealing in the employment context, *Missouri Law Review*, 57 (Fall), 1233, 1992.
26. *Monge v. Beebe Rubber Co.*, 316 A.2d 549, 551 (1974).

27. *Cleary v. American Airlines, Inc.*, 111 Cal. App. 3d 443, 454 (Cal. Ct. App. 1980).
28. *Foley v. Interactive Data Corp.*, 765 P.2d 373 (Cal. 1988).
29. *Fortune v. Nat'l Cash Register Co.*, 364 N.E.2d 1251 (Mass. 1977).
30. Burke, D., and Little, B., At-will employment: Just let it go, *Journal of Individual Employment Rights*, 10(2), 119, 2002–2003.
31. Issacharoff, S., The difficult path from observation to prescription, *New York University Law Review*, 77, 36, 2002.
32. Schwab, S. J., Life-cycle justice: Accommodating just cause and employment at will, *Michigan Law Review*, 92 (Oct.), 8, 1993.
33. St. Antoine, T. J., A seed germinates: Unjust discharge reform heads toward full flower, *Nebraska Law Review*, 67, 56, 1988.
34. Peck, C. J., Unjust discharges from employment: A necessary change in the law, *Ohio State Law Journal*, 40, 1, 1979.
35. Hepple, B., European rules on dismissal law? *Comparative Labor Law and Policy Journal*, 18, 204, 1997.
36. Maltby, L. L., Private justice: Employment arbitration and civil rights, *Columbia Human Rights Law Review*, 30 (Fall), 29, 1998.
37. Berger, V., Employment mediation in the twenty-first century: Challenges in a changing environment, *University of Pennsylvania Journal of Labor and Employment Law*, 5 (Spring), 487, 2003.
38. Estlund, C. L., Free speech and due process in the workplace, *Indiana Law Journal*, 71, 101, 1995.
39. Pascale, R. T., and Athos, A. G., *The Art of Japanese Management: Applications for American Executives*, Simon & Schuster, New York, 1981.
40. Foulkes, F. K., Large non-unionized employers, in *U.S. Industrial Relations 1950-1980: A Critical Assessment,* Industrial Relations Research Association, Madison, WI, 1981, 129.
41. Roehling, M. V., and Winters, D., Job security rights: The effects of specific policies and practices on the evaluation of employers, *Employee Rights and Responsibilities Journal*, 12, 1, 2000.
42. Devine, D. J., and Dunford, B. B., Employment at will and employment discharge: A justice perspective on legal actions following termination, *Personnel Psychology*, 51(4), 903, 1998.
43. Wayland, R. F., Clay, J. M., and Payne, S. L., Employment at-will statements: Perceptions of job applicants, *International Journal of Manpower*, 14, 2222, 1993.
44. Schwoere, C., and Rosen, B., Effects of employment at-will policies and compensation policies on corporate image and job pursuit intentions, *Journal of Applied Psychology*, 74, 653, 1989.
45. Verkerke, J. H., An empirical perspective on indefinite term employment contracts: Resolving the just cause debate, *Wisconsin Law Review*, 838, 1995.
46. Roehling, M. V., The good cause norm in employment relations: Empirical evidence and policy implications, *Employee Rights and Responsibilities Journal*, 14, 91, 2002.
47. Estlund, C. L., How wrong are employees about their rights, and why does it matter? *New York University Law Review*, 77, 6, 2002.
48. Kim, P. T., Norms, learning, and law: Exploring the influences on workers' legal knowledge, *University of Illinois Law Review*, 447, 1999.

49. Sunstein, C. R., Rights, minimal terms, and solidarity: A comment, *University of Chicago Law Review*, 51, 1041, 1984.
50. Korobkin, R., The status quo bias and contract default rules, *Cornell Law Review*, 83, 608, 1998.
51. Edelman, L. B., Abraham, S. E., and Erlanger, H. S., Professional construction of the law: The inflated threat of wrongful discharge, *Law & Society Review*, 26, 47, 1992.
52. Maltby, L. L., The projected economic impact of the model employment termination act, *The Annals of the American Academy of Political and Social Science*, 536 (Nov.), 103, 1994.
53. Stone, K. V. W., Legal regulation of the changing employment contract, *Cornell Journal of Law and Public Policy*, 13, 563, 2004.
54. *Employee Tenure in the Mid-1990s*, U.S.D.L. 97-25, Current Population Survey Publications, 1997, retrieved January 31, 2006, from http://www.bls.census.gov/cps/pub/tenure_0296.htm.
55. Rock, E. B., and Wachter, M. L., The enforceability of norms and the employment relationship, *University of Pennsylvania Law Review*, 144, 1913, 1996.
56. Posner, R. A. *Economic Analysis of Law*, 6th ed., Aspen, New York, 1992.
57. Freed, M. G., and Polsby, D. D., Just cause for termination rules and economic efficiency, *Emory Law Journal*, 38, 1097, 1989.
58. Epstein, R. A., In defense of the contract at will, *University of Chicago Law Review*, 51, 947, 1984.
59. Dertouzos, J. N., and Karoly, L. A., Labor-market responses to employer liability, RAND, Institute for Civil Justice, Santa Monica, CA, 1992.
60. Dertouzos, J. N., Holland, E. and Ebener, P., The legal and economic consequences of wrongful termination, RAND, Institute for Civil Justice, Santa Monica, CA, 1998.
61. Autor, D. H., Donahue, J. J., and Schwab, S. J., The costs of wrongful-discharge laws, MIT, 2005, retrieved January 31, 2006, from http://econ-www.mit.edu/faculty/download_pdf.php?id=407.
62. France abolished the requirement that public authorities give prior authorization for economic dismissals; Belgium, Germany, Sweden, Spain, and Italy granted employers greater flexibility to use fixed-term contracts; Germany, Portugal, and Spain relaxed or removed restrictions on the use of temporary work agencies; Belgium reduced the notice employers must give discharged employees; Germany and the United Kingdom removed some categories of workers from protection from unfair dismissal; and Belgium and the United Kingdom reduced legal support for workers' representatives. Hepple, B., European rules on dismissal law? *Comparative Labor Law and Policy Journal*, 18, 204, 1997.
63. Montana wrongful discharge from Employment Act of 1987, *Mont. Code Ann.* §§ 39-2-901 to 39-2-915 (2003).
64. Tomkins, J., Legislating the employment relationship: Montana's wrongful-discharge law, *Employee Relations Law Journal*, 14, 387, 1998.
65. 29 P.R. Laws Ann. Tit. 29, §§ 185a (2003).
66. V.I. Code Ann. Tit. 24, §§ 76-79 (2003).
67. Model Employment Termination Act, 7A U.L.A. 428.
68. Cappelli, P., Comment: What will the future of employment policy look like? *Industrial and Labor Relations Review*, 55, 724, 2002.
69. *Gilmer v. Interstate/Johnson Lane Corp.*, 500 U.S. 20 (1991).

70. *Wright v. Universal Maritime Serv. Corp.*, 525 U.S. 70 (1998).
71. Several studies show that employees prevail more often in arbitration than in court. The American Arbitration Association found a winning rate of 64 percent for arbitral claimants; by contrast, claimants' success rates in separate surveys of federal courts (14.9 percent) and EEOC cases (16.8 percent) were much lower (although these figures omit pretrial settlements). St. Antoine, T. J., Labor and employment law in two transitional decades, *Brandeis Law Journal*, 5 (Spring), 495, 2004.
72. Sutton, J. R., et al., The legalization of the workplace, *American Journal of Sociology*, 99 (4), 944, 1994.
73. *Croslin v. Bush* (Case No. 02-20189-CIV-HUCK)(S.D. Fla., Sept. 3, 2002).
74. *Florida Public Employees Council 79, A.F.S.C.M.E. v. Bush* (Case No 01-1900)(Fla. Cir. Ct., Jan. 22, 2002).
75. *Muldrow v. Bush* (Case No. 4:01-CV-167-RH)(N.D. Fla., April 25, 2002).
76. *Department of Corrections v. Florida Nurses Ass'n.*, 508 So.2d 317, 320 (Fla. 1987).
77. *Croslin v. Bush*; *Weglarz v. Metropolitan Dade County* (Case No. 97-1876-CIV-DAVIS)(S.D. Fla., Dec. 12, 1997); and *Wilson v. Metropolitan Dade County* (Case No. 93-0076-CIV-MORENO)(S.D. Fla., Nov. 22, 1993).
78. *Gattis v. Gravett*, 806 F.2d 778,781 (8th Cir. 1986).
79. *Wilkinson v. State Crime Laboratory Commission*, 788 A.2d 1129, 1140 (R.I. 2002).
80. *Clark and Stephenson v. State Personnel Board*, 314 S.E.2d 658 (Ga. 1984).
81. *Declue v. City of Clayton*, 540 S.E.2d 675 (Ga. Ct. App. 2000).
82. *Declet v. Department of Children and Families*, 15 FCSR 152 (2000), 776 So.2d 1000 (2001).
83. *Career Service Report Month Ending June 30, 1999*, Florida Department of Management Services, Public Employees Relations Commission, Tallahassee, 1999; *Career Service Report Month Ending June 30, 2000*, Florida Department of Management Services, Public Employees Relations Commission, Tallahassee, 2000; *Career Service Report Month Ending June 30, 2001*, Florida Department of Management Services, Public Employees Relations Commission, Tallahassee, 2001; *Career Service Report Month Ending June 30, 2002*, Florida Department of Management Services, Public Employees Relations Commission, Tallahassee, 2002; *Career Service Report Month Ending June 30, 2003*, Florida Department of Management Services, Public Employees Relations Commission, Tallahassee, 2003; and *Career Service Report Month Ending June 30, 2004*, Florida Department of Management Services, Public Employees Relations Commission, Tallahassee, 2004.
84. *State of Florida Annual Workforce Report, January through December 1999*, Florida Department of Management Services, Division of Human Resource Management, Tallahassee, 2000, http://dms.myflorida.com/dms/workforce/human_resource_management/human_resource_programs_and_information/reports.
85. *State of Florida Annual Workforce Report, January through December 2004*, Florida Department of Management Services, Division of Human Resource Management, Tallahassee, 2005, http://dms.myflorida.com/dms/workforce/human_resource_management/human_resource_programs_and_information/reports.

86. *A Due Process Protocol for Mediation and Arbitration of Statutory Disputes Arising out of the Emploiyment Relationship*, May 9, 1995, retrieved July 10, 2006 from http://www.ilr.cornell.edu/alliance/resources/Guide/Due_process_protocol_empdispute.html.
87. Cotterell, B., State Elder Affairs Chief Fired, *Tallahassee Democrat,* 1B, January 26, 2005.

PART II

IS PATRONAGE A PROBLEM?

4

BRINGING BACK BOSS TWEED: COULD AT-WILL EMPLOYMENT WORK IN STATE AND LOCAL GOVERNMENT AND, IF SO, WHERE?

Robert Maranto
Villanova University

Jeremy Johnson
Brown University

INTRODUCTION

Bureaucracies at all levels of government are seeking to reform and even eliminate their traditional civil service systems. Since 1996 Georgia has ended tenure for new hires and for those promoted to management positions, so far to mixed reviews.[1] Florida has eliminated tenure for middle- and high-level managers.[2]

In the U.S. government the new Department of Homeland Security and, since its latest reauthorization bill passed in late 2004, the Defense Department have begun the process of developing new personnel systems with reduced civil service protections and with broad banding, a practice that increases management discretion over pay.[3] The Defense Department personnel reforms, put in the annual budget authorization in the fall of 2004, received relatively little attention despite their revolutionary quality. As a Washington journalist who covers the U.S. civil service commented, "[I]t's really just a matter of time before this goes government-wide. There's not a lot of people left outside the unions who think the old [personnel] system was worth anything" (anonymous personal phone conversation, April 7, 2005). When the final regulations are written, employees will likely be essentially at-will, and managers will have the discretion to determine pay through performance.[4]

This chapter summarizes why it may make sense to end tenure in the U.S. civil service, outlining arguments presented by the lead author in numerous works.[5] However, all administrative reform is fundamentally *political*, and the very political factors that make reforming the U.S. civil service system relatively low risk make reforming most state and local civil service systems relatively risky. What works in Washington may not play in Peoria, much less Philadelphia.

The second part of this chapter presents hypotheses predicting which states can reform their civil service systems to end tenure and increase managerial discretion with relatively little risk of large-scale spoils-based patronage, and conversely which states cannot. Factors hypothesized to influence these results are state party organization, state-level corruption, the capacity of state government bureaucracies, media scrutiny, and minority party strength. Finally, states will be ranked for their preconditions for such successful civil service reform.

THE CASE FOR REFORMING THE U.S. CIVIL SERVICE

As the lead author has argued for some years,[6] a case can be made for reforming the U.S. civil service system to end civil service tenure. Currently, tenure protects significant numbers of "turkeys" who do little or no work, and are often disruptive. Managers cannot separate low performers without investing enormous time. Accordingly, managers work around low performers, or place them in "turkey farms" where little work is expected or done. This costs little monetarily, but undermines respect for the public service and damages morale among the vast majority of servants who serve the people.[7]

Civil service tenure once made sense. Tenure was originally developed mainly to protect the civil service from the depredations of the political parties. In the 1800s, before the Pendleton Act and to some degree thereafter, citizens could not normally gain U.S. civil service jobs without at least a recommendation from a politician. New hires were typically required to pay assessments (often up to 5 percent of their salary) to the party in power, or to individual politicians. Actual civil service turnover when a new political party won the presidency was low, because politicians realized that disrupting the civil service was not a winning electoral strategy. Still, assessments and the need for political credentials tarnished the reputation of the public service.[8]

Fortunately, that Washington is long gone. Before the 1950s, U.S. political appointments were primarily to help the incumbent party win elections as "spoils" patronage, reflecting the views of 19th-century Tammany Hall boss William Marcy (aka Boss Tweed), who was famed for saying, "To the victor goes the spoils."[9] Accordingly, political appointees concentrated in such organizations as the U.S. Postal Service, where relatively little expertise was required, and where appointees could help the incumbent party win elections. In sharp contrast, since at least the Eisenhower administration (and arguably since Franklin D. Roosevelt) political appointments have served to put the president's policy imprint on an ever growing U.S. government; accordingly, presidents have increasingly focused more on the *expertise* of political appointees than on their political credentials.[10] Appointment power has moved from the political parties to the White House.[11] Although spoils and policy patronage are often linked together, the two are fundamentally different. Spoils patronage can be considered a form of corruption, used by parties to help assure reelection. In contrast, policy patronage plays a vital role in keeping government bureaucracies accountable and assuring executive leadership, in accord with American democratic traditions.

On the macro level, increases in the numbers of political appointees have been driven largely by growth among Washington policy makers generally. As Maranto[12] points out, from the early 1960s to the early 1990s the number of presidential political appointees roughly doubled, but congressional staffs more than *tripled*. Washington-based interest groups and media outlets increased even more rapidly, and political appointees spend much of their time representing the president to these and other political actors. In short, the numbers of Washington political appointees have increased not for patronage reasons, but because the amount of *political work* has gone up exponentially.

On the agency level, presidents make more political appointments to controversial agencies. Highly technocratic agencies with missions the two parties agree on (e.g., the Nuclear Regulatory Commission, the Patent Office, the Federal Bureau of Investigation, and until recently the Central Intelligence Agency) have few or no political appointees. Since the 1960s, regulatory and social welfare agencies have become controversial, leading presidents to seek increased control over their policy making by increasing the numbers of political appointees. There are, after all, Democratic and

Republican ways to do education, healthcare reform, affirmative action, workplace safety, and environmental protection.[13]

Fortunately, whereas controversy has increased, corruption and quasi-corruption (such as spoils appointments) have not. Since the 1960s Washington politics has become more ideological: traditional material-based politics have receded, representing changes in the broader society.[14] This decreases the likelihood that presidents will use executive branch jobs for material rewards; rather, political posts are for policy. Indeed, evidence suggests that U.S. political appointees are ideological, dedicated to their visions of the public interest.[15]

A more ideological Washington has meant a more conflicted Washington.[16] Political appointees and their management of the executive branch have received ever greater scrutiny from the media, interest groups, and Congress. This shift has been reinforced by increasingly complex and pervasive ethics rules for U.S. officials, a new legal regime used by interest groups, the media, congress members, and prosecutors (special and otherwise) to attack wayward political appointees.[17] Washington has become a "hyperpluralistic" environment in which constant scrutiny and conflict make it difficult to get anything done.[18] Or, as one successful political appointee recalled, for years the official started each day by grabbing the *Washington Post* as soon as it arrived at 5:30 A.M., "and I looked at the front page and looked at the government affairs page and prayed to God my name wasn't there" (anonymous personal phone conversation, November 18, 1999). Further, the typical political appointee works so much—typically 70 hours a week—doing his or her political work as to leave little time and energy for managing, much less micro-managing, lower-level agency personnel decisions.[19]

In short, a moralistic political culture combines with external political pressures to preclude widespread reward-based patronage in the U.S. civil service. As the civil service system grows more flexible, this will likely make it possible for career managers to hold their employees accountable; it will not significantly increase the likelihood that political appointees will raid agencies for patronage jobs. The U.S. civil service is and will remain a policy machine, not a patronage machine. But would the same hold for state and local public bureaucracies?

WHY WHAT WORKS IN WASHINGTON MAY NOT PLAY IN PHILADELPHIA: A POLITICAL THEORY OF STATE PUBLIC PERSONNEL REFORM

There are some good reasons to reform state and local bureaucracies to end civil service tenure and generally increase managerial discretion. As such writer-practitioners as Anechiarico and Jacobs,[20] Savas,[21] and

Lasseter[22] point out, state and local civil service systems move very slowly. They keep government from hiring the best and make it unduly difficult to separate low performers. Indeed, Hamilton[23] reports that after court orders forced Chicago to move from a spoils system to a merit system, public managers faced

> time delays in filling vacant positions and [requiring] additional time and paperwork on the part of hiring officials. Nonpatronage systems are not designed to attract the best and the brightest but rather to keep patronage-oriented applicants out.

Although reform did end patronage hiring in Chicago—no mean feat—Hamilton fears that "antipatronage systems are an overreaction to past excesses of patronage."[24] Seeking a middle ground, he suggests that reformers rely less on complex civil service processes to defeat spoils; instead "[u]nions, court decisions, the media, and public demands for quality public services should mitigate the excesses of patronage."[25] But in what cases might these prove insufficient protections of the integrity and capability of the public service? As discussed above, recent increases in the number of Washington political appointees seemingly have not increased corruption, but this might not hold in all states and localities. Where would civil service reform pose risks?

As explained above, civil service reform is fundamentally political; thus successful reform depends on political factors. The very idealism of the national political class, combined with scrutiny from an active news media and from the opposing party, limits the degree to which national politicians can use civil service jobs as spoils. Indeed, the most notable spoils scandals occurred in state and local governments with less moralistic political cultures, less political competition, and less media scrutiny: thus, arguments for civil service reform lose much of their force when applied to state and (especially) local governments.[26]

All this suggests several independent variables likely to preclude patronage in a reformed public service. These may be categorized as *patronage demand variables*, *political environment variables*, and *bureaucratic capacity variables*.

Patronage Demand Variables

As Fenton,[27] Elazar,[28] Mayhew,[29] and Barone and Cohen[30] report, some state political cultures tolerate corruption. In states with an individualistic political culture, the political class sees politics as a series of individual and intergroup struggles for material gain: individualistic politicians lack scruples about using government jobs to reward friends, and indeed voters accept patronage and corruption. Such tendencies may be reinforced by the relatively nonideological character of state and local politics. Although there are Democratic and Republican ways to regulate the environment, there are not yet Democratic and Republican ways to pave roads or collect trash. In contrast to individualistic states, voters and political elites in moralistic states are relatively intolerant of such uses of public resources for private purposes. Laws in moralistic states reflect these values. Accordingly, it will be relatively risky to the integrity and capacity of public service to make civil service systems more flexible in states that are relatively tolerant of corruption.

A related demand variable is the nature of the state party organizations. Some state parties are "machines" held together by material incentives such as patronage. Others are less hierarchical, united by purposive (idealistic) incentives rather than patronage.[31] Reforming civil service in states with machine parties will hold greater risks to the public service.

Political Environmental Variables

In politics, sunlight is the best disinfectant. Yet sunlight depends on a news media with the capacity to report efforts by politicians to use the public service for patronage. Local TV news stations are notoriously ineffective investigators,[32] but major newspapers do better. They may inhibit state political elites from using widespread patronage. Accordingly, reforming civil service in states without major newspapers will hold greater risks.

Secondly, some states have an active two-party system, whereas others are essentially one-party. Ideally, a strong minority party that seriously contests elections and scrutinizes government helps assure that civil service reform is used to improve public service rather than to install patronage; thus, reforming civil service in one-party states will hold greater risks to the public service. Notably, the most significant departures from the merit system in the U.S. government in the 20th century took place during the early and middle New Deal period, a time of one-party domination in Washington.[33]

Bureaucratic Capacity

Finally, some bureaucracies are simply easier to "raid" for patronage than others. Within the U.S. civil service, the strong organization cultures, dedication to mission, and administrative capacity of defense agencies make them relatively immune to patronage demands. The Pentagon, the U.S. Forest Service, and other well-regarded public organizations have the legitimacy to deny significant patronage demands. Until at least the 1990s, however, this could not be said of the U.S. Office of Personnel Management, nor of the U.S. Federal Emergency Management Agency.[34] Even in an at-will employment environment, state and local politicians will not attempt to use for patronage high-capacity public agencies; indeed, the career executives of such agencies may have the political clout to resist such demands. Thus, ironically, reforming civil service in states with relatively less effective public bureaucracies will hold greater risks.

THE BEST AND WORSE STATES FOR CIVIL SERVICE REFORM

This section presents measures of independent variables, ranking states. It culminates in two scales predicting which states should and should not reform their civil service systems to allow more flexibility generally and at-will employment in particular.

Patronage Demand Variables

Corruption

Perhaps the key variable is whether a state has a known culture of and tolerance for political corruption. In more corrupt states, tenure protection matters more for effective governance. Unfortunately, there is no ideal way to measure political corruption. Researchers cannot ask elected officials or lobbyists how many corrupt transactions they have engaged in. Such measures as the percentage of public officials indicted are similarly suspect, because some prosecutors are more aggressive than others and because state laws vary. Perhaps the best measure of state-level corruption is that of Boylan and Long,[35] who surveyed state house reporters about corruption in state government. The *corruption* measure ranges from 1.5 to 5.5, with a mean of 3.52 and a standard deviation of 1.16. As Table 4.1 shows, *corruption* has high face validity, with Colorado, the Dakotas, Maine, and Minnesota particularly clean in contrast to the most corrupt states: Rhode Island, Louisiana, and New Mexico. In accord with Fenton,[36] Minnesota, Wisconsin, and Michigan rate low on corruption, contrasting Ohio, Indiana, and Illinois. Unfortunately, Boylan and Long cannot rank Massachusetts, New Hampshire, and New Jersey. Given the import of this variable, these states have been assigned the mean corruption measures of their nearest and most similar neighbors: thus Massachusetts is ranked midway between Connecticut and Rhode Island, New Hampshire between Maine and Vermont, and New Jersey between Pennsylvania and New York. (In each case, the neighboring states themselves have similar corruption rankings.)

Table 4.1 State Corruption Scores

Rank[a]	*State*	*Score*
1–10		
1	Colorado	1.5
1	North Dakota	1.5
1	South Dakota	1.5
4	Maine	1.67
5	Minnesota	2
5	Oregon	2
5	Vermont	2
8	Montana	2.14
9	Iowa	2.25
10	Kansas	2.43
11–20		
11	Idaho	2.5
12	Wisconsin	2.6
13	Nebraska	2.67
13	Virginia	2.67
15	Michigan	2.96
16	Alaska	3
16	Texas	3
16	Washington	3
16	Wyoming	3
20	Tennessee	3.25
21–28		
21	California	3.33
22	North Carolina	3.35
23	Florida	3.5
23	Georgia	3.5
23	Nevada	3.5
23	South Carolina	3.5
27	Arkansas	3.67
28	Missouri	3.69

Table 4.1 State Corruption Scores (continued)

Rank[a]	*State*	*Score*
29–38		
29	Hawaii	4
29	Indiana	4
29	Mississippi	4
29	New York	4
33	Maryland	4.05
34	Utah	4.33
35	Pennsylvania	4.45
36	Connecticut	4.5
37	Illinois	4.67
37	Ohio	4.67
39–47		
39	Arizona	4.71
39	West Virginia	4.71
41	Kentucky	4.86
42	Alabama	4.91
43	Delaware	5
43	Oklahoma	5
45	New Mexico	5.3
46	Louisiana	5.4
47	Rhode Island	5.5
	Rated via Nearest Neighbors	
Massachusetts	5	
New Hampshire	1.83	
New Jersey	4.23	

Source: Boylan, R. T., and Long, C. X., A survey of state house reporters' perception of public corruption, *State Politics & Politics Quarterly*, 3(4), 2003. With permission.

[a] Rank number 1 is least corrupt, and number 47 is most corrupt.

Traditional Party Organizations

The traditional party organization (TPO) index developed by Mayhew[37] denotes parties with substantial autonomy, stability, hierarchy, influence over candidate nominations, and reliance on material rather than purposive (idealistic) incentives. By definition, such parties are relatively likely to see government jobs as rewards for supporters;[38] thus, civil service reform holds more risk in high-TPO states. This measure has high face validity, with Illinois, New York, and Rhode Island holding high TPO scores. As expected, TPO correlates with corruption (r = .40; p = .004).

Political Environmental Variables

Media Capacity

As explained above, states with large newspapers with the capacity to do investigative journalism seem less susceptible to spoils. Presumably, more large newspapers mean more government accountability. Therefore, the list of the 150 largest daily papers in the United States, those with reported circulation over 80,000 (see Audit Bur eau of Circulators, http://www.accessabc.com), is used. States get one point for each such newspaper they have, with an additional half-point for any such newspaper in the state capital; thus, higher scores suggest more media scrutiny. *Media capacity* ranges from 0 to 3, with a mean of 1.73 and a standard deviation of .82.

Media capacity correlates with *corruption* (r = .33; p = .02) and (barely) with TPO (r = .23; p = .10). It seems unlikely that having major newspapers increases corruption and traditional party organization; rather the correlation is most likely spurious because more urban states have both more corruption and larger media outlets. Indeed, a dummy variable denoting the sparsely populated Rocky Mountain and Great Plains states correlates negatively with all three of these variables.

Party Competition

As explained above, states dominated by one party might be more apt to suffer spoils, because party competition will be less likely to hold the major party accountable. Accordingly, *partycomp* denotes the mean percentage of seats held by the minority party in the two houses of the state legislature. Where Democrats control one chamber and Republicans another, this variable is assigned a .6 value; it thus ranges from .15 to .6, with a mean of .41 and a standard deviation of .12. This variable seems preferable to party control of the governorship because the latter is a less stable measure, with gubernatorial elections often depending on candidate personality. (See Table 4.2.)

Bureaucratic Capacity

Finally, states whose public bureaucracies have greater capacity can better resist spoils demands. For this, the measures of effective management developed by Ingraham et al.[39] are used. These authors rated all 50 states on financial management capacity, capital and infrastructure management capacity, human resources management capacity, information technology, and managing for results. The researchers assigned letter grades from A– to F on each item. Notably, states that do well on one tend to do well on others. The mean letter grade and concomitant mean grade point average (*govperf*) for each state are calculated, as reported in Table 4.3. *Govperf* ranges go from D+ for Alabama to A– for Virginia, Utah, and Washington. This measure thus has high face validity. *Govperf* does not correlate with any other item, save for a weak relationship with *partycomp* ($r = .28$; $p = .05$).

As Table 4.4 and the discussions above show, most of the variables intercorrelate weakly or not at all, and the correlations of media with corruption and TPO are probably spurious. Corruption and TPO, in contrast, correlate relatively strongly. Notably, controlling for region, *govperf* correlates negatively with corruption ($r = -.25$; $p = .08$). As one might expect, less corrupt states seemingly have somewhat more effective state bureaucracies.

SUMMARY MEASURES: WHICH STATES RANK WHERE?

Two summary indexes of the preconditions of successful civil service reform have been developed. *Reform1* employs three variables that involve patronage demand variables and bureaucratic capacity: *Corrupt*, *TPO*, and *Govperf*. Because this theory does not specify which independent variables will yield the strongest relationships, each variable has been weighted equally so that each will run on roughly a 1–5 scale, save for outliers. To do this *Corrupt* and *TPO* are used in their raw forms, whereas we multiply *Govperf* by 1.25. Because *Govperf* correlates negatively with the other two variables, the measure *Reform1* as *Corrupt* + *TPO* – *Govperf* is calculated; thus, higher numbers mean that reform is more risky. As Table 4.5 shows, *Reform1* ranges from –.85 for Minnesota to 8.28 for Rhode Island, with a mean of 2.38 and a standard deviation of 2.43. *Reform1* has high face validity, with the most reform-friendly scores going to Western or Midwestern states with progressive traditions. The least reform-friendly states tend to be Northeastern states with individualistic traditions, along with

Table 4.2 State Party Competition

Rank[a]	*State*	*Score*
1–11		
1	Delaware	0.6
1	Georgia	0.6
1	Indiana	0.6
1	Kentucky	0.6
1	Minnesota	0.6
1	Nevada	0.6
1	New York	0.6
1	Vermont	0.6
1	Washington	0.6
10	Maine	0.48
10	New Jersey	0.48
12–22		
12	North Carolina	0.47
13	Colorado	0.46
13	Oregon	0.46
13	Tennessee	0.46
16	Illinois	0.45
16	Montana	0.45
16	Oklahoma	0.45
19	Iowa	0.44
19	Pennsylvania	0.44
19	South Carolina	0.44
19	Wisconsin	0.44
23–31		
23	Michigan	0.43
23	Missouri	0.43
25	New Mexico	0.41
26	Connecticut	0.4
26	Texas	0.4
28	Alaska	0.39

Table 4.2 State Party Competition (continued)

Rank[a]	*State*	*Score*
28	Arizona	0.39
28	California	0.39
28	Virginia	0.39
32–41		
32	Mississippi	0.36
33	Alabama	0.35
33	Ohio	0.35
35	Florida	0.34
36	Louisiana	0.33
36	South Dakota	0.33
38	North Dakota	0.32
39	Kansas	0.31
39	Maryland	0.31
39	West Virginia	0.31
42–50		
42	Nebraska	b
43	Wyoming	0.29
44	New Hampshire	0.28
45	Arkansas	0.27
46	Hawaii	0.25
46	Utah	0.25
48	Idaho	0.22
49	Rhode Island	0.16
50	Massachusetts	0.15

Source: Barone, M., and Cohen, R.E., *The Almanac of American Politics: 2004*, National Journal Group, Washington, DC, 2003. With permission.

[a] States ranked 1 are the most competitive states as determined through partisan control of seats in the state legislature; number 50 is the least competitive, as derived from the percentage of minority party seats in both houses of the state legislature.

[b] Nebraska's unicameral legislature is officially elected on a nonpartisan basis, yet the state is clearly dominated by the Republican Party, so it has been given the above placement on the list.

Table 4.3 State Government Performance, GPA, and Letter Grade

Rank	*State*	*GPA*	*Grade*
1–10			
1	Alabama	1.28	D+
2	Rhode Island	1.78	C–
3	Hawaii	1.84	C/C–
4	Arkansas	1.89	C
4	Connecticut	1.89	C
6	Oklahoma	1.95	C
7	New Mexico	1.97	C
8	Alaska	2	C
8	New York	2	C
10	California	2.03	C
11–20			
11	Wyoming	2.06	C
12	New Hampshire	2.11	C
13	Arizona	2.17	C+/C
14	Nevada	2.19	C+
15	West Virginia	2.22	C+
16	Idaho	2.31	C+
17	Colorado	2.33	C+
17	Mississippi	2.33	C+
19	Maine	2.36	C+
20	Massachusetts	2.44	C+
21–31			
21	Georgia	2.45	C+
22	South Dakota	2.47	B–/C+
23	Indiana	2.5	B–/C+
24	Montana	2.53	B–/C+
25	Florida	2.58	B–
25	Oregon	2.58	B–
27	North Dakota	2.59	B–

Table 4.3 State Government Performance, GPA, and Letter Grade (continued)

Rank	*State*	*GPA*	*Grade*
28	Tennessee	2.61	B–
29	Vermont	2.64	B–
30	Louisiana (tie)	2.67	B–
30	New Jersey	2.67	B–
32–40			
32	Illinois	2.69	B–
33	Kansas	2.83	B/B–
33	Nebraska	2.83	B/B–
33	Wisconsin	2.83	B/B–
36	Ohio	2.97	B
37	North Carolina	3	B
37	Texas	3	B
39	Minnesota	3.08	B
40	South Carolina	3.14	B+/B
41–50			
41	Maryland	3.16	B+/B
42	Delaware	3.17	B+/B
43	Iowa	3.22	B+
43	Kentucky	3.22	B+
45	Pennsylvania	3.25	B+
46	Michigan	3.44	B+
47	Missouri	3.5	A–/B+
48	Virginia	3.56	A–
49	Utah	3.58	A–
50	Washington	3.67	A–

Source: Ingraham, P. W., Joyce, P. G., and Donahue, A. K., *Government Performance: Why Management Matters*, Johns Hopkins University Press, Baltimore, 2003, 72–73.

Table 4.4 Intercorrelations of Key Independent Variables

	Media	*TPO*	*Corrupt*	*Govperf*
Media	1.0			
TPO (party organization)	.23*	1.0		
Corrupt	.33**	.40***	1.0	
Govperf	.19	.12	–.19	1.0
Partycomp	.11	.18	–.15	.28**

*Statistically significant at .10.

**Statistically significant at .05.

***Statistically significant at .01.

Louisiana, Indiana, and West Virginia. The two states that have most reformed their civil service systems, Florida and Georgia, rank in the middle of the distribution at 21st and 28th respectively.

Although *media* and *partycomp* do not generally seem related to the other variables, they theoretically exert independent impacts affecting reform-readiness, as detailed above. Accordingly, a second index using all these measures is offered. To rescale media for the index, media (which, save for one outlier, ranges from 0 to 2.5) is multiplied by two. Similarly, *partycomp* (ranging from .15 to .6) is multiplied by ten. Then, *Reform2* is calculated as *Reform1 – partycomp – media*. *Reform2* ranges from –11.85 for Minnesota to 3.68 for Rhode Island with a mean of –5.17 and a standard deviation of 2.92, again with higher scores indicating that civil service reform is more risky. Naturally, the two indexes are similar, correlating at .70. Five states score among the ten most reform-friendly in both indexes: Minnesota, Iowa, Washington, Michigan, and Kansas (and Wisconsin just misses). Similarly, six states are among the ten least reform-friendly by both measures: Rhode Island, Illinois, West Virginia, New Jersey, Maryland, and Delaware (and Louisiana just misses). Again, this measure has high face validity.

DISCUSSION

Some states remain within an antiquated political culture conducive to spoils, making radical civil service reform risky. In contrast, states that meet certain criteria are much safer candidates for reform. Although Rhode Island apparently remains a haven for cronyism,[40] some (mainly Midwestern) states steeped in the Progressive tradition seem far better able to handle the responsibilities and temptations that an end to tenure would provide.[41] These should be the first attempt at-will employment because

Table 4.5 Summary Indexes of Reform Readiness

Rank	*Index*	*State*
	Reform 1 (Corrupt, TPO, and Govperf)	
1–10		
1	–0.85	Minnesota
2	–0.78	Iowa
3	–0.74	North Dakota
4	–0.59	South Dakota
5	–0.59	Washington
6	–0.34	Michigan
7	–0.3	Vermont
8	–0.28	Maine
9	–0.23	Oregon
10	–0.11	Kansas
11–20		
11	–0.02	Montana
12	0.06	Wisconsin
13	0.13	Nebraska
14	0.19	New Hampshire
15	0.22	Virginia
16	0.57	South Carolina
17	0.6	North Carolina
18	0.61	Idaho
19	0.86	Utah
20	1.25	Texas
21–30		
21	1.27	Florida
22	1.42	Wyoming
23	1.76	Nevada
24	1.79	California
25	1.99	Tennessee
26	2.09	Mississippi
27	2.31	Arkansas
28	2.44	Georgia
29	2.5	Alaska
30	2.95	Massachusetts

-- *continued*

Table 4.5 Summary Indexes of Reform Readiness (continued)

Rank	*Index*	*State*
31–40		
31	3	Arizona
32	3.14	Connecticut
33	3.31	Missouri
34	3.56	Oklahoma
35	3.59	Colorado
36	3.7	Hawaii
37	4.31	Alabama
38	4.83	Kentucky
39	4.87	New Mexico
40	4.96	Ohio
41–50		
41	5.04	Delaware
42	5.06	Louisiana
43	5.1	Maryland
44	5.39	Pennsylvania
45	5.88	Indiana
46	5.89	New Jersey
47	5.94	West Virginia
48	6.31	Illinois
49	6.5	New York
50	8.28	Rhode Island
	Reform 2 (using all proposed independent variables)	
1–10		
1	–11.85	Minnesota
2	–10.59	Washington
3	–9.64	Michigan
4	–9.34	Wisconsin
5	–9.10	North Carolina
6	–8.68	Virginia
7	–8.56	Georgia
8	–8.21	Kansas
9	–8.18	Iowa
10	–7.83	South Carolina

-- *continued*

Table 4.5 Summary Indexes of Reform Readiness (continued)

Rank	*Index*	*State*
11–20		
11	–7.75	Texas
12	–7.61	Tennessee
13	–7.11	California
14	–7.08	Maine
15	–6.83	Oregon
16	–6.30	Vermont
17	–6.24	Nevada
18	–6.13	Florida
19	–6.01	Colorado
20	–5.90	Arizona
21–30		
21	–5.86	Connecticut
22	–5.17	Kentucky
23	–5.13	Indiana
24	–5.10	Nebraska
25	–4.99	Missouri
26	–4.64	Utah
27	–4.61	New Hampshire
28	–4.59	Idaho
29	–4.55	Massachusetts
30	–4.52	Montana
31–40		
31	–4.51	Mississippi
32	–4.50	New York
33	–4.01	Pennsylvania
34	–3.94	North Dakota
35	–3.94	Oklahoma
36	–3.89	South Dakota
37	–3.54	Ohio
38	–3.40	Alaska
39	–3.39	Arkansas
40	–3.24	Louisiana

-- *continued*

Table 4.5 Summary Indexes of Reform Readiness (continued)

Rank	*Index*	*State*
41–50		
41	–3.19	Alabama
42	–2.96	Delaware
43	–2.91	New Jersey
44	–2.19	Illinois
45	–1.80	Hawaii
46	–1.48	Wyoming
47	–1.23	New Mexico
48	–.16	West Virginia
49	.00	Maryland
50	3.68	Rhode Island

they have many of the preconditions for success, whereas such states as Rhode Island, Illinois, West Virginia, New Jersey, Maryland, Delaware, and Louisiana should instead tighten ethics laws as a precondition to state and local civil service reform.

Notably, the question of reform for the myriad local governments is not addressed here. Measures for local governments are more difficult to come by, though obviously such variables as party competition and newspaper scrutiny will yield less sanguine predictions for most local governments. Also, local governments hold a wide range of political cultures. Many cities are individualistic, as are some rural areas, whereas the suburbs are somewhat more likely to be moralistic.[42] This political theory of administrative reform may apply to local governments, but the data needed to make predictions is lacking.

Although predictions can be made as to where civil service tenure could most profitably be eliminated, these predictions cannot be tested until more states decide to implement at-will employment, and until the early reforms in Georgia and Florida (which rank as moderately conducive to reform by our measures) are more thoroughly examined. In general, this theory warns that many and perhaps most states should not reform their civil service systems.

One disturbing possibility, as an anonymous reviewer pointed out, is that in the very states where corruption is more common, party competition is limited, media scrutiny is inadequate, and bureaucratic professionalization and unionization are less developed, political pressures to reform will be strongest. This is precisely because these settings are more conducive to playing political games with government employment.

Future research should examine how well reform works in different states, to begin to test whether the hypotheses presented here are accurate. Second, scholars need to consider which of the variables in the theory have the most explanatory power, and why. Third, scholars need to consider which additional variables need inclusion. For example, one anonymous reviewer suggests that states with powerful public sector unions will be less likely to misuse appointment powers inherent to a reformed civil service, because unions will provide additional scrutiny of personnel policy. Perhaps unions might play roles contingent on the dominant state political party. In Republican-dominated states like Ohio, powerful unions may in fact help keep political leaders in check. In contrast, in Democratic states like Rhode Island, powerful unions may join with the dominant party to use the civil service for spoils-oriented patronage.[43]

Ideally, civil service innovations will be road-tested in Minnesota rather than Rhode Island. However, even in the Minnesotas of the world, reform could lead to unanticipated consequences that need to be carefully monitored. For better or worse, however, at-will government employment may be the wave of the future. Accordingly, scholars and policy makers need to consider the preconditions for its success.

ACKNOWLEDGMENTS

The authors thank Eric M. Uslaner, Craig M. Wheeland, Leonard Shyles, Matthew Baird, and three anonymous reviewers for their assistance. The usual caveats apply.

REFERENCES

1. Condrey, S. E., Reinventing state civil service systems: The Georgia experience, *Review of Public Personnel Administration*, 22(2), 114, 2002; Gossett, C. W., Civil service reform: The case of Georgia, *Review of Public Personnel Administration*, 22(2), 94, 2002; Lasseter, R. W., Georgia's merit system reform 1996–2001: An operating agency's perspective, *Review of Public Personnel Administration*, 22(2), 125, 2002; Kellough, J. E., and Nigro, L. G., Pay for performance in Georgia state government: Employee perspectives on GeorgiaGain after 5 years, *Review of Public Personnel Administration*, 22(2), 146, 2002.
2. West, J. P., Georgia on the mind of radical civil service reformers, *Review of Public Personnel Administration*, 22(2), 79, 2002; Bowman, J. S., Gertz, M. G., Gertz, S. C., and Williams, R. L., Civil service reform in Florida: Employee attitudes 1 year later, *Review of Public Personnel Administration*, 23(4), 286, 2003.
3. Barr, S., New personnel systems have much in common, *Washington Post*, February 13, 2005, C02.

4. Under broad banding, a civil servant will not know the salaries of peers unless he or she files a Freedom of Information Act Request, something few are likely to do; thus, managers can use pay for performance without facing widespread complaints from their direct reports. Although in the short term long-standing traditions might keep managers from exercising their new discretion, it seems plausible that over time new managers will adjust to the new administrative regime.
5. These arguments are not fully accepted by the second author of this chapter. In particular, he doubts that ending civil service tenure will increase public respect for government bureaucrats.
6. Maranto, R., Rethinking the unthinkable: Reply to Durant, Goodsell, Knott, and Murray on "A case for spoils in federal personnel management," *Administration and Society*, 30(1), 3, 1998. Reprinted in *Radical Reform of the Civil Service*, Condrey, S., and Maranto, R., eds., Lexington, Lanham, MD, 2001; Maranto, R., Thinking the unthinkable in public administration: A case for spoils in the federal bureaucracy, *Administration and Society*, 29(6), 623, 1998. Reprinted in *Radical Reform of the Civil Service*, Condrey, S., and Maranto, R., eds., Lexington, Lanham, MD, 2001; Maranto, R., Turkey farm: Why we can't delay civil service reform, *Washington Monthly*, (November), 27, 1999; Maranto, R., Praising civil service but not bureaucracy: A brief against tenure in the U.S. civil service, *Review of Public Personnel Administration*, 22(3), 175, 2002.
7. Maranto, R., Turkey farm: Why we can't delay civil service reform, *Washington Monthly*, (November), 27, 1999.
8. Maranto, R., Rethinking the unthinkable: Reply to Durant, Goodsell, Knott, and Murray on "A case for spoils in federal personnel management," *Administration and Society*, 30(1), 3, 1998. Reprinted in *Radical Reform of the Civil Service*, Condrey, S., and Maranto, R., eds., Lexington, Lanham, MD, 2001; Maranto, R., Thinking the unthinkable in public administration: A case for spoils in the federal bureaucracy, *Administration and Society*, 29(6), 623, 1998. Reprinted in *Radical Reform of the Civil Service*, Condrey, S., and Maranto, R., eds., Lexington, Lanham, MD, 2001; Van Riper, P. P., *History of the United States Civil Service*, Row, Peterson, Evanston, IL, 1958.
9. Callow, A., *The Tweed Ring*, Oxford University Press, London, 1965.
10. Van Riper, P. P., *History of the United States Civil Service*, Row, Peterson, Evanston, IL, 1958; Fowler, D. G., *The Cabinet Politician: the Postmasters General, 1829–1909*, Columbia University Press, New York, 1943; Maranto, R., *Beyond a Government of Strangers: How Career Executives and Political Appointees Can Turn Conflict to Cooperation*, Lexington, Lanham, MD, 2005; Morone, J. A., *The Democratic Wish: Popular Participation and the Limits of American Government*, Yale University Press, New Haven, CT, 1998.
11. Weko, T. J., *The Politicizing Presidency*, University Press of Kansas, Lawrence, 1995.
12. Maranto, R., Praising civil service but not bureaucracy: A brief against tenure in the U.S. civil service, *Review of Public Personnel Administration*, 22(3), 175, 2002; Maranto, R., *Beyond a Government of Strangers: How Career Executives and Political Appointees Can Turn Conflict to Cooperation*, Lexington, Lanham, MD, 2005.

13. Harris, R. A., and Milkis, S. M., *The Politics of Regulatory Change*, Oxford University Press, New York, 1989; Maranto, R., *Politics and Bureaucracy in the Modern Presidency: Appointees and Careerists in the Reagan Administration*, Greenwood, Westport, CT, 1993.
14. Dionne, E. J., Jr., *Why Americans Hate Politics*, Simon & Schuster, New York, 1991; Hunter, J. D., *Culture Wars: The Struggle to Define America*, Basic Books, New York, 1991; Uslaner, E. M., *The Decline of Comity in Congress*, University of Michigan Press, Ann Arbor, 1993.
15. Brewer, G. A., and Maranto, R., Comparing the roles of political appointees and career executives in the U.S. federal executive branch, *American Review of Public Administration*, 30(1), 69, 2000.
16. Uslaner, E. M., *The Decline of Comity in Congress*, University of Michigan Press, Ann Arbor, 1993.
17. Maranto, R., *Beyond a Government of Strangers: How Career Executives and Political Appointees Can Turn Conflict to Cooperation*, Lexington, Lanham, MD, 2005; Ginsberg, B., and Shefter, M., *Politics by Other Means*, 3rd ed., Norton, New York, 2002; Mackenzie, G. C., ed.. *Innocent until Nominated*, Brookings Institution, Washington, DC, 2001; Mackenzie, G. C., and Hafken, M., *Scandal Proof: Do Ethics Laws Make Government Ethical?* Brookings Institution, Washington, DC, 2002.
18. Rauch, J., Government's end: Why Washington stopped working, *PublicAffairs*, New York, 1999.
19. Maranto, R., *Beyond a Government of Strangers: How Career Executives and Political Appointees Can Turn Conflict to Cooperation*, Lexington, Lanham, MD, 2005.
20. Anechiarico, F., and Jacobs, J. B., *The Pursuit of Absolute Integrity*, University of Chicago Press, Chicago, 1996.
21. Savas, E. S., *Privatization and Public-Private Partnerships*, Chatham House, New York, 2000.
22. Lasseter, R. W., Georgia's merit system reform 1996–2001: An operating agency's perspective, *Review of Public Personnel Administration*, 22(2), 125, 2002, 126.
23. Hamilton, D. K., Is patronage dead? The impact of antipatronage staffing systems, *Review of Public Personnel Administration*, 22(1), 3, 2002, 3.
24. Ibid., 21.
25. Ibid., 23.
26. Maranto, R., Rethinking the unthinkable: Reply to Durant, Goodsell, Knott, and Murray on "A case for spoils in federal personnel management," *Administration and Society*, 30(1), 3, 1998. Reprinted in *Radical Reform of the Civil Service*, Condrey, S., and Maranto, R., eds., Lexington, Lanham, MD, 2001; Maranto, R., Thinking the unthinkable in public administration: A case for spoils in the federal bureaucracy, *Administration and Society,* 29(6), 623, 1998. Reprinted in *Radical Reform of the Civil Service*, Condrey, S., and Maranto, R., eds., Lexington, Lanham, MD, 2001.
27. Fenton, J. H., *Midwest Politics*, Holt, Rinehart, & Winston, New York, 1966.
28. Elazar, D. J., *American Federalism: A View from the States*, Harper & Row, New York, 1972.
29. Mayhew, D. R., *Placing Parties in American Politics*, Princeton University Press, Princeton, NJ, 1986.

30. Barone, M., and Cohen, R. E., *The Almanac of American Politics: 2004*, National Journal Group, Washington, DC, 2003.
31. Mayhew, D. R., *Placing Parties in American Politics*, Princeton University Press, Princeton, NJ, 1986; Sorauf, F. J., *Party and Representation*, Atherton, New York, 1963.
32. Kerbel, M. R., *If It Bleeds, It Leads: An Anatomy of Television*, Westview, Boulder, CO, 2000.
33. Maranto, R., *Politics and Bureaucracy in the Modern Presidency: Appointees and Careerists in the Reagan Administration*, Greenwood, Westport, CT, 1993.
34. Ibid.
35. Boylan, R. T., and Long, C. X., A survey of state house reporters' perception of public corruption, *State Politics & Politics Quarterly*, 3(4), 2003.
36. Fenton, J. H., *Midwest Politics*, Holt, Rinehart, & Winston, New York, 1966.
37. Mayhew, D. R., *Placing Parties in American Politics*, Princeton University Press, Princeton, NJ, 1986, 18–23, 239.
38. Elazar, D. J., *American Federalism: A View from the States*, Harper & Row, New York, 1972; Sorauf, F. J., *Party and Representation*, Atherton, New York, 1963; Riordan, W. L., *Plunkitt of Tammany Hall*, Dutton, New York, 1963 (originally published 1916).
39. Ingraham, P. W., Joyce, P. G., and Donahue, A. K., *Government Performance: Why Management Matters*, Johns Hopkins University Press, Baltimore, 2003, 72–73.
40. Stanton, M., *The Prince of Providence: The True Story of Buddy Cianci, America's Most Notorious Mayor, Some Wiseguys, and the Feds*, Random House, New York, 2003.
41. Unger, N. C., *Fighting Bob La Follette: The Righteous Reformer*, University of North Carolina Press, Chapel Hill, 2000.
42. Elazar, D. J., *American Federalism: A View from the States*, Harper & Row, New York, 1972; Gaventa, J., *Power and Powerlessness*, University of Illinois Press, Urbana, 1980; Jackson, K. T., *Crabgrass Frontier: The Suburbanization of the United States*, Oxford University Press, New York, 1985.
43. Data on union strength comes from Hirsch, B. T., and Macpherson, D., *Union Membership and Earnings Data Book*, Bureau of National Affairs Inc., Washington, DC, 1997. The percentage of public sector employees covered by collective bargaining agreements was coded, which ranged from under 17 percent for South Carolina, Mississippi, and Virginia to more than 67 percent for Connecticut, Rhode Island, and New York. This variable did not correlate with other hypothetical independent variables; rather, the South and West have few union members relative to other regions.

5

THE DEMONIZATION OF PATRONAGE: FOLK DEVILS AND THE *BOSTON GLOBE'S* COVERAGE OF THE 9/11 TERRORIST ATTACKS

Domonic A. Bearfield
Texas A&M University

INTRODUCTION

> Patronage, in all of its forms, has eroded public confidence in Massport, created morale problems for qualified and dedicated employees, and contributed to the inefficiency of the organization.
>
> ***Report of the Special Advisory Task Force on Massport*, December 4, 2001**

Although many years have passed since the heyday of civil service reform, there is still a negative valence associated with patronage. Although it is uncommon to hear patronage described as evil, as it was frequently described during the Progressive era, in the contemporary mind, patronage has become an "administrative unthinkable,"[1] a sickness of bureaucracy,[2] or quite simply tainted with corruption.[3] In this respect, the victory of

Progressive era civil service reformers has been twofold: the emergence and growth of the civil service system, and a demonized concept of patronage.

As a result, a biased view of patronage has developed. This biased view has become so pervasive that it largely goes unchallenged. Yet, as Ostrom[4] reminds us, "[the] fact that something is widely believed does not make it correct."[5] Such broadly held beliefs, or what she describes as self-evident truths, are an impediment to empirical examination. When an idea is so widely accepted that it has become simply "common sense," there is little incentive to question that belief.

In this chapter, it is argued that the negative view of patronage that pervades the public culture in Massachusetts (and elsewhere) resulted in its use as a "folk devil" following the terrorist attacks of 9/11. More specifically, the patronage folk devil was used to initiate a moral panic that implied an unsubstantiated causal link between personnel practices and the hijacking of two airplanes out of Logan Airport. The discussion begins with an explanation of moral panic theory and a definition of the folk devil concept. This is followed by a brief overview of the historical development of the patronage folk devil, followed by the relationship between Boston and patronage. The second part of the chapter discusses the specific moral panic initiated after the 9/11 attacks and its consequences by examining the *Boston Globe*'s coverage of Massport, the independent public authority that manages Logan Airport, following 9/11. The analysis concludes with a discussion of the implications of moral panics and how empirical research can help to retard the development of future folk devils, as well as the abuse of old ones such as patronage.

FOLK DEVILS AND MORAL PANICS

The term *moral panic* has been used to describe the exaggerated reaction of a society to events and phenomena that challenge or upset traditional norms and values. The concept first emerged in Stanley Cohen's[6] landmark study of "Mods and Rockers" in the United Kingdom during the 1960s. Since then, the concept has been used to examine public reaction to a range of phenomena, including random violence,[7] sex and AIDS,[8] and illegal drug use.[9]

In his original work, Cohen offered the following description of a moral panic:

> A condition, episode, person or group of persons emerges to become defined as a threat to societal values and interests; its nature is presented in a stylized and stereotypical fashion by the mass media; the moral barricades are manned by editors,

> bishops, politicians and other right-thinking people; socially accredited experts pronounce their diagnoses and solutions; ways of coping are evolved or (more often) resorted to; the condition then disappears, submerges or deteriorates and becomes more visible. Sometimes the object of the panic is quite novel and at other times it is something which has been in existence long enough but suddenly appears in the limelight. Sometimes the panic passes over and is forgotten, except in folklore and collective memory; at other times it has more serious and long-lasting repercussions and might produce such changes as those in legal and social policy or even the way the society conceives itself.[10]

At the center of the moral panic is the "folk devil," an object of fear or contempt, which becomes the focus of the citizen backlash and governmental intervention. Folk devils are "visible reminders of what we should not be."[11] Heir describes Cohen's conceptualization of folk devils as "the personification of evil . . . which are stripped of all positive characteristics and endowed with pejorative evaluations."[12] The folk devil is seen as the source of the societal threat, and the actual threat posed during the moral panic is largely exaggerated. Although the folk devil is a product of social construction, one should not conclude that it is wholly fantasy or make-believe.[6, 13]

The Patronage Folk Devil

Anne Freedman notes, "No one wants to admit to a practice that bears the taint of corrupt machine politics."[14] Although patronage was once the dominant method of personnel selection in the United States, following the emergence of civil service reform the view of patronage has been a negative one. This is largely explained by the very nature of the U.S. civil service reform movement. According to Mosher,[15] "[The] enthusiasm and dedication which the movement came to command may perhaps best be explained by the fact that its essence was moral, at a time when American thinking was heavily moralistic . . . [the civil service reform movement] was a campaign *against evils*" (italics in original).[16] With increased efficiency but a secondary consideration,[17] the battle against patronage was largely framed as one of good versus evil.[15, 18] A combination of progressive and social gospel reformers, muckrakers, scholars, and political actors used this newly demonized construction of patronage as a justification for civil service reform.[19–28]

Reformers shaped the definition of patronage, providing it with an inherently negative valence.[29] As Edelman states, "[P]olitical language is political reality."[30] Language and the construction of meaning are essential to the development of public policy making. Once an image has been constructed, or meaning established, political actors are able to use the newly defined image in the construction of narratives. Narratives are then used to determine the course of political action. Narratives are also used to establish the recipients of rewards and sanctions.[31, 32]

Patronage emerged from the civil service debate as a synonym to corruption. It is a view that is still widely held,[1] despite evidence refuting the existence of widespread corruption during the 1800s.[33, 34] Recent attempts to reform the federal civil service have been met with familiar criticism. Opponents argued that changes would produce a return to patronage, increased inefficiency, nepotism,[35, 36] cronyism,[37] and hiring "based on who you know rather than what you know."[38] These phrases, similar to the phrases used by Progressive era reformers, are an attempt to stimulate the same sense of moral indignation that proved successful 100 years ago.

Boston and Patronage

Although the negative view of patronage remains pervasive, its power as a folk devil is often defined locally. According to Bosso's "potency of localism,"[39] America's fragmented federal system results in "problems inevitably get[ting] framed in local and state terms." By extension, political machines, bosses, and patronage must be understood in a local context.[40] Unlike in the West, where progressive reformers enjoyed much greater success, in the Northeast, reform produced only temporary losses for the machines, which were later regained.[41] In fact, Boston is even unique from its northeastern neighbors outside of Massachusetts with a history of candidate-centered organizations based on a personal following, as opposed to more party-based machines.[3]

> Boston is a heterogeneous city, a city of neighborhoods and tightly knit ethnic groups. Political followings have historically been personal followings and have lasted only as long as individuals have been able to hold them together.[42]

Quite often, those personal machines were held together by the use of patronage. One of the most famous Boston-style machines was built by James Curley during the first half of the 20th century. Using a combination of patronage and rhetoric, Curley constructed a "Robin Hood-like" image that resonated in the city's older ethnic communities.[43–45] Later in the century, "meal ticket seekers," or those in pursuit of the material gains of patronage, were an important subculture during the tenure of Mayor Kevin White (1968–1983).[42] Given the real or imagined rewards of patronage, it has been viewed in many neighborhoods as a tool for social mobility.

> In Boston, the working class and ethnic populations tend to see politics as a means for achieving individual goals rather than an instrument for public policy. There is an assumption the individuals are in politics for what they can get out of it and the populace expects (and generally tolerates) backroom deals and corruption. Such a culture provides a fertile soil for patronage; it is simply considered a normal part of politics.[46]

The view of politics as a pathway to individual and material gain has long been a source of intense conflict. This conflict extends beyond the city limits and into the political life of the entire state of Massachusetts. Elazar[47] traces the roots of this conflict to political culture clashes between Irish immigrants and older, established Yankee families beginning in the 19th century. Unlike the individualistic political culture of the Irish immigrants, the Yankees represented a moralistic political culture, with a focus on advancing the common good.

Although the combatants are no longer divided into Irish and Yankee camps, there is still a strong negative reaction in the Boston area to patronage. As Hogarty[48] points out, the use of patronage at independent public authorities in Massachusetts has often erupted into very public controversies in the media.[49] Often intense, these controversies serve as a reminder that the conflict between the two political cultures still exists.

MORAL PANIC: MASSPORT AND THE *BOSTON GLOBE*'S COVERAGE AFTER 9/11

On the morning of September 11, 2001, two planes were hijacked after leaving Logan International Airport. That same morning, two additional planes, one from Dulles International Airport near Washington D.C., and the other from Newark International Airport in Newark, N.J., were also hijacked. Following the hijackings, questions were raised in the Boston media concerning security procedures at Logan. Although nearly simultaneous hijackings at multiple airports could be an indication of a systemwide security weakness, the attention in Boston was focused on Massport.[50] The next section details how the negative view of patronage, reflected in the *Boston Globe*'s[51] coverage of Massport after 9/11, effectively created a moral panic.

The Case of the Convenient Whipping Boy

American Airlines Flight 11 and United Airlines Flight 175, both out of Boston's Logan Airport, were hijacked by terrorists and flown into the north and south towers of the World Trade Center in New York City. Coverage by the *Boston Globe* on the day of the attacks did not assign blame to any particular entity or individual. Stories ranged from questions of how the hijackers were able to breach security at multiple airports,[52] to the possibility that the attacks may have occurred without any breach in security.[53] Another article noted that Boston had recently become a desirable destination for terrorist organization members and sympathizers due to the city's proximity to New York and the ability of foreign terrorists to blend into the local immigrant community.[54]

The following day, a few articles reported a history of security violations at Logan, including over 136 violations discovered by the Federal Aviation Administration (FAA) from 1997 to 1999.[55, 56] Despite this history, many believed that security problems were not unique to Logan. Quoting an airline pilot, Matthew Brelis, the paper's aviation writer, wrote, "[E]very airport is vulnerable. I don't imagine that Logan is any worse than any other airport, and it may be better."[57] In another article, former Massport Executive Director Peter Blute[58] and others argued that the use of multiple airports on the day of the attacks provided evidence against singling out Logan as a target for blame. The article also noted several problems with airline security, including low morale among FAA security staff and a federal policy that fragmented responsibility for security between airports and airlines.[56, 59]

On the same day, an editorial appeared rejecting the premise that Logan's security lapses were typical among major airports. The editorial claimed that "the terrorist masterminds who planned yesterday's carnage probably didn't pick the names of airports out of a hat. From cargo bay to check-in gate, Logan had been exposed as a soft target."[60] In the days to follow, the management of Massport, particularly the agency's hiring practices, would receive considerable attention.

On September 14, under the headline "Political Ties Strong at Airport," the authors declared that "the focus is now on the leadership of the Massachusetts Port Authority, an agency long run by political appointees without aviation or security backgrounds."[61] Described as a "destination for patronage appointees through many gubernatorial administrations,"[62] the focus was soon on Massport's executive director, Virginia Buckingham, and the agency's public safety director, Joseph Lawless.

Buckingham, a chief of staff and campaign manager to former Governor William Weld, was appointed to the authority by Governor Paul Cellucci following a scandal involving the previous executive director, Peter Blute. Although there had been controversy surrounding the political nature of the appointment (she was also Cellucci's chief of staff), the paper noted that Buckingham had "generally gotten high marks for her performance [at Massport]."[63]

Lawless had been a state trooper for 13 years, including periods in the Middlesex County district attorney's office and as the head of Governor Weld's personal protection team before his appointment to Massport. He worked at the authority for eight years prior to the terrorist attacks.[62, 64] Although described as "a shining star in the DA's office" and "a good homicide investigator,"[64] Lawless did not have any aviation experience prior to his appointment. He would eventually serve as a member of the World Committee for Public Safety and Security, the Airports Council International North American Steering Committee, and the FAA Security Equipment Product Team.[65]

Despite advice from aides who urged her to blame the airlines for the attacks,[66] Buckingham showed faith in the developing investigation. On September 16, Buckingham stated that the "ongoing investigation is going to point out insufficiencies in the system at all airports, including Logan. If there are specific flaws that are unique to Logan, people here, including myself, will accept responsibility and whatever consequences there are."[67]

In lieu of waiting for the results of the investigation, two days later the *Globe* printed a strong antipatronage piece in the op-ed section under the headline "Massport Needs Leadership, Not Patronage" by columnist Joan Vennochi.[68] It was the first of several articles and editorials connecting the use of patronage at Massport to the terrorist acts.

> In the aftermath of the Sept. 11 tragedy, Massport public safety director Joseph Lawless emerges as the perfect illustration of the professionalism you don't get when you hire a man whose distinguishing characteristic is his former job as Governor William F. Weld's chauffeur. But the problem is bigger and deeper than the holes in Lawless's resume or his pitiful response to last week's calamity. It reflects a long-term political culture in the Commonwealth that not only accepts patronage, but begins with this hiring premise for public employees: It's not what you know, it's who you know.[69]

Vennochi proceeded to call for Buckingham's removal, urging then-Acting Governor Jane Swift to "declare the death of the culture of patronage at Massport and the dawn of a new culture of professionalism."[69]

Sensing the pursuit of "another agenda" by critics, including many who opposed Buckingham's initial appointment to Massport, on September 24 reporter Adrian Walker wrote that "there is no evidence that failures on the part of Massport personnel led to the hijackings. . . . That doesn't seem to matter, somehow."[70] Walker suggested that more facts and evidence were needed before deciding who should be forced to resign. Still, the negative, antipatronage articles, many of which directly called for the resignation of Buckingham and Lawless, continued.

An article announcing the formation of a panel by Swift, "charged with overhauling operations at Logan Airport," referenced the "mounting criticism that [Massport] has served as a patronage dumping ground."[71] Shortly after, under the headline "Patronage Still Rules the Roost at Logan," Derrick Jackson wrote,

> If the deaths of 6,000 people and the destruction of two airplanes, two 110-story skyscrapers, and freedom as we knew it were not enough to end patronage, then nothing will. So far, they have not been enough. It has been two-and-a-half weeks since the greatest attack on the American mainland was launched from Logan airport, and Virginia Buckingham is still running Logan.[72]

With the agency under increased political pressure and scrutiny, several personnel changes were made at Massport during the month of October 2001. On October 2, Massport Public Safety Director Lawless was demoted from his position and placed in charge of security for Massport facilities in the Port of Boston. Swift declared the change was caused by "continued security breaches."[73] Shortly after, on October 12, the Massport board of directors agreed to lay off 180 workers from the authority due to "growing financial and political pressures." Included in the layoffs were "three high profile patronage hires," although none of the positions involved airport security.[74] By the end of the month, Buckingham would resign from her position as executive director of Massport.

According to the *Boston Globe*, by the time of Buckingham's resignation she "had become increasingly isolated at Massport . . . and [Acting Governor] Swift had not spoken to her in weeks."[75] The article noted that "Buckingham's allies . . . mounted an effort to save her, suggesting that only in Boston, with its famously rough-and-tumble political climate, were people calling for firings after the terrorist attack."[75] However, in "Assessing the Undoing of Buckingham," reporters Yvonne Abraham and Frank Phillips offered a different take on the events that forced her to resign: "A decade of Republican administrations using Massport as a patronage dumping ground landed in Buckingham's lap."[76]

Analysis

The relevance of moral panic analysis to the Massport patronage case can be assessed using the framework established by Goode and Ben-Yehuda.[77] They identified five criteria that must be present for a moral panic to exist: concern, hostility, consensus, disproportionality, and volatility.

Concern

Goode and Ben-Yehuda state that "there must be a heightened level of concern over the behavior . . . of a certain group or category and the consequences that that behavior presumably causes for the rest of the society."[78] Although it has been argued that concern is often difficult to measure,[79] Goode and Ben-Yehuda suggest that concern can be measured in a variety of ways, including "public opinion polls, media attention, proposed legislation, action groups or social movement activity."[80]

To measure the level of concern during the time period relevant to the Massport case, a hybrid approach has been adopted. Using the Lexis-Nexis database, a search of full-text articles in the *Boston Globe* was conducted using the keyword *patronage*. The search was set for three months before and three months after the terrorist attacks. Using 9/11 as the triggering event, the intent is to capture the spontaneous and often volatile nature of moral panic attacks. To measure both general media coverage and direct public opinion, after the initial results were produced, *a search within results* was conducted using the term *Letters to the Editor*. Only articles addressing patronage as it relates to hiring in the public sector were included in the results. Articles addressing other forms of patronage, such as support of the arts or local business, were excluded. Counting the number of articles and the letters to the editor produced a measure of the *Globe*'s coverage and a measure of public concern during the relevant time period.[81]

6/11/01 to 9/11/01

During the three months prior to 9/11, the *Boston Globe* ran five articles dealing with the use of patronage in the public sector. Of the five articles, three articles addressed the use of patronage in the state of Massachusetts, whereas the other two articles addressed patronage usage in New Hampshire and France. Also, there were no letters to the editor concerning the use of patronage. This would indicate that patronage was not a pressing issue among the *Boston Globe*'s staff or readership during this time period.

9/12/01 to 12/11/01

During the three months after 9/11, the *Boston Globe* printed 97 articles dealing with the issue of patronage. A search within the results indicated that 68 of those articles mentioned the use of patronage at Massport. Other articles address the use of patronage by the Massachusetts Court, the Massachusetts Bay Transportation Authority, the Watertown Police Department, and the Massachusetts Low Level Radioactive Waste Management Board.

Of the 97 articles printed by the *Boston Globe* during this period, nine of the articles were letters to the editor. The rise in letters from zero to nine during the two search periods indicates that there was an increased level of public concern surrounding the use of patronage in the state of Massachusetts. It should be noted that the letters to the editor were not clustered in any given month during this three-month period, but spread out evenly over the course of the three months reviewed. There were two letters printed in September, three printed in October, one letter printed in November, and three printed in December. The sharp increase in both newspaper articles and letters to the editor addressing the issue of patronage during the three months following the terrorist attacks strongly suggests an increase in concern.

Hostility

Along with an increase in concern over the issue, there must also be increased levels of hostility toward those who support or participate in the offending activity. "Members are collectively designated as the enemy of respectable, law-abiding society; their behavior is seen as harmful or threatening to the values, interests, way of life, possibly the very existence, of the society, or a sizable segment of the society."[80] It is during the hostility phase that battle lines are drawn, setting the stage for the emergence of Cohen's folk devil.[6]

There are several indicators that illustrate an increase in hostility concerning the use of patronage. Two days prior to the terrorist attack, an article by columnist Alan Lupo appeared in the *Boston Globe* offering a lighthearted take on local colloquialisms. In the article, local terms were translated for new transplants to the region. Among the many terms included, several references to patronage were made along with the author's corresponding definitions:

Pols—politicians
Patronage—jobs pols give to their friends
Good patronage—occurs when their friends show up to work at the jobs

Bad patronage—when they don't, or they do, but you wish they hadn't
Appointments—jobs that reformers give to their friends[82]

Although the satirical, cynical definitions presented in the article may hint at latent feelings of resentment over the way that patronage has been used in the local area, given the lighthearted nature of the article it would be difficult to characterize the feelings toward patronage as hostile. However, this sense of lightheartedness prior to the terrorist attacks is in stark contrast to the angry, antipatronage tone of many of the articles that appeared after the attacks.

In the Vennochi and Jackson op-ed essays, readers are reminded of the many lives that were lost as a result of the terrorist hijackings, with the implicit suggestion that the use of patronage was in some way connected to those deaths. Both called for an end of the use of patronage at Massport, implying that by driving out the folk devil, future terrorist attacks would be avoided. "Misguided Blame" provides further evidence of the increase in hostility. Stressing the need for additional information, Walker writes, "No one in this terrible time is defending business as usual. But I think one can deplore the rush to judgment. . . . I think it is important to posses[s] more facts before debating who should resign, or who should replace them."[83]

The increased hostility was also reflected in the letters to the editor mentioned in the previous section. Of the nine letters printed following the attacks, all of them were highly critical of the use of patronage. One claimed that the use of patronage made the writer "physically ill" and that "the political misappointees that are running Massport" made him afraid to fly out of Logan Airport.[84] Another bluntly declared that "patronage is corruption."[85]

Consensus

According to Goode and Ben-Yehuda, "[T]here must be a certain minimal measure of agreement in the society as a whole or in designated segments of the society that the threat is real, serious, and caused by the wrongdoing of group members and their behavior."[80] The *Boston Herald*, a competing newspaper in the city, will be used to measure consensus. In the three months prior to the terrorist attacks, the *Herald* printed five articles dealing with the issue of patronage. Of those five articles, only one was from the letters to the editor section. In the three months following the attack, the *Herald* printed 67 articles dealing with the issue of patronage, including four letters to the editor.

The increase of articles and letters concerning patronage in the three months following the attacks is quite similar to the spike in coverage at the *Globe*. This indicates a degree of consensus that the threat posed by the use of patronage in Massachusetts government was serious and resonated throughout segments of the Boston community.

Disproportionality

To meet criterion for disproportionality, the perceived threat must be greater than the actual evidence. In a moral panic there is a sense that the disruptive behavior in question is eminent and great. However, a review of the relevant data connected to the threat does not support the sense of impending doom caused by the panic. As Goode and Ben-Yehuda point out, "[M]ost of the figures cited by moral panic claims makers are wildly exaggerated."[86] In this case, a causal linkage was inferred between the use of patronage at Massport and a weakness in aviation security at Logan. As a result, media coverage focused on three key local items: Logan was targeted due to its unique history of security violations, there was weak checkpoint screening at Logan, and Massport employed unqualified patronage appointees.

Logan Is Unique

In the days following the attack, the *Boston Globe* ran several stories detailing a history of security lapses at Logan Airport. Prior to the conclusion of the federal investigation, it was speculated that this caused the hijackers to target Logan. However, according to *The 9/11 Commission Report*, although "Logan was selected for two of the hijackings . . . we found no evidence that the terrorist targeted particular airports or airlines."[87] The report also stated, "Despite [previous] security problems at Logan . . . no evidence suggests that such issues entered into the terrorists' targeting."[87]

Checkpoint Screening

Many of the security lapses at Logan Airport involved the screening of passengers and baggage commonly known as *checkpoint screening*. At the time of the attacks, the airlines were responsible for checkpoint screening, a duty often handled by private contractors. On September 26, 2001, after reviewing checkpoint screening data from 1991 through 2000, the *Boston Globe* asserted that "FAA security statistics suggest that [Logan] is—by a substantial margin—the nation's most porous."[88] However, in a review of more recent checkpoint data, gathered from September 11, 1999, to September 11, 2001, the 9/11 Commission declared, "At the primary checkpoints, in aggregate, screeners met or exceeded the average for overall physical search, and X-ray detection, while falling below the norm for metal detection."[87, 89] Although Logan was below the norm for metal detection, the committee offered the following assessment on the history of checkpoint security, the only layer of security deemed relevant to the hijackings, for all three airports: "Nothing really stands out about any of them."[87]

Praise the Professional; Purge the Appointee

Schneider and Ingram argue that value-laden terms can be used in the social construction of groups to elevate one group, while stigmatizing another.[31] Maranto notes that appointees are often stigmatized by the myth of "appointee incompetence" and the suggestion that they add little value to their organizations.[90] Following the attacks, the *Boston Globe* invoked value-laden terms to make a clear distinction between career professionals and recipients of patronage.

In articles and editorials, Thomas Kinton was described as "the airport's respected aviation director,"[91] "the agency's experienced director of aviation,"[92] and "career port authority manager" in charge of the aviation division, which was "generally off-limits to patronage."[62]

By contrast, descriptions of Lawless signaled a tacit approval to diminish his professional experience. A day after the attacks, the *Globe* offered the following description: "Massport security director Joseph Lawless, a longtime state trooper who was former William F. Weld's chauffe[u]r in the early 1990's."[93] In later articles, the term *chauffeur* was sometimes replaced by the slightly more respectable *driver*[61, 65, 92] for *one-time bodyguard*.[94] All three terms served to undermine his stature as a professional.[95]

The coverage of these three issues is best described as the search for a "Boston-specific problem." This occurred even though there was no evidence to show that any of these issues played into the hijackers' decision to fly out of Logan. However, the disproportionate media attention given to these three issues helped to raise the public's level of anxiety during the moral panic.

Volatility

Moral panics tend to be fairly volatile in nature. Moral panics may be connected to long-standing historical issues or concerns, or they may "erupt fairly suddenly . . . and, nearly as suddenly, they subside."[86] In this case, patronage appears to be an instant folk devil, ready to be called upon during any crisis. Given Boston's long history with patronage,

patronage has been, and will continue to be, a folk devil capable of instigating a moral panic.

A three-month search of the *Boston Globe* using September 11, 2002, as the beginning date produced 85 articles concerning patronage. Despite Swift's withdrawal from the Republican Primary, patronage was a factor in the 2002 gubernatorial election. Republican Mitt Romney, who eventually became governor, ran as a reformer pledging to end patronage on Beacon Hill.

CONCLUSION

> This need to blame people, it's not happening in Newark, it's not happening in Dulles, where the other planes were hijacked. It's only happening here in Boston. . . . What does that say about Boston?
>
> **Joseph Lawless, quoted in the *Boston Globe*, September 26, 2001**[64]

> It had been five days since I had spoken to the governor. On September 21, I was summoned to attend Swift's daily security meeting. . . . Swift asked me to stay after the meeting ended. She said she knew that there was nothing Massport could have done to stop the hijackings. "But you also know politics," she continued, "and I can't guarantee you how this is going to turn out. The only way that I can sleep at night is that I know you understand how the media works." This would be the last time I talked to the governor before I resigned.
>
> **Virginia Buckingham, "My Side of the Story," *Boston Globe*, September 8, 2002**[96]

On December 4, 2001, *The Report of the Special Advisory Task Force on Massport* (The Carter Commission Report) was released, which declared "Patronage in all forms and at all levels is unacceptable."[97] The subsequent endorsement of the report by Swift was headlined on the front page of the *Boston Globe* as "Swift Declares Patronage Must End at Massport."[75] However, it is impossible to believe that this moral panic could have produced any other conclusion. As the case demonstrates, following the events of 9/11, the intense negative valence toward patronage emerged to produce a folk devil that invoked feelings in the Boston community bordering on visceral disgust.

As a result of a moral panic, and prior to the completion of any formal investigation, two well-respected administrators, Virginia Buckingham and Joseph Lawless, were forced out of their positions largely because they were portrayed as "patronage" hires in the most negative sense of the term. The conclusion reached by the Carter Commission, that patronage in all forms is bad, treats the negative view of patronage as a self-evident truth. As it has since the days of Progressive reform, patronage remains a perceived evil that cannot be tolerated.

However, acceptance of this narrow negative view of patronage poses a challenge that extends beyond Massport and Boston. As Ostrom argues, reforms "based on overly simplified views of the world have led to counterintuitive and counterintentional results."[98] In the case of patronage, the unchallenged negative view has been particularly problematic for the study and practice of public administration. For example, Hamilton notes that antipatronage policies in Illinois, a state with its own history of moral panics based on patronage folk devils, have failed to stop use of patronage in hiring, but instead, it has resulted in a cumbersome hiring system that limits the state's ability to hire talented employees.[99] On the federal level, Maranto argues that myths concerning the qualifications and work motivations of political appointees have limited our ability to maximize their capability.[90] These two examples speak to a history of folk devil narratives, which promoted a view of patronage as an inherently unproductive or destructive ("evil") activity. The power of these narratives precluded any empirical examination of patronage's functionality and its potential contribution to the progress or improvement of society or social conditions.[100] Recent research exploring the possibility of a positive role for patronage[1, 90, 99, 101] represents an important step toward removing the patronage folk devil of some of its potency.

However, the point of this analysis is not to advocate for an increase in patronage hires. Rather, it is to argue that the uncritical, unchallenged negative view of patronage has consequences beyond the challenge it poses to scholars and policy makers. In the case of Massport, in the period immediately following the tragic events of 9/11, it helped to fuel a moral panic by providing a powerful folk devil that did considerable damage to the morale of a relatively well-functioning public agency and did a considerable injustice to the careers and reputations of at least two committed public service professionals. Negatively constructed concepts such as patronage require great and consistent empirical examination to thwart their development into folk devils. Or, as Ostrom states, "[T]heoretically driven empirical research is an essential element of improving the operation of a democratic system."[98]

ACKNOWLEDGMENTS

This article was originally prepared for presentation at the 2004 Ethics Forum, 65th Annual Meeting of the American Society of Public Administrators, Portland, Oregon, March 26, 2004, and revised for presentation at the 36th Annual Meeting of the Northeastern Political Science Association, Boston, November, 11–13, 2004. The author would like to thank Melvin Dubnick, Laina Niemi, Trey Baker, David Rochefort, Christopher Bosso, Jonathan West, James Bowman, and the two anonymous reviewers.

ENDNOTES

1. Maranto, R., Thinking the unthinkable in public administration: A case for spoils in the federal bureaucracy, *Admin. Soc.*, 29, 623, 1998.
2. Caiden, G. E., What really is public maladministration?, *Publ. Admin. Rev.*, 51, 486, 1991.
3. Freedman, A. E., *Patronage: An American Tradition*, Nelson-Hall, Chicago, 1994.
4. Ostrom, E., The danger of self-evident truths, *Political Science & Politics*, 33, 33, 2000.
5. Ibid., 33.
6. Cohen, S., *Folk Devils and Moral Panics: The Creation of the Mods and Rockers*, MacGibbon and Kee, London, 2002.
7. Best, J., *Random Violence: How We Talk about New Crimes and New Victims*, University of California Press, Berkeley, 1999.
8. Thompson, K., *Moral Panics*, Routledge, London, 1998.
9. Heir, S., Conceptualizing moral panic through a moral economy of harm, *Critical Sociology*, 28, 311, 2002.
10. Cohen 2002, 1.
11. Ibid., 2.
12. Heir 2002, 313.
13. Waddington, P., Mugging as a moral panic: A question of proportion, *Brit. J. Sociol.*, 37, 245, 1986.
14. Freedman 1994, vii.
15. Mosher, F. C., *Democracy and the Public Service*, Oxford University Press, New York, 1982.
16. Ibid., 68.
17. Van Riper, P., *The History of the United States Civil Service*, Row Peterson, Evanston, IL, 1958.
18. For classic examples of how the morality argument was used as a justification for municipal and civil service reform, see Steffens, L., *The Shame of the Cities*, McClure Phillips, New York, 1904; and Parkhurst, C., *Our Fight with Tammany*, New York, 1895.
19. Addams, J., *Democracy and Social Ethics*, Macmillan, New York, 1902.
20. Bryce, J. B., *The American Commonwealth*, Macmillan, New York, 1899.
21. Bryce, J., The relations of political science to history and to practice: Presidential address, fifth annual meeting of the American Political Science Association, *Amer. Polit. Sci. Rev.*, 3, 1, 1909.

22. Fairlie, J., State administration in New York., *Polit. Sci. Quart.*, 15, 50, 1900.
23. Gitterman, J. M., The council of appointment in New York, *Polit. Sci. Quart.*, 7, 80, 1892.
24. Powers, F. P., The reform of the federal service, *Polit. Sci. Quart.*, 3, 247, 1888.
25. Simkhovitch, M., Friendship and politics, *Polit. Sci. Quart.*, 17, 189, 1902.
26. Snow, F., Cabinet government in the United States, *Ann. Amer. Acad. Polit. Soc. Sci.*, 3, 1, 1892.
27. Whitridge, F., Rotation in office, *Polit. Sci. Quart.*, 4, 279, 1889.
28. Wilson, W., The study of administration, *Polit. Sci. Quart.*, 2, 197, 1887.
29. For example, following the assassination of President James Garfield by Charles Guiteau, a frustrated office seeker, reformers transformed Garfield into a strong civil service reform advocate despite his weak record on the issue. The image of the martyred president was used to solidify the idea that patronage was evil. See [17] and [33].
30. Edelman, M., Political language and political reality, *PS*, 18, 10, 1985.
31. Schneider, A., and Ingram, H., *Policy Design for Democracy*, University Press of Kansas, Lawrence, 1997.
32. Stone, D., Causal stories and the formation of policy agendas, *Polit. Sci. Quart.*, 104, 281, 1989.
33. Hoogenboom, A. A., *Outlawing the Spoils: A History of the Civil Service Reform Movement, 1865–1883*, University of Illinois Press, Urbana, 1968.
34. Nelson, M., A short, ironic history of American national bureaucracy, *J. Polit.*, 44, 747, 1982.
35. Lee, C., House panel launches civil service overhaul, *Washington Post*, May 9, 2003, A33.
36. Lee, C., Overhaul of federal workforce is sought, *Washington Post*, June 8, 2003, A01.
37. Lee, C., Hill urges caution in civil service changes, *Washington Post*, January 28, 2005, A25.
38. Barr, S., Big, bold plan headed at defense bureaucracy, *Washington Post*, April 27, 2003, C02.
39. Bosso, C., The contextual bases of problem definition, in *The Politics of Problem Definition*, Rochefort, D., and Cobb, R., eds., University of Kansas, Lawrence, 1994, 182.
40. Colburn, D., and Pozzetta, G., Bosses and machines: Changing interpretations in American history, *History Teacher*, 9, 445, 1976.
41. Shefter, M., Regional receptivity to reform: The legacy of the progressive era, *Polit. Sci. Quart.*, 98, 459, 1983.
42. Weinberg, M., Boston's Kevin White: A mayor who survives, *Polit. Sci. Quart.*, 96, 87, 1981.
43. Beatty, J., *The Rascal King*, Da Capo, Cambridge, 2000.
44. Bruner, J., and Korchin, S., The boss and the vote: Case study in city politics, *Public Opin. Quart.*, 10, 1, 1946.
45. Connolly, J., Reconstituting ethnic politics: Boston, 1909–1925, *Soc. Sci. Hist.*, 19, 478, 1995.
46. Freedman 1994, 173–174.
47. Elazar, D., *American Federalism: A View from the States*, 2nd ed., Crowell, New York, 1972.

48. Hogarty argues that public authorities in Massachusetts are often torn between trying to maintain their independence while remaining responsive to citizens and elected officials. See Hogarty, R., The paradox of public authorities in Massachusetts, *New England Journal of Public Policy*, 17, 19, 2002.
49. Hogarty 2002.
50. Massport is also responsible for operating L. G. Hanscom Field, Worcester Regional Airport, the Port of Boston, and the Tobin Memorial Bridge.
51. The *Boston Globe* was selected as the paper of record for this case study given its local and national reputation. The *Globe* is considered the leading newspaper in the city, and was ranked in a tie for sixth place nationwide in the *Columbia Journalism Review*'s 1999 survey of America's best newspapers.
52. Donnelly, J., How could this have happened? *Boston Globe*, September 11, 2001, A7.
53. Barry. E., and Lewis, R., A fateful journey from Logan, *Boston Globe*, September 11, 2001, A1.
54. Cullen, K., Task force probing hub link to attacks, *Boston Globe*, September 11, 2001, 2nd ed., A6.
55. Bailey, S., Would you fly today? *Boston Globe*, September 12, 2001., 3rd ed., F1.
56. Howe, P., and Brelis, M., Crashes in NYC had grim origins at Logan, *Boston Globe*, September 12, 2001, 3rd ed., A1.
57. Brelis, M., Attack on America/airborne scenario, *Boston Globe*, September 12, 2001, 3rd ed., A11.
58. Blute was fired as executive director when he was caught by a *Boston Herald* photographer hosting a lunchtime party cruise paid for by Massport. See Hogarty 2002.
59. The airlines often contracted with private security companies to handle passenger and baggage screening.
60. Editorial, A war comes home, *Boston Globe*, September 12, 2001, 3rd ed., A16.
61. Mooney, B., and Kowalczyk, L., Political ties strong at airport, *Boston Globe*, September 14, 2001, 3rd ed., B1.
62. Ibid.
63. Phillips, F., and Klein, R., Post-attack Logan leadership could boost or hurt Swift, *Boston Globe*, September 13, 2001, 3rd ed., B3.
64. Cullen, K., America prepares/the investigation of Massport, *Boston Globe*, September 26, 2001, 3rd ed., A14.
65. Ebbert, S., and Kowalczyk, L., Logan security directory sought free rein, ex-driver for Weld balked at oversight, *Boston Globe*, September 15, 2001, 3rd ed., B1.
66. Buckingham, V., My side of the story, *Boston Globe Magazine*, September 8, 2002, 3rd ed., 10.
67. Robinson, W., Massport chief pledges accountability, *Boston Globe*, September 16, 2001, 3rd ed., A17.
68. Vennochi, J., Massport needs leadership, not patronage, *Boston Globe*, September 18, 2001, 3rd ed., A15.
69. Ibid., A15.
70. Walker, A., Misguided blame, *Boston Globe*, September 24, 2001, 3rd ed., B1.

71. Phillips, F., Noted figures are tapped for Logan review, *Boston Globe*, September 27, 2001, 3rd ed., B1.
72. Jackson, D., Patronage still rules the roost at Logan, *Boston Globe*, September 28, 2001, 3rd ed., A21.
73. Murphy, S., America prepares air safety, *Boston Globe*, October 4, 2001, 3rd ed., A34.
74. Lewis, R., and Mooney, B., Massport board ok's new fees, 180 layoffs, *Boston Globe*, October 12, 2001, 3rd ed., B1.
75. Phillips, F., and Lewis, R., Swift declares patronage must end at Massport, *Boston Globe*, December 4, 2001, 3rd ed., A1.
76. Abraham Y., and Phillips, F., Assessing the undoing of Buckingham, *Boston Globe*, October 27, 2001, 3rd ed., B4.
77. Goode, E., and Ben-Yehuda, N., Moral panics: Culture, politics, and social construction, *Annu. Rev. Sociol.*, 20, 149, 1994.
78. Ibid., 156–157.
79. Ungar, S., Moral panic versus the risk society: The implications of the changing sites of social anxiety, *Brit. J. Sociol.*, 52, 271, 2001.
80. Goode and Ben-Yehuda 1994, 157.
81. According to *Boston Globe* Services, "The globe receives an average of 350 letters to the editor every week and publishes only six or seven everyday because of limited space" (https://bostonglobe.com/newsroom/Editorial-Opinion/letterstoeditor.stm). Because the Lexis-Nexis search only reveals the number of letters printed, it is understood that the actual number of letters received could be higher.
82. Lupo, A., Here's how youse can learn the lingo, *Boston Globe*, September 9, 2001, 3rd ed., North Weekly 3.
83. Walker 2001, B1.
84. Rabbitt, S., Fix Logan now, *Boston Globe*, September 29, 2001, 3rd ed., A14.
85. Hruby, M., Patronage is corruption, *Boston Globe*, December 5, 2001, 3rd ed., A22.
86. Goode and Ben-Yehuda 1994, 158.
87. National Commission on Terrorist Attacks upon the United States, *The 9/11 Commission Report*, Norton, New York, 2004.
88. Brelis, M., and Carroll, M., FAA finds Logan security among worst in U.S., *Boston Globe*, September 26, 2001, 3rd ed., A1.
89. By comparison, Dulles exceeded the national average for physical search, but was below average for metal detector and X-ray. However, Newark exceeded or met the national average in all three areas. See [87].
90. Maranto, R., Praising civil service but not bureaucracy: A brief against tenure in the U.S. civil service, *Review of Public Personnel Administration*, 22, 175, 2002.
91. Ebbert and Kowalczyk 2001, B1.
92. Editorial, Crisis at Massport, *Boston Globe*, September 19, 2001, 3rd ed., A20.
93. Howe and Brelis, 2001, A1.
94. Phillips, F., and Lewis, R., America prepares impact on New England/former governor's legacy, *Boston Globe*, September 21, 2001, 3rd ed., B8.

95. An article detailing attempts by Lawless to defend his professional background, printed days prior to his demotion, confirmed this perception. The reporter noted that "Lawless's law enforcement career and the qualifications for his job have been reduced by some to this: He was Weld's chauffer." See [54]. Buckingham's professional background was also questioned. Although Buckingham was chief of staff to two governors, the perception was that she possessed "little administrative experience" prior to her appointment. See [49]. However, when asked about Buckingham's role in the oversight of 60,000 state employees during his administration, former Governor William Weld was quoted asking, "Who do you think was managing them, me?" See [93].
96. Buckingham, 2002, 10.
97. Special Advisory Task Force on Massport, *Report of the Special Advisory Task Force on Massport*, Commonwealth of Massachusetts, Boston, 2004.
98. Ostrom 2000, 42.
99. Hamilton, D., Is patronage dead? The impact of antipatronage staffing systems, *Review of Public Personnel Administration*, 22, 3, 2002.
100. Bearfield D., A critical examination of the use of patronage in U.S. public administration, Ph.D. diss., Rutgers University, Newark, NJ, 2004.
101. Goodsell, C., A radical idea welcomed but with some buts, *Admin. Soc.*, 29, 653, 1998.

PART III

STATE CASES OF CIVIL SERVICE REFORM

6

ENDING CIVIL SERVICE PROTECTIONS IN FLORIDA GOVERNMENT: EXPERIENCES IN STATE AGENCIES

James S. Bowman
Florida State University

Jonathan P. West
University of Miami

INTRODUCTION

Private companies and public agencies have been transformed in recent years as managerialism—an ideology emphasizing deregulated, decentralized, downsized organizations driven by market-style imperatives—propelled change. Corporations reengineered and governments reinvented. (1, 2) As a result, the management of human resources is undergoing profound transition in both concept and practice. A key component of this transformation is the dissolution of the traditional social contract at work—job security with good pay and benefits in exchange for employee commitment and loyalty. In the process the long-standing American employment at-will business doctrine, which was eroded in the latter part of the 20th century, has been revitalized and has spread to the public sector through civil service reform.

Fueled by entrepreneurial strategies, budget cutbacks, and devolution, the contemporary reform movement (3) has gained exemptions from merit systems across the nation by expanding management prerogatives and restricting employee rights. (4, 5) By the turn of the 21st century, a variety of federal departments (e.g., the Federal Aviation Administration, Internal Revenue Service, General Accountability Office, and National Aeronautics and Space Administration) had received full or partial waivers from Title 5 of the U.S. Code, which defines the merit system. In the wake of September 11, 2001, the Transportation Security Agency established at-will employment for its personnel, and subsequently the Departments of Homeland Security and Defense were authorized to create new human resource management systems. The Bush administration later announced that it would seek congressional approval to use these approaches as templates for governmentwide change. At the state level, major reform examples also exist. In 1996 Georgia law mandated that all new civil servants be hired on an at-will basis, and in 2001 Florida eliminated job tenure for most incumbent middle managers (and made it easier to discipline remaining career employees and harder to appeal adverse actions). South Carolina and Arkansas recently abolished their merit systems; less dramatically, a number of states (e.g., Indiana, Delaware, and Kansas) are reclassifying career service positions to unclassified ones as a consequence of reorganizations, reductions in force, and/or retirements.

This study examines the impact of the Florida law on state agencies. The objective is to ascertain the extent to which the elimination of the defining characteristic of the merit system—job protection from partisan interference—has affected employees. After reviewing pertinent literature and background material, the third section describes the study methodology. This is followed by the presentation of findings and a discussion of their implications for the future of reform.

SCHOLARLY LITERATURE AND BACKGROUND MATERIAL

Scholarly Literature

Although there is little research on the impact of employment at-will on career employees, a useful body of civil service reform literature has emerged in the last decade. (6) Kettl and his colleagues outlined many of the themes—decentralization, performance measurement, contracting out, and civil service deregulation—echoed in subsequent work. (7) For instance, Ingraham and her coauthors offered a vision for the 21st-century public service, (8) and Denhardt and Denhardt contrasted components of the "new public service" with those of New Public Management and "old public administration." (9) Schultz and Maranto provided a history of the nation's civil service reforms. (10; see also 11, 12) Condrey and Maranto presented historical, comparative, and point-counterpoint material on radical reform, (13) and Thompson examined institutional consequences of civil service disaggregation during the Clinton years. (14)

In the last several years, West edited a journal symposium on Georgia's legislation, (15) Bowman critiqued Florida's changes, (16) Walters described changes in three states, (17) Maranto maintained that opposition to reform was based on misconceptions about political appointees as well as careerists, (18) West and Bowman investigated Florida's initiative using stakeholder analysis, (19) and Kellough and Nigro collected studies in 2002 on state-level reforms. (20)

Overall, this work is theoretical, descriptive, and normative, as it posits frameworks to understand change, describes those reforms, and develops arguments about them. There is, however, a paucity of evaluative research in most jurisdictions. Very little systematic data exists, although there are several examples of empirical research. Kellough and Nigro found that Georgia employees had reservations about the purpose of reform and its daily administration, but the system "had little of the desired impact on agency performance beyond redefining workers' . . . job security." (21) Bowman et al. surveyed affected Florida personnel and found that respondents doubted assumptions made by both reformers and their critics, were concerned about downsizing, and rejected claims made by change advocates about the effects of at-will employment on productivity, morale, and pay. (22)

What is lacking in the extant corpus of knowledge are analyses of the impact of reform on staff in individual departments. Indeed, scholars often appeal for such work to provide knowledge unavailable in survey research. The present study, therefore, contributes to the literature by examining the effect of these changes on employees in three state agencies. To provide a context for the Florida experience, the section below briefly reviews at-will employment and then the state's civil service system.

Background Material

Employment at-Will

In the private sector, employment at-will as a management proprietary right predominates; an adverse action can be taken against an employee for any or no reason not contrary to law. In the public sector, courts recognize that most employees (except those in policy-making positions) have legislative, contractual, and constitutional protections against unjust discharge; notably, the Fifth Amendment (concerning denial of life, liberty, and property without due process of law) applies to federal staff, and the parallel Fourteenth Amendment to state and local personnel.

Although these guarantees apply to government employees, they have influenced the private sector. Over the years, three exceptions to at-will employment emerged—labor contracts, antidiscrimination laws, and public policy statutes—which may provide protection from unjust discharge in selected states. (23) By the end of the last century, these limitations led commentators to predict the demise of the at-will doctrine. (24, 25) Most workers, however, remain susceptible to arbitrary termination because they are not covered by contract or may discover that statutory or judicial protections do not include the numerous reasons that can be found to discharge someone.

Moreover, at-will employment has been revitalized both in the private and public arenas. In the private sphere, the landmark 2000 *Guz vs. Bechtel National, Inc.* ruling by the California Supreme Court vitiated a leading exception to the doctrine in a case likely to have nationwide impact. (26) In the public sector, reform advocates in Florida and elsewhere believe that public servants have no need of job tenure because modern civil rights, whistle-blowing retaliation, and related laws are said to provide adequate protection. (27) The emergence of contingent workers as a large, growing proportion of the workforce in both sectors suggests that employees are increasingly viewed as "disposable." (28) Furthermore, to the extent that American-style capitalism is emulated in other countries, U.S. management practices like employment at-will also may be adopted.

Reform in Florida

Governor Jeb Bush was elected by a wide margin in 1998, promising CEO-like efficiency and no-nonsense management. (29) Consistent with private sector cutbacks characteristic of that decade, he directed all agencies to plan to reduce their workforces by 25 percent in five years. Issues such as education, crime, tax cuts, the environment, and affirmative action were the focus of his first two years in office, but the governor believed that his policy initiatives would be jeopardized if the state's employment system was not changed.

Accordingly, Service First was announced in the March 2001 State of the State Address. The governor contended that the merit system had changed from protecting the public to protecting employees without regard for performance. He wanted to relieve managers of cumbersome personnel processes (by removing job protections) and give agencies more flexibility to compensate high performers (by instituting a bonus program). In response to predictions that the state would revert to patronage practices, Bush argued that partisanship, cronyism, nepotism, and favoritism could corrupt the existing career service system; because job safeguards impeded flexibility and did not solve the problems they were designed to solve, they should be abolished. (30)

The most contentious part of the reform was the conversion of a substantial number of Career Service (CS) personnel to Selected Exempt Service (SES; an existing category immediately below the Senior Executive Service), thereby abolishing their job security. The secretary of the Department of Management Services spoke of irritation with "we-bes" (career public servants who believe that "we be here when you come and we be here when you're gone"), and suggested that they should lose job security. (31) Critics observed that this was consistent with what would become the governor's decisive "my way or the highway" management style. (32) To achieve greater responsiveness, the new legislation made 16,300 managers, supervisors, and confidential employees (of the 118,064 state career personnel) "at-will," serving at the pleasure of the appointing official. Although those shifted to SES lost job security, they received fully paid health, life, and disability insurance as well as additional leave time. The legislation (http://www.myflorida.com/dms) did not mandate evaluation of the effects of the changes.

In an initiative paralleling Service First, Productivity First made personnel management staff at-will through privatization. By eliminating 900 career service positions, the state's entire personnel system (responsible for administrating the pay and benefits for over 200,000 current and retired employees) was thereby outsourced. Programs such as these build upon contemporary federal and state trends intended to reinvigorate, and limit the size of, government. (33, 34)

In short, the national civil service reform movement has been successful in achieving a multitude of changes, including employment at-will, in recent years. Various commentators have suggested that the movement is politically derived and increasingly partisan. Reformers believe that differences between the public and private sector are to be reduced by (1) "running government like a business"; (2) emphasizing the classic "theory of the firm" that organizations have a duty to their immediate principals with few obligations to employees or other stakeholders; (3) providing limited evidence for change or acknowledgement of potential weaknesses, as open dialogue is not necessarily seen as useful; and (4) favoring fundamental, not incremental, changes. (35, 36, 37)

METHODOLOGY

Between October 2004 and March 2005, over fifty 10–45-minute, semi-structured telephone interviews were conducted with staff converted from Career Service to Selected Exempt Service in the Departments of Transportation, Environmental Protection, and Children and Families.

Respondents were chosen from agency-supplied randomized lists of managerial, supervisory, and confidential employees, one-half located in state capital headquarters (home to a substantial proportion of the workforce) and one-half in Miami-Dade County field district offices (home to the state's largest population center). (38) The agencies represent the broad range of governmental distributive, regulatory, and redistribution functions. (39)

Questioning generally began by asking why respondents believed the reform bill was passed, and then focused on whether Service First positively or negatively affected activities such as department recruitment, employee productivity, managerial flexibility, service provision, staff morale, employee compensation, workforce loyalty, and the nonpartisan character of public service. Several additional items addressed (1) whether the participant believed that Service First was either a successful or unsuccessful application of the "business model" to government, and (2) whether employees are generally seen as an asset to be developed or as a cost to be controlled.

In addition to these confidential interviews, the authors conducted semistructured in-person interviews in February–June 2005 with departmental human resource managers in central or district offices (n = three), as well as selected gubernatorial staff, legislative personnel, as well as current and former agency personnel (n = five). Participants were selected on the basis of their expertise, policy-making roles, and availability. These sessions lasted approximately 45–75 minutes each and also focused on the program deployment issues discussed with the middle managers. (40)

A potential problem with qualitative methods is the difficulty in generalizing to a larger environment. Yin suggests examining the context in which actions take place and using multiple sites to increase generalizability, a reason why several departments were selected for this research. (41) One limitation of this work is its reliance on telephone interview data; despite guarantees of anonymity, information was not easily obtained from some SESers due to the sensitive nature of the topic, (42) a problem not encountered in the face-to-face sessions with other stakeholders. In addition, with few exceptions, potentially important secondary material such as departmental publications and raw personnel data did not contain relevant information. Despite such concerns, it proved possible to achieve a reasonable understanding of each agency under Service First, thus enabling an evaluation of the reform's impact. The results below provide a useful perspective on reform as the findings examine the effects of the law in the workplace. After presenting these data, the analysis concludes with comments on civil service reform in Florida and elsewhere in the years ahead.

FINDINGS

To ascertain each department's implementation of reform and its impact on employees, the discussion first describes the views of the agency personnel directors, and then turns to those employees affected by Service First. Included are respondent beliefs on why the law was enacted and its effects on agency processes and people (recruitment, service provision, responsiveness, productivity, pay, morale and loyalty, political neutrality, and public employment appeal). This is followed by whether employees are seen as an asset or a cost, and if reform is considered a successful or unsuccessful application of business practices. The department discussions conclude with a case study. Last, a broad comparison of the findings of this research to results from an all-agency, statewide sample of SESers one year after passage of Service First (43) is presented. Due to the nature of the cases and the wide-ranging interview format, the data below is not expressed in percentage terms.

Transportation

The Department of Transportation (DOT), responsible for highway, railroad, airport, and seaport systems, addresses the state's transportation needs with a budget over $6 billion. It employs 7,450 people, down from over 10,000 in 2000 in response to the governor's goal of reducing the state workforce by 25 percent. In so doing, it has become one of Florida's most privatized agencies. The central office in the capital oversees seven districts.

Human Resource Management View

Congruent with reform objectives, the personnel chief in the capital city believed that the program was "to provide more flexibility to managers by cutting civil service red tape, and offering more benefits to employees to achieve a smaller, smarter, better government" (personal communication, February 3, 2005). Compared to some human resource initiatives, she pointed out that Service First was "cut and dried" as it was readily implemented by converting career employees into the extant SES personnel classification.

One major focus of Service First—recruitment—was quickly affected by change. Prior to the law, "we had to honor the process," which took six weeks from position advertisement to job offer, a process that now takes one month. Although a principal reform rationale was to improve citizen service by increasing responsiveness, the respondent felt that it has had little effect because employees have routinely been responsive and service-oriented.

Reform was also to make government more productive. This official said, "We may be more productive now because we do more with less, but it is hard to determine if it is because of Service First which ran concurrently with downsizing." Although employee morale and loyalty were, initially, negatively affected, agency personnel saw that "SESers were not terminated at [a] greater rate than others." The manager believed that concerns about the neutrality of civil service were not germane to DOT because SES officials still benefit from career service–like job protections—that is, the agency requires termination for cause.

Overall, the interviewee saw public employment as more attractive today because managers get free benefit coverage without any waiting period, do not have to be concerned about increasing health insurance costs, and immediately become eligible to use leave time. Employees are regarded as both a cost (insurance, retirement, workers' compensation) and an asset (the department's philosophy is to invest in every person and to expect a return on that investment). The latter view has included denials of dismissal recommendations to transfer the individual to a suitable position (personal communication, February 3, 2005). He or she recognized the political appeal of "running government like a business," but believed that public and private operating principles are different, and doubted that outsourced services save the state money.

SES Views

When respondents (ten from the central office and nine from district offices) were queried about the passage of Service First, most indicated that the governor wanted more management flexibility and accountability to streamline and downsize government, answers similar to the HR responses above. However, approximately one-half also commented that the objective was to "erode the civil service" by removing employees at the pleasure of their superior; as one district supervisor said, "It was a political smokescreen; we call it Service Last."

Although many informants saw no difference (or did not know), five felt that recruitment was easier because "the state paying for benefits is a plus under Service First" (a district confidential employee). However, several believed that hiring was more difficult now, although "Service First is not the only factor explaining it," as continued low pay (something reform was to address) is the principal problem according to a district supervisor. Like the HRM head in Tallahassee, most saw no change in service provision and responsiveness; a Miami-based supervisor said, "[G]ood people do a good job and provide good service."

Concerning productivity, once again most officials found that reform had no effect. However, "downsizing has impacted substantially on the volume of work," in the words of a district manager, and those remaining do more work, according to a central office manager. A Tallahassee supervisory SESer stated that "initially Service First decreased productivity because of time lost in discussion and questions about it," a view echoed by a confidential employee also in the capital. Ultimately, though, impact on productivity depends on the work unit (in the opinion of a district supervisor) and the "quality of the person" (a district confidential employee). And reform does make it easier to let nonperformers go, in the view of a state capital confidential worker. In response to questioning about compensation, most saw no change, although nearly as many believed that there had been a negative impact. Thus, a district supervisor said that this was "sad because we have some really good people," who are trained by the state and then hired away.

Regarding workforce morale and loyalty, "there were initial misgivings as people felt that their status was jeopardized" (a district supervisor). One central office confidential employee indicated that "there was a perception that something was taken away (job protection) while we still had the same responsibilities and pay (but better benefits)." A confidential employee from the Miami district office said, "During the first year after Service First passed, there was concern that it was a play for power that would allow leaders to work their will," a view echoed by a manager in the capital city. Although some of these concerns apparently have moderated, several respondents noted that "paltry" rewards adversely affected morale, and valuable employees who left the department "often felt unappreciated" (a field supervisor). In the end, though, "who you work for and how you feel about your job" are decisive, said a confidential employee from the Miami district office. A minority believed that morale and loyalty were unaffected by reform.

With respect to political neutrality of public service, approximately one-half of the sample thought that nothing changed. For example, several SES personnel acknowledged reluctance to "speak truth to power," but believed that "someone could always be gotten rid of" (a Tallahassee supervisor) and that "the reaction of elected officials was always in the back of your mind" (a field office manager). These concerns, however, were more evident in politically vulnerable agencies, at higher levels of management, and in the state capital.

Among those perceiving a change in the nonpartisan civil service, a capital confidential employee said that "Service First creates an environment for abuse," and that it "led to a decline in efficiency as good ideas are not expressed and problems not addressed." A Tallahassee-area manager asserted that "people are more timid, less eager to call attention to controversial areas"; "You do not want to p--- off people who could cost you your job," a Miami confidential employee claimed. One respondent stated flatly that "there is more fear under Service First and you think twice about blowing the whistle" (a district manager). Another believed that civil service is more partisan and that even career service staff work in fear (a Miami supervisor). A district supervisor said, "There is concern about the 'shoot the messenger' syndrome. People are more careful about how and what they say and do" to avoid, in the words of a Miami supervisor, "getting burned. Before Service First, we had watchdogs looking out for the public interest."

Many study participants felt that reform had no effect on the attractiveness of public employment. However, one field supervisor indicated that "for a new college graduate, it won't matter if you are SES or CS, as many do not appreciate the difference until they have been here for several years." Others replied that job appeal diminished due to loss of job security, whereas several thought it increased because of the benefit/leave package. In response to whether employees are seen as an asset or cost, many said it depends on whose opinion is asked; as a Tallahassee supervisor observed, "for politicians, they are costs, for managers, assets." A capital city confidential official stated, "In the current environment, employees are seen as necessary, but only until it can be figured out how to farm them out." A Miami supervisor indicated that personnel "are assets—but not under Service First philosophy."

Finally, when asked if the reform law, as an application of the "business model," was successful or not, a supervisor in Tallahassee replied that it was successful because short- and long-term planning has been pushed down to appropriate levels and most are in a better position financially because of SES benefits. Another supervisor at the same location was appreciative of recruitment process streamlining and the ability to work on personnel issues (with just a temporary negative effect on morale); a Miami-area supervisor concurred that the change provides more management flexibility and ways to improve processes. A headquarters supervisor held that Service First could have been more successful if all employees were placed at-will. But most agreed with a district manager who emphasized that "you can't run government like a business. We don't have the flexibility of a corporation because of budget constraints and bureaucratic limitations." Others echoed a capital city manager who said that "business does not work the same as government and there are enough 'disbenefits' in Service First that we were better off before." Indeed, several SESers characterized the law as completely unsuccessful. "If you are going to apply the business model [and] take away job security, then increase salaries too" (a district confidential worker).

To summarize, DOT is a major state agency whose personnel director largely agreed with the governor's reform goals. Recruitment takes less time today, productivity may have increased, service and responsiveness have always been present, morale and loyalty have not been greatly impacted, and the civil service remains nonpartisan (no empirical data is maintained on such matters). Hiring SES officials is easier now because of the benefit package, employees are seen as a departmental asset, and business practices, although not without value, are different than those found in government.

On the part of those converted (Table 6.1), many officials agreed with the announced goals of reform, but approximately one-half thought that they were politically derived. They also split on the effect of change on recruitment, but like the HR managers, believed that no change occurred in service provision, responsiveness, or productivity. Most saw an adverse effect, especially in the beginning, on morale and loyalty. The majority did not see any change in pay, although nearly as many thought that reform had a negative impact on respondent attitudes about compensation. Concerning the nonpartisan character of public service, one-half saw no change but many others alluded to increased fear at work. Personnel also were not in agreement on the appeal of public employment after reform,

Table 6.1 Predominant Views on Service First (n = 51 SES officials)

Reform Dimension	*DOT*	*DEP*	*DCF*
Reform goals	Positive/negative	Negative	Negative
Recruitment	No change	Negative	No change/negative
Service provision	No change	No change	No change/negative
Responsiveness	No change	Positive/no change	Positive/no change
Productivity	No change	No change	Positive/no change
Morale and loyalty	Negative	Negative	Negative
Pay	No change/negative	Negative/no change	Negative
Nonpartisan service	Negative	Negative	Negative
Employment appeal	No change/negative	Negative	Negative
Cost or asset	Cost	Cost	Cost
Business model	Unsuccessful	Unsuccessful	Unsuccessful

and many thought that elected officials see employees as a cost to be controlled. Finally, whereas some believed Service First was a successful application of the corporate model, most felt that government cannot be run by business principles. A case study of how reform impacted one DOT employee is found in Appendix 1 at the end of this chapter.

Environmental Protection

The Department of Environmental Protection's (DEP) mission is to protect, restore, and manage the state's natural resources and to enforce environmental laws. With a budget of over $2 billion, it employs 3,500 people. The department may be unique because in 1995 approximately 100 career service engineers and environmental administrators were placed into SES. This was done for reasons similar to those advanced by Service First with apparently few untoward results.

Human Resource Management View

The reason Service First was enacted was to provide "greater managerial flexibility, discretion, and benefits," according to the state capital agency human resource manager (personal communication, February 3, 2005). In "real and practical terms," it had no effect on the recruitment process, service provision, or responsiveness. Reform, similarly, had neither a positive nor negative impact on morale, as many personnel took the attitude of "Oh well, another change." The same was true for workforce loyalty, as employees were described as "very dedicated," long in agency tenure, and believing that work with DEP is not just another job.

Concerning a politically neutral public service, the official also saw no repercussions as a result of reform. "Some say that personnel are not as comfortable in enforcement actions because of the changed status, but contrary to what one might think most are not hesitant to go into SES because we have a lot of professional people who do a good job." Indeed, the interviewee indicated that civil service protections have no effect. "When the agency needs to do what it needs to do, the safeguards have more to do with managers just doing management's job by fulfilling a few more procedural requirements." All staff, he or she continued, are entitled to fair treatment and are protected by federal law. The number of SES dismissals is very low, with no increase since Service First.

With respect to employees as an asset or cost, "It's sad, but to be seen as an asset, the state would have to have a 'real' pay philosophy" to ensure marketplace competitiveness (personal communication, February 3, 2005). "Instead, raises are decided at the end of the legislative session, the 'last crumb on the table.'" Overall, this manager sees value in Service

First private sector principles, such as managerial flexibility in selection and retention, but reform did not provide business-like rewards.

SES Views

Although several of the 15 officials (eight from the central office, seven from the district office) answered that they "had no idea" why Service First was enacted or that it was to create more accountability, the rest seemed to agree with the Tallahassee supervisor who opined that it was "to make downsizing easier." Elaborating, a Miami confidential employee claimed that "the governor had to make it possible for people who were 'locked in' to their state jobs to lose protections so that positions could be privatized."

Respondents also doubted the positive impact of reform on recruitment as just three believed that it was enhanced, four saw no change, and the rest felt that the result was adverse. A district manager believed that it was easier before because "now SESers have less job security and they may be cynical about what it takes to succeed in the job." A Miami supervisor said, "We used to meet applicants . . . and find out whether they would fit into our organization. Now it is done all on-line. . . . Losing the personal touch has been frustrating to employees and applicants."

Most thought that there had been no change in service provision, as a district supervisor said they remain attentive to the public. Another Miami supervisor, however, believed that it was poorer because employees were unhappy about Service First. In replies to whether reform affected responsiveness, a district supervisor stated that "SES status has increased the attentiveness and speed with which employees respond to requests from elected officials," a view shared by several others. Yet, approximately the same number of administrators believed that no change had occurred since 2001. A capital city manager stated that they are "a little more vulnerable, yes, but does it affect behavior, no. I am lucky because I trust my supervisors; everything depends upon the integrity of people above you."

Two capital city participants who suggested that reform had "slight or limited" positive repercussions captured minority views on whether productivity increased or decreased. One district manager added, "People were reluctant to become SES because they serve at-will, but it does put stress on people to perform better." Most officials, though, mentioned that reform had no effect, and several believed that the impact was negative. For instance, one Tallahassee supervisor observed that "we lost people with experience and the replacements had none," and a district manager contended that "it takes longer to get things done because people are very careful to avoid making mistakes or offending the wrong person."

Respondents were divided on the reform's results on pay as most believed it to be negative, but nearly as many saw no change. For example, a Tallahassee-based supervisor indicated, "Broadbanding opened a Pandora's Box, but we fill at the minimum, so what's the point of Service First?" A Miami confidential official pointed out, "We were supposed to see an increase in salary accompanying our conversion. It has not happened."

Workforce morale and loyalty, in the opinion of several officials, "depends on where you are and who your superiors are" (a Tallahassee manager), or there was no reform impact because "in this day and age, you are just glad to have a job" (a headquarters confidential employee). Everyone else, in contrast to the HR view, perceived that Service First had adverse consequences. "It used to be that we belonged to a fraternity of public service. People never considered job offers to leave. Now they are actively looking," according to a district manager. A Miami-based confidential employee said, "While many remain loyal, it is no longer a two-way street because we can be easily replaced."

Such perceptions were reflected in answers on civil service impartiality. Whereas three respondents indicated no change or "don't know," the remainder thought the impact was negative. "Before people made recommendations that might be controversial, but not now; before employees liked to help people, but now they worry about antagonizing the current political party" (a Tallahassee supervisor). Another person at the same location and rank said, "Employment at-will causes us to be very judicial in how we deal with citizens who have political connections; the individual, independent public servant is gone." On the attractiveness of government employment, the sample again offered largely adverse responses. No one thought that Service First improved public employment appeal, and just a small number believed that it resulted in no change, perhaps because the overall compensation package was still not competitive. One capital city supervisor said, "Someone might as well work for business for more money as there is no security in government."

In reply to whether employees are regarded as an asset or a cost, a manager in Tallahassee said, "An asset. I try to develop my employees and I have been treated well," a view supported by three other respondents. Another stated, "It depends. In my unit, we view employees as an asset; higher ups view them as a cost" (a district confidential employee). The rest of the sample, however, emphasized the latter view; for instance, "Politicians see employees as 'lard bricks,' and government as a drain on state resource" (a capital city supervisor), "SES makes it seem like employees are viewed as more of a cost to be controlled" (a Miami manager), and "the rhetoric is that they are assets; the problem is the absence of funds to invest in employee development" (a district manager).

Last, do personnel see reform as a successful application of the business model? A Miami confidential official thought it was and said, "People who thought they couldn't be touched are now out of the public service. I came from the private sector, so this was not new to me." A Tallahassee confidential staffer indicated both positive and negative consequences of Service First, but thought the results will be more positive in the future. The balance of interviewees regarded the reform initiative as an unsuccessful application of corporate practices:

- "The question's premise is not true because successful businesses *have* employee protections" (a Tallahassee manager).
- "Public service is not a business as it does not make money from services; outsourcing does not save money, but instead just gets rid of employees" (a capital city supervisor).
- "I don't think it works well in government. It is ironic that I did not fear losing my job in the private sector, but in the state sector I have been more concerned. In business, you can get resources and supplies when needed, but in government it is much more difficult" (a district confidential employee).
- "The business approach assumes 'profits' are more important than people. One of the insulting things are names right out of '1984' like Service First" (a headquarters supervisor).

To summarize, the Department of Environmental Protection plays a significant role in husbanding and regulating the state's natural resources. The human resource office saw reform objectives in gubernatorial terms as improving managerial flexibility. Service First did not, however, have substantial positive or negative effects on recruitment, services, productivity, morale and loyalty, or the nonpartisan character of government employment. The data suggests that personnel can be seen as costs to be controlled and the implementation of the corporate model as incomplete. Officials converted to Selected Exempt status had largely different interpretations on most issues (Table 6.1). They did not accept the official reform goal and thought Service First negatively affected recruitment, morale and loyalty, public service neutrality, and governmental employment appeal. Roughly one-half of the respondents thought that responsiveness improved, but the other half did not think any change occurred. They were also divided on pay issues as one-half saw negative consequences and the other half discerned no difference. These SESers believed that reform had no impact on productivity, but thought employees were regarded as costs and saw an unsuccessful implementation of corporate-style practices. A case on the effect of Service First in DEP is found in Appendix 2.

Department of Children and Families

The Department of Children and Families' (DCF) mission is to partner with communities to ensure the well-being of children and families in areas such as child care services, developmental disabilities, economic self-sufficiency, mental health services, and substance abuse. DCF, an agency with a budget of $3.8 billion, over 22,000 positions, and eight service districts plus a regional office, is shifting from being a direct provider to an overseer as a result of privatization. In response to considerable political scrutiny and public controversy, it also has been undergoing organizational restructuring to improve operational effectiveness.

HRM View

The reform law was passed because it was "in line with the governor's push for privatization. There was a perception of the civil service that they were more interested in protection than serving the customer. Service First was a way to 'refresh' the workforce," in the view of this official (anonymous, personal communication, May 19, 2005).

Recruitment has been improved because the new system appeals to those "who really want to serve clients," with the result that service provision is enhanced. The director indicated that political accountability and responsiveness remain unchanged; according to the interviewee, "[I]f someone is asked by a politician to do something against the rules, you can't break the rules. It probably gets kicked up the ladder to someone else to handle it." Although the impact of change on morale has been both "good and bad, those who are more likely to be productive are more positive as a result of reform"; in any case, there "has not been a marked increase in employee complaints."

Overall the new legislation has been a success in the application of business techniques to government, but this executive would like to see more investment in staff "as an organizational value that is institutionalized rather than something that may change when leadership changes."

SES Views

Some two-thirds of these 17 officials (eight from headquarters, seven from the district office) believed that the objective of Service First was to downsize government. A supervisory employee from Tallahassee indicated that "they said it was to improve accountability; in reality it was to cut positions." A capital city confidential official thought that reform was passed "just so employers could fire employees easier, at any time for any reason; I have seen it happen." "The governor has been against public employees since taking office," according to a Miami manager. "He started with middle managers because they had no union protection, but it was part of a broader plan to cut all categories of public employees." One field manager, however, said Service First "was Governor Bush's initiative to downsize government and make managerial positions more accessible to those outside state government" (the balance of the interviewees did not know why Service First was enacted).

There was a division among the respondents on the reform's impact on recruitment, as one-half felt that it had no effect and one-half felt that it had negative repercussions. A district manager said, "State government used to be a career where people came out of school and continued to work to retirement. Now there is no respect, no raises, and demoralized staff." Several people, however, thought that recruitment had improved. A Miami confidential interviewee, for example, said that "it is easier to hire and fire," and a Tallahassee confidential employee noted that it is easier to recruit by "placing 'whoever' into SES."

Concerning service provision, most agreed it was the same as before; one district supervisor put it this way: "I don't think public service has suffered as a result of Service First." But a Tallahassee manager asserted, "[H]ow can it [reform] not affect service provision negatively? Downsizing and increased work load is a no-win situation." "Staff is so unmotivated [to provide service]," claimed a Miami-based manager, "that almost everyone is looking for employment elsewhere." On whether reform has enhanced responsiveness, the sample was divided between those who thought it was increased and those who saw no difference.

Nearly half of the officials mentioned no change in productivity, and one-half believed it was enhanced. Reform "increased fear and therefore productivity," according to a capital city confidential employee. Representing the remaining five people who believed that productivity declined was a Miami manager claiming that "the workforce is totally demoralized. There is no motivation, no promotions, they eliminated overtime, no comp time—why work harder?" Echoing this view, approximately two-thirds of the sample felt morale and loyalty decreased under Service First. "Morale is down the drain," a district confidential staffer stated. A Tallahassee manager added, "There is no loyalty in the workforce; everyone feels like a free agent. There is no real difference between Career Service and Selected Exempt as all work at-will. We are 'day labor.'"

With respect to compensation issues, one person noted the fully paid benefits that accompanied conversion to unclassified status, but most thought that reform had a negative impact (three saw no change). A headquarters supervisor observed, "Service First promised more competitive pay and performance bonuses, but this has not happened." According to a district manager, "We are losing ground every year. This year they said they would give everyone a bonus of $1,000; it will actually be about $675 [after taxes]. This is a slap in the face to our hard-working employees."

On the impartiality of civil service, many employees felt that reform encouraged political mischief. A capital city manager said that it "is no longer neutral for anyone" as instances of reprisal occur. A Tallahassee confidential employee believed that "most perceive that if they don't tow the party line that their job is at risk." However, six of the officials thought that the legislation had no effect at all, and two people stated it had a positive result.

Concerning the appeal of government employment, one Miami confidential worker indicated that Service First may have enhanced it. A Tallahassee manager said that "it depends on the level; for entry-level, it might have increased appeal but not for long-serving employees." In addition, four respondents noted no impact. Everyone else, however, thought attractiveness diminished as "it has to be less given the drift to spoils" (a capital city manager). A field manager said, "If I knew then what I know now, I would never have taken this job. It used to be an attractive place to work." Another Miami manager thought, "The only thing it has done for us is pay health insurance. It would be better for us to pay health insurance and retain job security and seniority rights."

Responding to the query about personnel as an asset or cost, four affirmed that they are seen as an asset. One, though, observed that "maybe employees are assets, as business likes state employees when they apply [for private enterprise jobs]." Most interviewees believed that personnel are a cost to be controlled. For instance, a Tallahassee manager said, "Bush's plan was to cut costs by reducing 25 percent of the workforce—regardless of cost. Service First costs more with worse outcomes." Another manager, this one from the district office, believed that high officials see personnel as costs:

> One of our employees had her computer break five times in a two or three day period. No replacement was available so some of the work was delayed. 'Upstairs' may have felt some job action needed to take place because of low performance. But the lack of tools and resources—not slacking off—was the explanation for the problem.

Finally, several SESers considered the reform initiative to be a successful implementation of business practices; one Miami confidential official said that "it worked for me" and another indicated that she had greater support to complete tasks. Three officials saw a mixed impact or no impact. Most of the sample, though, perceived problems. A district manager said that it was "[n]ot remotely successful. Service First does not use the free market structure. Businesses would honestly and objectively research whether to 'do' in house or contract out. Jeb [Bush] purchases everything outside no matter what." A Tallahassee supervisory employee, also dubious, provided a different explanation: "Well, talk about running government like a business, but look at the way business does things: underhanded deals, hiring cronies, and so on."

The Department of Children and Families, in summary, is a politically salient agency subject to leadership turnover, investigations, and controversy, some of which involves the authorities affected by Service First (see the case in appendix 3). The HRM official saw reform as successful, as an opportunity for change that improved recruitment and services but did not affect responsiveness. The majority of the exempt personnel (Table 6.1) thought that the objective of reform was to downsize government. One-half believed that it had no effect on recruitment, and one-half indicated a negative impact. Most thought that service provision remained as before, whereas they were divided between no difference and an increase in responsiveness. Regarding productivity, half did not see any change, and the other half discerned improvement. Over two-thirds of the sample felt that morale and loyalty declined, and the legislation had an adverse effect on attitudes toward pay. Most believed that the neutrality of public administration was impaired, the appeal of government employment diminished, employees are regarded as a cost, and Service First was a flawed implementation of business practices.

COMPARING SURVEY AND CASE DATA

One year after Service First was enacted in 2001, a random statewide survey was conducted of all those transferred to SES (50); the questionnaire consisted of agree-disagree statements and several multiple-choice items. At that time, many SESers did not believe that they were fully informed about the provisions of the new law, although most accepted the official rationale that it was to increase flexibility to manage employees. However, over 60 percent indicated that an important objective was to downsize government, a finding that remains true in the agencies today (especially DEP and DCF). A similar proportion believed earlier that Service First would not enhance hiring processes, an opinion still endorsed in DEP (DOT respondents see no change, and DCF officials are divided between no change and a negative effect). Most employees surveyed previously did not think that reform would enhance responsiveness, a view that continues, especially in DOT (personnel in the other two agencies see more responsiveness, although many contend there has been no change).

Nearly one-half of the respondents earlier contended that reform would make government less productive (18 percent said more productive, and

29 percent indicated no change would occur). But today DOT and DEP employees believe that there has been no impact on productivity; DCF officials see some positive effect, whereas others see no change. Earlier, just over one-half of the governmentwide survey participants rejected the claim that morale was high in their agencies (19 percent were neutral, and 30 percent agreed); now morale is low in the three departments. In the prior research, most informants did not think that money was available to reward employees, and just 10 percent thought that reform would lead to better pay. SESers in the agencies in late 2004–2005 find that reform either made things worse or there has been no change (in descending order of negative attitudes from most to least: DCF, DEP, DOT). Finally more than 80 percent of the statewide sample believed that employees were regarded as a cost to be controlled, a view that endures today in the three departments.

In short, although some employees have come to realize that Service First "is not the end of the world" (in the words of a DEP district manager), reform is nonetheless seen "as imposed by higher ups on an unwilling workforce" (the same official). Another DEP district manager put it this way: "In exchange for ten years of service, I was put on the chopping block. When I was converted to SES, all my co-workers breathed a sigh of relief that it was me and not them."

CONCLUSION

The dawn of the new century witnessed 9/11 terrorism and corporate scandals, and the reform debate is over how government can best deal with external and internal threats to the nation. The outcome will determine whether the public service can effectively respond, and in the process perhaps regain its historical role as a model employer. Reformers, using a "see no evil" strategy, believe that the public sector should be modernized by reinstituting employment at-will, last used in government in the 19th century. Critics fear that this reinvents the spoils system, a system without merit that, through the pursuit of political self-interest and neglect of the common good, contained the seeds of its own destruction.

Civil service reform in Florida, as elsewhere, was prompted by the idea that corporate employment practices are inherently superior and therefore civil service protections against corruption should be abolished. Yet, there is simply no record to support the need for employment at-will in government—or business. Instead, there are powerful illusions about how things work in the private sector and that its techniques can be easily used in government irrespective of cost, consequence, or corruption. Reformers further seemed to believe that political appointees would be highly qualified, unbiased professionals who would seek the public interest above all. This might be called the "Goldilocks effect": that everything is just right and nothing will go wrong, a pleasant, if dubious, assumption in light of the spoils system of yesteryear and the Enron era of today.

Some five years after the enactment of Service First, the Selected Exempt Service corps—officials occupying critical linchpin roles in their departments—see reform as being of little consequence at best and as harmful at worse. Whereas selected interviewees perceived modest, if any, change in the public service, many others saw the independent civil servant being neutralized and services jeopardized by the reluctance "to speak truth to power." The human resource officials, in contrast, generally held a more sanguine view of Service First. Although not necessarily prepared to declare it a success, they agreed with its goals, found that it positively affected some processes, and thought that it was an incomplete application of the business model.

As institutional knowledge and ethical norms decay, the politicization of the civil service is likely to accelerate, for at least two reasons. First, baby boomers will retire in large numbers in the near future. Second, their replacements are not expected to have a career, much less a calling, in public service; rather, working for government simply will become a place to "be" for a short stint before they move on (statements attributed to DOT and DEP personnel officials). (51) The corporatization of the public sector and the erosion of a higher purpose embodied in government employment together ensure that the society will help serve the economy instead of the other way around.

Contemporary reform, then, is an example of the "wrong problem 'problem.'" The problem, advocates maintain, is bad management, a convenient diversion from substantive issues facing the polity. The real problem is political leadership, one that claims a "crisis" exists, provides little or no evidence of it, presents an ersatz solution, dismisses questions as carping, and ultimately makes the problem worse.

There is nothing automatic about the public service ethos—that employment practices will be reasonably free of political influence and that commonweal will prevail when confronted by partisan intrigue. Instead, it must be continuously nurtured, and reformers who would denigrate it would do well to honor Hippocrates' oath, "First do not harm." Devaluing public servants through at-will employment, privatization, and downsizing is a peculiar way to improve government and to address the very real problems that it confronts.

ENDNOTES

1. Hammer, M., and James, C., *Reengineering the Corporation*, HarperCollins, New York, 1994.
2. Osborne, D., and Gaebler, T., *Reinventing Government: How the Entrepreneurial Spirit Is Transforming the Public Sector*, Addison-Wesley, Reading, MA, 1992.
3. Condrey, S., and Maranto, R., *Radical Reform of the Civil Service*, Lexington Books, New York, 2001 (hereinafter "Condrey").
4. Kellough, J. E., and Nigro, L., eds., *In Civil Service Reform in the States*, State University of New York Press, Albany, 2006 (hereinafter "Kellough").
5. Bowman, J., and West, J., Removing employee protections: A "see no evil" approach to civil service reform, unpublished paper, Florida State University and University of Miami, 2005 (hereinafter "Bowman 2005").
6. The next several paragraphs are updated, modified, and expanded from Bowman, J., Gertz, M., Gertz, S., and Williams, Civil service reform in Florida state government: Employee attitudes one year later, *Review of Public Personnel Administration*, 32(4), 286, 2003 (hereinafter "Bowman 2003").
7. Kettle, D., Ingraham, P., Sanders, R., and Horner, C., *Civil Service Reform: Building a Government That Works*, Brookings Institution, Washington, DC, 1996.
8. Ingraham, P., and Moynihan, D., People and performance: Challenges for the future of public service—the report from the Wye River Conference, *Public Administration Review*, 60, 1, 54, 2000 (hereinafter "Ingraham").
9. Denhardt, R., and Denhardt, J., *The New Public Service: Serving, Not Steering*, Sharpe, Armonk, NY, 2002.
10. Schultz, D., and Maranto, R., *Politics of Civil Service Reform*, Lang, New York, 1998.
11. Light, P., *The Tides of Reform: Making Government Work 1945–1995*, Yale University Press, New Haven, CT, 1997.
12. Ingraham, P., *The Foundation of Merit: Public Service in American Democracy*, Johns Hopkins University Press, Baltimore, MD, 1995.
13. Condrey, supra note 3.
14. Thompson, J., The civil service under Clinton: The institutional consequences of disaggregation, *Review of Public Personnel Administration*, 21(2), 87, 2001.
15. West, J., Georgia on the mind of radical civil service reformers, *Review of Public Personnel Administration*, 21, 2, 79–93, 2002.
16. Bowman, J., At-will employment in Florida: A naked formula to corrupt public service, *WorkingUSA*, 6(2), 90, 2002 (hereinafter "Bowman 2002").
17. Walters, J., *Life after Civil Service Reform: The Texas, Georgia, and Florida Experiences*, IBM Endowment for the Business of Government, Arlington, VA, 2002.
18. Maranto, R., Praising civil service but not bureaucracy: A brief against tenure in the U.S. Civil Service, *Review of Public Personnel Administration*, 22(3), 175, Fall, 2002.
19. West, J., and Bowman, J., Stakeholder analysis of civil service reform in Florida: A descriptive, instrumental, normative human resource management perspective, *State and Local Government Review*, 36(1), 20, 2004.
20. Kellough, supra note 4.

21. Kellough, J., and Nigro, L., Civil service reform in Georgia: Findings of a survey of state employees' view about GeorgiaGain and Act 816, unpublished manuscript, University of Georgia, 2001.
22. Bowman 2003.
23. Muhl, C., The employment at-will doctrine: Three major exceptions, *Monthly Labor Review*, 124, 1, 3–12, 2001.
24. Hines, A., The postmodern shift in values and jobs and the implications for HR, *Employment Relations Today*, 26, 35, Winter, 2000.
25. Martucci, W., and Place, J., Employment law at the dawn of the millennium, *Employment Relations Today*, 26, 109, Winter, 2000.
26. Cottone, E., Employee protection from unjust discharge: A proposal for judicial reversal of the terminable-at-will doctrine, *Santa Clara Law Review*, 42, 1259, 2001–2002.
27. Hamilton, D., Is patronage dead? The impact of antipatronage staffing systems, *Review of Public Personnel Administration*, 22, 3, March, 2002.
28. Autor, D., Outsourcing at will: Unjust dismissal doctrine and the growth of temporary help employment, *National Bureau of Economic Research*, Working Paper 7557, NBER, Cambridge, MA, 2002.
29. The next two paragraphs are adapted from Bowman 2005.
30. Cotterell, B., People First could use disaster aid, *Tallahassee Democrat*, 1B, July 4, 2005.
31. Secretary Henderson speaks to FPA, *FPA News*, 2(3), 1, Spring, 2001.
32. Fineout, G., Bush remains mum about potential political plans, *Tallahassee Democrat*, June 15, 2005, 6B.
33. Condrey, supra note 3.
34. Coggburn, J., Personnel deregulation: Exploring differences in the American states, *Review of Public Personnel Administration*, 22, 114, 2001.
35. Ingraham, supra note 8.
36. Bowman 2002, supra note 16.
37. Lane, L., Wolf, J., and Woodard, C., Reassessing the human resource crisis in the public service, *American Review of Public Administration*, 33, 2, 123–145, 2003.
38. The interviewees approximated the profile of the entire SES corps, a group that is roughly gender-balanced, well educated, experienced in state government, advanced middle-aged, moderate to liberal in political philosophy, and predominantly Democratic in party registration. Confidential employees differed from other SES members as they were more likely to be female and have less education; they also seemed to be generally less knowledgeable about Service First, perhaps because their duties are less management-oriented and more secretarial in character. The demographic commonalities and knowledge levels between SES supervisors and managers were greater than their differences.
39. Lowi, T., *The End of Liberalism; Ideology, Policy, and the Crisis of Public Authority*, Norton, New York, 1969.

40. Many of the questions posed to participants in this research were based on a statewide survey of new SESers one year after passage (Bowman 2003), the findings of which provide a context for the agencies analyzed here. The purpose of the present project (and the relatively informal nature of the telephone and in-person interviews that support it) do not, however, permit rigorous comparisons between the two studies partly because not all respondents in the two studies were asked exactly the same questions.
41. Yin, R., *Case Study Research: Design and Methods*, 3rd ed., Sage, Thousand Oaks, CA, 2002.
42. Thus, selected respondents were concerned about the purpose of the study. The authors were also asked whether the agency and their universities authorized it, and if the interview was confidential (and whether they would be quoted). Some said that they had to close their door before participating. Others stated that the authors had to obtain permission from their superior for a confidential interview. One respondent only agreed to participate after reviewing one of the author's published articles on a related subject. A key executive, who had promised to participate, later declined because of an agency leadership change. In the view of one high-level anonymous source in the same department, the current secretary upon assuming office "locked things down as much as possible." In addition, the secretary was known to be "vindictive, so why take any chances granting interviews with outsiders?" Although a number of interviewees were expansive, cautious answers to some queries, such as "I'd rather not say" or "No comment," were encountered (follow-up probes were not always successful in eliciting additional information).
43. Muhl, supra note 23.
44. Zuckerman, L., Whistle-blower laws protect woman's job, state commission says, *Daytona Beach News Journal*, sec. A, 1A, July 4, 2002.
45. Ibid.
46. Brad Blog, http://residentbush.com/Aftermath2004_BradBlog.html (hereinafter "Brad Blog").
47. Madsen, W., Special report: Texas to Florida: White House–linked clandestine operation paid for "vote switching" software, http://www.onlinejournal.com/Special_Reports/120604Madsen/120604Madsen.html.
48. Brad Blog, supra note 46.
49. Cotterell, supra note 30.
50. Bowman, 2003, supra note 22.
51. Walters, supra note 17.

APPENDIX 1

Department of Transportation Terminations

Mavis Georgalis was a specialized technologies manager; part of her job was to oversee DOT's contract with software producer Yang Enterprises International (YEI). While the contract was under her supervision, the corporation's billing practices and relationship to the then-Florida House Speaker Tom Feeney (R-Oviedo) became known. Feeney, Jeb Bush's former running mate, served as corporate counsel and lobbyist for Yang, and was a Florida congressman while remaining closely associated with YEI. Georgalis informed investigators that Yang demanded payment for contract work not performed or already paid for (44). The firm met with Roy Cales, the governor's technology "czar" and other high officials, and Cales asked her supervisor, "Do we have a new contract manager yet?" (45)

Clint Curtis, a DOT employee and former YEI programmer terminated the same day as Georgalis, uncovered most of the malfeasance. During his employment with YEI, Curtis had been approached by Feeney and YEI CEO Li-Woan Yang. They asked for a "vote fraud software prototype," specifying that the programming for this needed to stay hidden even if the source code was inspected. Feeney and YEI executives wanted it to be "undetectable to voters and election supervisors." (46, 47)

After joining DOT, Curtis (with Georgalis) reported allegations of overbilling to the state inspector general in May 2001. They reportedly were harassed, and pressure mounted on DOT to have them fired. (48) In November 2001, they were sued by YEI (represented by Feeney's law firm) for stealing intellectual property. DOT refused to join their defense because it was not named as a defendant, although Georgalis was able to add them later as a co-defendant. In April 2002, both employees were discharged (Georgalis was offered a letter of resignation, which she signed under duress).

The Florida Human Rights Commission sought Georgalis's reinstatement; when refused, it filed suit. The trial court granted reinstatement pursuant to the Florida Whistleblower's Act. The department appealed on the grounds that she failed to comply within the notice and filing deadlines under the act. In 2003, the 1st District Court of Appeal affirmed the trial court's judgment. The department would later decide against awarding a $77 million contract to YEI.

APPENDIX 2

Human Resource Unit in Transition at the Department of Environmental Protection

Service First was followed by a second gubernatorial initiative, People First, a program to outsource the state's human resource function. Florida contracted with Convergys to provide these services with the result that many state employees in these roles were no longer needed. Service First made it possible to quickly implement People First because the removal of job security made employees easily expendable. In DEP, nearly one-half of the staff in human resources were downsized.

Florida is not alone in outsourcing services to Convergys as the latter has nearly 600 clients in more than 60 countries. The company claims that it delivers savings to clients, including reduced labor costs, lower open enrollment costs, reduced operating costs, improved employee case closures, and higher satisfaction scores. In Florida, service delivery quickly become contentious due to missed implementation deadlines, cost overruns, frequent paycheck mistakes and erroneous insurance cancellations, widespread employee complaints, multihour waits on customer service telephone lines, agency and legislative investigations, public hearings, and withholding of state payments to the contractor.

One state HRM official observed that the initiative was "implemented before the system was fully developed and tested; it hurts more than helps employees as 'people' were taken out of People First. It would have cost $80 million to update the old computer system; the People First system cost $350 million" (anonymous, personal communication, February 2, 2005). A state government newspaper columnist recently summarized the situation by indicating that "People First and Convergys have done for [employee personnel files] what [Hurricanes] Charlie and Ivan did for Fort Myers and Pensacola." (49)

Clearly, the combination of Service First and People First reflects a broader agenda of reducing state capacity in favor of private sector solutions. Although it may be too early to tell whether outsourcing benefits will be realized, the initial transition has been fraught with problems. A DEP line manager indicated, "We used to have someone who helped with recruitment, benefits, workers' comp and other procedures. We have lost most of the good people, and now one person is expected to perform many of these functions. We lack HR guidance to help us do our job effectively" (anonymous, personal communication, November 5, 2004).

APPENDIX 3

Terminations at Department of Children and Families

In March 2003, an aide to State Senator Rudy Garcia (R-Hialeah), took Garcia's grandmother to a service center to restore her food stamp benefits. The aide claimed that employees were rude, talked disrespectfully, and did not provide prompt service. Service center personnel pointed out that the aide insisted that she be helped before others who had been waiting for hours and cursed at personnel when she was refused immediate service. The aide complained to the agency deputy secretary. Six staff (including a receptionist, supervisors, and administrators), who would become known as the "Garcia Six," were terminated whether or not they were at-will employees.

After a series of articles in the *Miami Herald*, which documented conflicting accounts about who authorized what actions, DCF announced under threat of legal action that the dismissals would be reviewed. According to one former department executive, the agency was concerned not only that it might lose in court, but also that litigation would open up the departmental leadership to hostile legal discovery and deposition—"a clear public relations loser" (anonymous, personal communication, March 14, 2005). The agency secretary, who would later resign in the midst of ethics charges, maintained that the personnel were not discharged because of the complaint. Following the DCF evaluation, all employees were reinstated.

7

AT-WILL EMPLOYMENT IN GOVERNMENT: ITS IMPACT IN THE STATE OF TEXAS

Jerrell D. Coggburn
The University of Texas at San Antonio

INTRODUCTION

Language describing the state of affairs in the U.S. public service and the changes being undertaken in the name of civil service reform offers some indication as to the pervasiveness and seriousness of human resource (HR) challenges and to the boldness of some attempts to address these challenges. For example, civil service systems have been assailed as inefficient, archaic, cumbersome, moribund, meritless, disconnected from agency management and strategy, flat-footed, suffering from paralysis, constituting a straightjacket for managers, emphasizing employee protection over performance, or just plain broken.[1–8] Similarly, the announcement of an impending "quiet crisis" in the public service was no less dire in its attempt to draw attention to the trouble that employers face in attracting the "best and brightest" to public service careers.[9] More recently, the Government Performance Project (GPP) has warned of a "personnel tornado on the horizon" for state governments as they attempt to deal with large portions of their workforces becoming retirement-eligible, low employee morale, and antigovernment sentiment.[10] Together, these various assessments portend an ominous future.

On the reform side, the language and, indeed, the changes have been no less striking. Reformers have advocated—and in places have succeeded in—"blowing up" the civil service.[5] Observers have described going "to the edge"[11] with civil service reform, "radical reform,"[12] and a "civil service tsunami."[13] These labels serve as apt descriptions for various civil service reform efforts designed, largely, to increase executive control over workforces. One significant strategy, as evidenced by reforms in Georgia, Florida, and Texas, is to make the employment relationship "at will." The general argument states that governments gain a powerful management tool for ensuring employee productivity, enhancing managerial flexibility and control (e.g., by giving a free hand to terminate people for whatever the reason—or for no reason at all), and, as a result, improving performance.

Like reforms designed to decentralize and deregulate civil service systems, at-will employment can be taken as evidence of nothing short of a full-fledged attack on bureaucracy.[14] At a minimum, such reforms raise important questions to the public administration community. Bedrock employment principles like merit and due process, for example, appear compromised by employment relationships allowing employers to summarily dismiss civil servants. Proponents of at-will employment also reinforce negative images of civil servants when selling the need for reform: suggesting that the threat of immediate dismissal is a necessary tool for motivating employees plays into stereotypes, further undermines confidence in government, and may exacerbate difficulties faced in attracting employee talent. Troubling, too, is the naïveté with which proponents advance their arguments: there appears to be no appreciation for existing limits on at-will termination, and there is uncritical acceptance that this largely American private sector arrangement will work in the pubic sector.[4, 15, 16] In short, at-will employment appears to be gaining momentum as a method of reform despite a lack of critical inquiry into underlying issues.

This article examines at-will employment in Texas state government. Texas has received considerable attention in the literature because of its early acceptance of civil service reforms like decentralization, deregulation, and at-will employment. Such status led one observer to refer to Texas as the "grandfather of civil-service-free states."[5, p. 16] Given this, Texas employees, managers, and HR professionals have worked for some time under employment provisions only recently being adopted or considered by other state governments. This makes the state a prime candidate for case study investigation of at-will employment. The chapter is arranged into four sections. The first provides context for HR in Texas by briefly describing the state's status as an at-will employer. The second describes the methodology for a survey used to gather data from Texas's state agency HR directors. The third reports findings and analyzes their importance. Finally, the chapter concludes with a discussion of the findings' implications.

HR IN TEXAS STATE GOVERNMENT

The organization and administration of Texas's state government HR function have been described in some detail elsewhere,[5, 17] so discussion here is limited to describing at-will employment. This employment relationship has been summarized succinctly by the State Classification Office (SCO), a small HR entity within the Texas State Auditor's Office, in its *Texas Human Resource Management Statutes Inventory*: "Unless explicitly exempted by written contract, statute, or policy, all state employees are employed 'at will' and there is no implied contract of employment."[18, p. 57] The *Inventory* also discusses the state's stance on "probationary" versus "permanent" employment status:

> There is no legislation either requiring or prohibiting an employee probationary period. Agencies and institutions of higher education have complete discretion in this matter. If used, such a practice should be documented and communicated to employees as an internal policy. The existence of a probationary period should be structured such that it does not diminish the State's employment-at-will doctrine.[18, p. 59]

Although agencies have latitude to create policies like probationary periods and employee grievance processes, they are explicitly directed to preserve their status as at-will employers.

Exceptions to the at-will doctrine in Texas are both narrow and explicit. State agencies must adhere to state laws that prohibit terminations in a variety of circumstances[a] and to both state and federal employment and antidiscrimination laws. There is but one explicitly recognized judicial exception to the at-will employment doctrine in Texas. In *Sabine Pilot Services, Inc. v. Hauck* (1985), the Texas Supreme Court carved out a narrow "public policy exception" to the at-will employment doctrine. The case involved a deckhand (Hauck) fired for his refusal to pump the bilges on his employer's (Sabine Pilot Services) boat into open waters. Such activity is illegal, and Hauck, knowing this, refused to comply and was subsequently fired. In finding for Hauck, the court held that employees terminated for the sole reason of refusing to commit an illegal act that carries a criminal penalty can sue for wrongful termination. This, obviously, is a narrow exception to the at-will doctrine, especially when compared to other states' interpretation of "public policy." Moreover, Texas courts have not recognized "implied contract" or "good faith and fair dealing" exceptions to at-will employment, which often are found in other states.[19]

In sum, Texas has established itself as an at-will employer, a position that is tempered by state and federal law and by judicial interpretation ("common law"). Against this background, several questions arise: how do state agencies view the nature of the at-will employment relationship? How do they use the flexibility inherent in at-will employment? How do they view the effects of at-will employment on public employees and agency performance?

SURVEY OF STATE HR DIRECTORS

To examine how agencies view at-will employment, its use in practice, and its effects, data was gathered from a mail survey administered to 122 HR directors in Texas's state agencies. It asked respondents to offer their level of agreement or disagreement with a series of statements related to at-will employment. Names and addresses for the directors were obtained directly from the SCO. The anonymous survey was administered between January and March 2005 following Dillman's tailored design method.[20] Completed surveys were received from 77 directors, for an overall response rate of approximately 63 percent.

It is important to note at the outset that HR directors have perspectives on at-will employment that may differ from others in state government (e.g., employees, agency managers and directors, and elected officials). Moreover, these directors' attitudes, as reflected in their survey responses, are shaped in part by their own experiences: they too are employed at will, and most have not worked outside of an at-will employment setting. Still, the nature of HR management in Texas state government is such that HR directors play integral roles in designing and implementing HR programs for their agencies. They possess intimate knowledge of how the HR function is administered and the advantages and disadvantages of the state's approach to HR, including its status as an at-will employer. Additional perspectives are provided from several confidential interviews conducted with officials from the largest state employees' association, the Texas Public Employees Association (TPEA); from the largest state employees' union, the Texas Public Employees Union (TPEU);[b] and with the SCO. Although these additional perspectives—discussed in the conclusion—offer a modicum of balance, it is the survey of HR directors that forms the basis for analysis.

Findings and Analysis

Discussion of findings is arranged below into three sections considering, in order, HR directors' opinions on the at-will employment doctrine, agencies' use of at-will employment, and the effects of at-will employment.

The Doctrine

Calls for the adoption of at-will employment in the public sector center on a number of purported benefits. Generally, proponents argue that it assures more political responsiveness on the part of civil servants and provides managers with a more flexible and efficient approach to meeting changing organizational objectives and dealing with matters of employee misfeasance, malfeasance, and nonfeasance.

Political executives often complain about "bureaucratic resistance" on the part of agencies, particularly career civil servants. At-will policies enhance responsiveness, it is argued, because civil servants are compelled to act on policy initiatives lest they be terminated.[13, 21] The first item in Table 7.1 addresses responsiveness. As shown, 58.4 percent of state HR directors agreed that at-will employment "helps ensure that employees are responsive to the goals and priorities of agency administrators" (23.4 percent disagreed, and 18.2 percent were neutral). This suggests that there is general recognition of at-will employment's tendency to compel employee responsiveness.

Flexibility arguments are couched in the need to offer management greater latitude in HR decision making if they are to successfully adapt to changing organizational needs and expectations.[22] Although "flexibility" is often a euphemism for creating greater executive/political control, political executives and appointees may not be the only ones pleased with at-will employment. Indeed, HR professionals operating in other at-will states generally appear satisfied with the approach.[13, 23] As for efficiency arguments, they imply that organizational performance is impeded by costly and time-consuming HR processes (i.e., discipline and termination process) that protect poor performers at the expense of organizational performance. The second and third items in Table 7.1 tap into these arguments. Somewhat surprisingly, only pluralities agreed with statements related to greater efficiency and managerial flexibility. Specifically, 37.7 percent agreed (31.2 percent disagreed or were neutral, respectively) that "at-will employment in government makes the HR function more efficient," and a slightly higher percentage (44.2 percent) agreed that it "provides essential management flexibility over the HR function (28.6 percent disagreed, and 27.3 percent were neutral).

Next, respondents were presented statements related to employee motivation. An unfortunate—and empirically unsubstantiated—aspect of pro-at-will rhetoric suggests that stripping civil servants of the property rights held in their positions is a necessary tool of employee motivation. The argument contends that civil servants, hiding behind the protection of grievance and appeal procedures, are lazy, unresponsive, and underperforming.[but see 4, 21, 24, 25] The threat or use of termination at will is viewed as a tool to overcome such conditions. This is a "Theory X" approach to

Table 7.1 Texas HR Directors' Opinions on the at-Will Employment Doctrine

In General, at-Will Employment in Government . . .	*% Agree*	*% Disagree*	*% Neither Agree nor Disagree*
Helps ensure that employees are responsive to the goals and priorities of agency administrators	58.4	23.4	18.2
Makes the HR function more efficient	37.7	31.2	31.2
Provides essential managerial flexibility over the HR function	44.2	28.6	27.3
Provides needed motivation for employee performance	40.3	36.4	23.4
Gives an upper hand to employers relative to employees in the employment relationship	41.6	41.6	16.9
Represents an essential piece of modern government management	44.2	23.4	32.5
Is at odds with the public sector's traditional emphasis on merit in human resource decisions	28.6	44.2	27.3

Source: At-Will Employment in Texas State Government Survey, administered by the author January–March 2005.

Note: ($N = 77$) Figures in the table are percentages. The survey employed a five-point Likert scale. Response categories were coded as follows: 1 for *strongly agree*, 2 for *agree*, 3 for *neither agree nor disagree*, 4 for *disagree*, and 5 for *strongly disagree*. For ease of presentation, the *strongly agree* and *agree* categories were combined, as were the *strongly disagree* and *disagree* categories. Percentages may not sum to 100 due to rounding.

management that suggests civil servants must be forced to do work.[4] Here again, the level of agreement (40.3 percent) with the statement related to at-will employment's ability to provide motivation is less than what might be expected. Indeed, almost as many respondents (36.4 percent) disagreed with this statement as agreed (23.4 percent were neutral).

In addition to the efficiency, flexibility, and motivation arguments, at-will employment raises the question of who stands to gain and lose in a switch from traditional civil service systems to at-will employment relationships. A plain reading of the at-will doctrine would suggest that agency executives and civil servants are on even footing. This is because of the principle of mutuality that holds, theoretically, that either party has the ability to terminate the employment relationship at any time and for any or no reason.[19] Employers are free to seek additional hires, and employees are free to market themselves elsewhere. What this reading misses is that mutuality does not exist in today's workplace. Rather, the increasingly specialized nature of work means that employees' skills are likewise more specialized and, therefore, potentially less marketable.[19, 25] This may be especially true of government employment, where oftentimes a market failure has necessitated the public provision and (in most cases) production of a public good or service. In other words, there is no "market" for many public service jobs, thus civil servants may be even more beholden to their employers for continued employment.

On this aspect of at-will employment, respondents were equally divided: 41.6 percent agreed and 41.6 percent disagreed that it "gives an upper hand to employers relative to employees in the employment relationship" (16.9 percent were neutral). In this instance, the "tie" would appear to go to those who reject the idea of an even playing field for employers vis-à-vis employees. As Walters suggests, at-will employment is a powerful tool for managers.[13] In other words, aside from statutory and judicial exceptions, at-will employment leaves employees in Texas "totally at the mercy of the employer."[26, p. 14]

Finally, public sector application of the at-will doctrine would seem to challenge the fundamental principle of merit that has been a defining feature of civil service systems for over 120 years. Merit, in a nutshell, has traditionally denoted decision making based upon job-related criteria (e.g., technical competence) as opposed to political patronage considerations. In contrast, the private sector–inspired at-will model, just like other reforms sweeping across governments,[16] holds that modern government work has bypassed the era when traditional civil service systems were practicable.

The final two items in Table 7.1 address these issues. First, 28.6 percent agreed that at-will employment "is at odds with the public sector's traditional emphasis on merit in human resource decisions" (44.2 percent disagreed, and 27.3 were neutral). Second, a plurality of 44.2 percent agreed that at-will employment "represents an essential piece of modern government management" (23.4 percent disagreed, and 32.5 percent were neutral). Taken together, these findings seem to support Woodard's[27] contention that "merit" is no longer a driving or foundational value or, potentially, one that is even understood by these HR professionals.

The Application of at-Will Employment

The preceding section offered some indication as to how respondents generally view the at-will employment doctrine. This section analyzes survey items addressing how state agencies utilize the at-will employment relationship. Specifically, because the doctrine allows for the termination of the employment relationship at any time, for no reason or for any reason not contrary to law,[19] the survey asked respondents to indicate their levels of agreement or disagreement with statements on reasons why at-will termination has been used in their respective agencies (see Table 7.2).

The first six items speak to some of the reasons why agencies may exercise the ability to terminate employees at will.[c] As shown, majorities of respondents agreed with the first three items listed. First and most obvious, 72.4 percent of directors agreed that employees in their respective agencies have been terminated at will for poor performance (19.5 percent disagreed, and 7.8 percent were neutral). This finding supports the argument advanced by reformers that employers can use at-will termination to get rid of perceived poor performers; in Texas, a strong majority of HR directors agree that they have done precisely that.

Second, a majority (51.3 percent) agreed that "employees have been terminated at will to meet agency budget shortfalls" (33.8 percent disagreed, and 14.3 percent were neutral). Similarly, 52.6 percent agreed that "employees have been terminated at will to meet agency downsizing goals" (33.8 percent disagreed, and 13.0 percent were neutral). These findings offer evidence to corroborate perceptions that a goal of at-will employment is to cut costs and downsize government; whereas this was the perception of employees in Florida,[21] it appears to be a reality in Texas according to a majority of HR directors.

In contrast to items on performance, budget, and downsizing, the other three statements on reasons for terminating employees at will produced considerably lower levels of agreement among survey respondents. Interestingly, two of these three items dealt specifically with the exercise of managerial flexibility. First, 18.2 percent agreed (and 58.5 percent disagreed) with the statement that in their agencies, "employees had been terminated at will because of personality conflicts with management" (23.4 were neutral). Second, 35.5 percent agreed (and 44.2 percent disagreed) that "employees had been terminated at will because of changing managerial priorities/objectives" (19.5 percent were neutral). Given arguments that "management discretion" is needed to meet ever-fluctuating

Table 7.2 Texas HR Directors' Opinions on the Use of at-Will Employment

In My Agency . . .	% *Agree*	% *Disagree*	% *Neither Agree nor Disagree*
Employees have been terminated at-will because of poor performance	72.4	19.5	7.8
Employees have been terminated at-will in order to meet agency budget shortfalls	51.3	33.8	14.3
Employees have been terminated at-will in order to meet agency downsizing goals	52.6	33.8	13.0
Employees have been terminated at-will because of personality conflicts with management	18.2	58.5	23.4
Employees have been terminated at-will because of changing managerial priorities/objectives	35.5	44.2	19.5
Employees have been terminated at-will in order to meet mandated management-to-staff ratios	17.3	69.3	13.3
Even though employment is at-will, most employee terminations are for good cause	97.4	1.3	1.3
Even if an employee is terminated at-will, we maintain documentation that would justify the termination should a lawsuit arise	94.7	1.3	3.9
Concern about wrongful termination and discrimination lawsuits limits our use of at-will termination	57.1	26.0	16.9

Source: At-Will Employment in Texas State Government Survey, administered by the author January–March 2005.

Note: ($N = 77$) Figures in the table are percentages. The survey employed a five-point Likert scale. Response categories were coded as follows: 1 for *strongly agree*, 2 for *agree*, 3 for *neither agree nor disagree*, 4 for *disagree*, and 5 for *strongly disagree*. For ease of presentation, the *strongly agree* and *agree* categories were combined, as were the *strongly disagree* and *disagree* categories. Percentages may not sum to 100 due to rounding.

organizational needs and managerial objectives, larger percentages in agreement could have been expected. Still, the findings are sufficient to raise concern about management's power vis-à-vis civil servants.

The final three items attempt to see how the legal landscape affects decisions to fire employees at will. Here, at least, there may be some positive signs for those who worry about wholesale employment abuses of civil servants. According to an astounding 97.4 percent of respondents, "even though employment is at-will, most employee terminations are for good cause" (1.3 percent disagreed and 1.3 percent were neutral). Similarly, 94.7 percent agreed (1.3 percent disagreed, and 3.9 percent were neutral) that their agencies maintain documentation that would justify an at-will termination in the event of an employee lawsuit. Finally, a majority (57.1 percent) agreed that "concern about wrongful termination and discrimination lawsuits limits our use of at-will termination" (26 percent disagreed, and 16.9 percent were neutral). These findings suggest that agencies are cognizant of the prospects of litigation that accompany termination and that such prospects may serve as a check on termination decisions.

With this knowledge of how state agencies utilize at-will terminations, the natural question is how often do state agencies exercise their ability to fire employees at will? Statewide agency turnover data available from the SCO offers some insight.[28] As shown in Table 7.3, at-will terminations are relatively rare when compared to other reasons—both voluntary and involuntary—employees left state government in fiscal years 2002–2005. Generally, the vast majority of employees who left state service did so voluntarily. At-will terminations, in contrast, accounted for only small percentages—from a low of 0.3 percent (2004) to a high of 0.8 percent (2005)—of all employee turnover. As a percentage of all *involuntary* turnover (not shown in Table 7.3), at-will terminations accounted for 4.2 percent (2005), 3.5 percent (2004), 2.7 percent (2003), and 3.3 percent (2002). It is impossible to say from the SCO data how many employees who resigned in lieu of termination would have been fired at will or for cause, thus the precise figures should be interpreted with a degree of caution. The percentages, too, mask the reality that hundreds of state employees have been terminated at will in Texas in recent years. Finally, the survey's finding that HR directors believe the majority of terminations are for cause even though employment is at will is corroborated by the involuntary turnover data in Table 7.3 (i.e., the majority of involuntary turnover is due to dismissal for cause).

Perceived Effects of at-Will Employment

The final set of items is arguably the most important. Indeed, it is the potential effects of at-will employment on civil servants that drive most of the concern raised in the scholarly literature. With several states adopt-

Table 7.3 Annual Turnover in Texas State Government[a]

	2005	*2004*	*2003*	*2003*
Voluntary termination	22,002	54,732	20,671	17,791
	(81.8%)	(91.9%)	(78.2%)	(78.4%)
Voluntary separation	14,830	13,256	12,084	12,690
	(55.2%)	(22.3%)	(45.7%)	(55.9%)
Transfer to another	3,253	38,447[b]	1,812	1,590
agency	(12.1%)	(64.5%)	(6.9%)	(7.0%)
	3,919	3,029	6,775	3,511
Retirement	(14.6%)	(5.1%)	(25.6%)	(15.5%)
Involuntary	4,882	4,843	5,746	4,891
termination	(18.2%)	(8.1%)	(21.8%)	(21.6%)
	2,679	2,561	2,683	2,879
Dismissal for cause	(10.0%)	(4.3%)	(10.2%)	(12.7%)
	1,693	1,569	1,492	1,502
Resignation in lieu of	(6.3%)	(2.6%)	(5.6%)	(6.6%)
separation	90	354	1,184	132
	(0.3%)	(0.6%)	(4.5%)	(0.6%)
Reduction in force	217	189	230	219
	(0.8%)	(0.3%)	(0.9%)	(1.0%)
Death	203	170	157	159
	(0.8%)	(0.3%)	(0.6%)	(0.7%)
At-will termination				

Source: Texas State Classification Office (2005).

[a] Figures in the table reflect the number (and percentage) of state employees in each turnover category.

[b] This figure is high due to the consolidation of 12 Health and Human Services Commission agencies into five. Employees whose agencies were consolidated were counted as "transfers."

ing at-will employment and with others undoubtedly looking at the possibility of following suit,[25] it becomes all the more important to look at the effects of at-will employment (see Table 7.4).

The results show that directors have mixed assessments. First, consider the issue of job security. As discussed, the at-will doctrine takes a "Theory X" approach to management, suggesting that the best way to motivate employees is to compel them to perform. In contrast, ample research exists suggesting that job security is more important than job insecurity as a motivating factor, particularly in the public sector.[25, 29, 30] Moreover, having a sense of security serves as one aspect of strengthening employee commitment to the organization, a commitment that can lead to greater employee productivity.[31–35]

Several items in Table 7.4 are related to these issues. First, a plurality (40.3 percent) agreed that in general, at-will employment "makes employ-

Table 7.4 Texas HR Directors' Opinions on Effects of at-Will Employment

In General, at-Will Employment in Government . . .	*% Agree*	*% Disagree*	*% Neither Agree nor Disagree*
Makes employees feel less secure about their jobs	40.3	39.0	20.8
Makes state government jobs less attractive to current and future employees than would be the case if there was more job security	19.5	65.0	15.6
Discourages employees from taking risks that could lead to program or policy innovation	22.1	49.4	28.6
Discourages employees from freely voicing objections to management directives	20.8	63.6	15.6
Discourages employees from reporting agency wrongdoing (or "blowing the whistle")	19.5	68.8	11.7
Could—by not requiring a rationale or justification for terminating employees—negatively affect managers' decision making in other non-HR decisions	36.4	35.1	28.6
Could—by not requiring a rationale or justification for terminating employees—make public employees less sensitive to issues of procedural fairness	38.2	35.5	26.3
Is sometimes used to fire competent employees so that other people with friends or connections to government can be hired	20.8	63.7	15.6
In My Agency . . .			
Employees are more productive because they are employed at-will	22.1	36.4	41.6
The lack of job security is made up for with competitive compensation (salary and benefits)	11.7	62.4	26.0
The lack of job security makes recruiting and retaining employees difficult	10.4	70.1	19.5

Table 7.4 Texas HR Directors' Opinions on Effects of at-Will Employment (continued)

In General, at-Will Employment in Government . . .	*% Agree*	*% Disagree*	*% Neither Agree nor Disagree*
I know of a case where a competent employee was fired at-will so that another person with friends or connections to government could be hired	2.6	87.0	10.4

Source: At-Will Employment in Texas State Government Survey, administered by the author January–March 2005.

Note: ($N = 77$) Figures in the table are percentages. The survey employed a five-point Likert scale. Response categories were coded as follows: 1 for *strongly agree*, 2 for *agree*, 3 for *neither agree or disagree*, 4 for *disagree*, and 5 for *strongly disagree*. For ease of presentation, the *strongly agree* and *agree* categories were combined, as were the *strongly disagree* and *disagree* categories. Percentages may not sum to 100 due to rounding.

ees feel less secure about their jobs" (39 percent disagreed, and 20.8 percent were neutral). This is not a surprising finding because employees *are* less secure under an at-will arrangement than under merit system coverage, but the point is that this feeling of insecurity is acknowledged by a sizable percentage of respondents. As for the link between at-will employment and performance, the first item under the section entitled "In My Agency . . ." directly poses the issue. Here, more disagreed (36.4 percent) than agreed (22.1 percent) that "employees are more productive because they are employed at-will" (41.6 percent offered neutral opinions). If there is a direct linkage between at-will employment and employee performance, it is not readily apparent to the HR directors.

Respondents also were asked their levels of agreement or disagreement with statements related to the lack of job security's effects on the attractiveness of state jobs and their agency's ability to recruit and retain employees. Schwoerer and Rosen[29] demonstrate that applicants have more positive assessments of organizations purporting to follow due process policies as opposed to at-will policies.[see also 36] These differing assessments can be attributed in part to negative inferences applicants draw about at-will employers (e.g., they are not committed to their employees, and they treat them poorly) relative to those espousing good cause and due process policies. Such effects are not limited to applicants. Indeed, the theory of reciprocity suggests that an employer's lack of commitment to employees (as evidenced by at-will policies) can be met with a similar lack of commitment to the employer by employees.[24, 31, 32] The result can be higher voluntary employee turnover. As this demonstrates, the nature of the employment relationship is an important factor in staffing.

These issues are not trivial in Texas, where the state government's annual turnover rate has ranged in the 15 to 20 percent range over the last five years. The HR directors, however, did not view at-will employment as being an impediment to staffing: 19.5 percent agreed (and 65 percent disagreed) that at-will employment generally "makes state government jobs less attractive than would be the case if there was more job security." Similarly, 10.4 percent agreed that in their own agencies "the lack of job security makes recruiting and retaining employees difficult" (70.1 percent disagreed, 19.5 percent were neutral). It may be that the "employers' market" that has existed in recent years has mitigated the negative effects of at-will policies in attracting and retaining employees, or it may be that directors attribute high turnover to something other than the at-will employment relationship (e.g., better pay in the private sector).

One final aspect of at-will employment's effects on job security deals with compensation. Schwoerer and Rosen[29] also show that negative perceptions of at-will employers can be attenuated by organizations offering leading (high) compensation. This is important for present purposes because of the trade-off that proponents of at-will employment often offer employees: forego civil service protections, but in return gain the prospect of better compensation. Such a trade-off is possible in theory because management's enhanced flexibility to hire and fire should reduce administrative costs, thereby freeing up additional funds for compensation.[25] If this holds, then employers ought to be better able to attract would-be employees and to retain existing ones. To see how this plays out, respondents were asked their level of agreement or disagreement with the statement "In my agency, the lack of job security is made up for with competitive compensation (salary and benefits)." As shown in Table 7.4, 62.4 percent disagreed with the statement (11.7 percent agreed, and 26 percent were neutral). So, to the extent that potential applicants and current employees draw negative inferences about agencies as at-will employers, there does not appear to be the lure of market-competitive (much less market-leading) compensation to serve as a counterbalance.

Aside from these important issues of job security, there is the question of at-will employment's compatibility with more participatory and fluid forms of organizational management. Recent management theory suggests the need for employee participation in organizational decision making, entrepreneurial risk taking, and freedom to innovate. With a little luck and some "tolerance for error" by management, these approaches promise to unleash employee energy, creativity, and innovation with organizational performance and stakeholders being the prime beneficiaries. Employees' ability to act in these desired ways would seem to be compromised by at-will employment because it "prioritizes obedience over employee resourcefulness." [34, p. 252, 4]

Two survey items are related to this issue. First, respondents were asked to offer their level of agreement or disagreement with the statement that at-will employment "discourages employees from taking risks that could lead to program or policy innovation." As Table 7.4 shows, 22.1 percent of respondents agreed with the statement (49.4 percent disagreed, and 28.6 neither agreed or disagreed). Although the number disagreeing was twice as high as those agreeing, less than half disagreed with the statement. Moreover, the fact that more than one in five agreed suggests that adhering to at-will employment may present an opportunity cost to innovation. On the second item, 63.6 percent disagreed that at-will employment "discourages employees from freely voicing objections to management directives" (20.8 percent agreed, and 15.6 percent were neutral). Thus, although the level of disagreement was greater here than on the previous item, one in five still felt that at-will employment suppresses employee objections. Such a finding presents the possibility of groupthink or, more troubling, an agentic shift among employees as they suppress their own objections to management direction.

Related more directly to ethical considerations are the potential effects of at-will employment on whistle-blower behavior. The literature suggests that employees who work under at-will employment arrangements may be less likely to blow the whistle on organizational wrongdoing or to refuse to participate themselves in such behavior.[37, 38] The reason for this "chilling effect" on employee whistle-blowing is obvious: such behavior can and often does result in adverse actions, including termination.[38, 39] Despite these possibilities, a majority (68.8 percent) disagreed that at-will employment "discourages employees from reporting agency wrongdoing (or 'blowing the whistle')." Still, 19.5 percent did agree that at-will employment creates a chilling effect.

Concern also can be raised about the effects of at-will employment on other forms of organizational decision making. This includes non-HR decisions that managers make as well as decisions rendered and service provided by street-level bureaucrats. On the first aspect, Radin and Werhane contend that at-will employment sends the message "that virtually anything is permissible because there is no accountability" and that it "sanctions the questionable managerial practice of making employment decisions without having to justify them, a practice commonly considered 'poor management' with regard to other types of economic decisions."[34, p. 259] Such sanctioning "violates the managerial ideal of rationality and consistency" and is simply poor management.[40, p. 240, 26] The concern here, then, is whether the capacity for making poor employment decisions does in fact spill over to other areas of decision making.

Here, slightly more agreed (36.4 percent) than disagreed (35.1 percent) that at-will employment "could—by not requiring a rationale or justification for terminating employees—negatively affect managers' decision making in other non-HR decisions" (28.6 percent were neutral). In an era preoccupied with "better performance" and increasing "management capacity," this finding signals that at-will employment can be counterproductive; that is, it can condition managers to make poor decisions.

In a related fashion, the effects of poor HR decision making might encourage poor decision making and general insensitivity to matters of due process. Denhardt, for example, argues that how an agency acts internally spills over to interactions with those on the outside; if employees are treated as persons of significance within the organization, then they are likely to treat those outside the organization (e.g., the public and agency clientele) in a similar fashion.[41] One can assume that the obverse holds as well: employees who are treated poorly by the organization (e.g., subject to arbitrary termination) will tend to treat poorly those outside the organization. On this aspect, too, survey findings give reason for pause. More HR directors agreed (38.2 percent) than disagreed (35.5 percent) that at-will employment "could—by not requiring a rationale or justification for terminating employees—make public employees less sensitive to issues of procedural fairness" (26.3 percent were neutral). Such a finding suggests that at-will employment can have a deleterious effect on the fairness of agency practices. This raises the possibility that a lack of consciousness about due process and procedural fairness could affect public employees' interaction with the public they are charged with serving.

Finally, two items in Table 7.4 speak to perhaps the most basic concern raised by opponents of at-will employment. The concern is that otherwise competent and professional civil servants will be terminated so that those with political or personal connections can be hired in their place. The occurrence of such practices represents an abuse of the civil service of the first order. And among HR directors, there is a moderate level of recognition—at least in the abstract—that at-will employment can produce such abuses. Specifically, 19.5 percent agreed that at-will employment "is sometimes used to fire competent employees so that other people with friends or connections to government can be hired" (63.7 percent disagreed, and 15.6 percent were neutral). On the more intrusive statement about one's personal knowledge of such abuses within their own agency, respondents were, predictably, less likely to agree: only 2.6 percent of respondents agreed that they knew of such an abuse, whereas 87 percent disagreed (10.4 percent were neutral). Regardless, there remains a recognition among some directors that at-will employment not just can be, but is, used in unsavory ways.

DISCUSSION

Implications of Survey Findings

There is strong and growing interest among civil service reformers in adopting private sector approaches to HR management, many of which ease or eliminate employee protections designed to protect civil servants from arbitrary or politically motivated treatment.[42] The clearest examples of this are efforts to strip civil servants of merit system protections and to replace them with at-will employment policies. Concern has been raised in the literature about the quick and uncritical acceptance of these private sector models, especially in light of the challenges they pose to long-held tenets of public sector employment.

In several instances, the survey findings reported here offer reason for concern about the appropriateness, use, and effects of at-will employment. On items related to the concept of at-will employment, respondents expressed strong agreement that it increases employee responsiveness to agency administrators, but levels of agreement about the doctrine's ability to produce greater efficiency, essential management flexibility, and needed employee motivation were much more tepid. This suggests that many of the espoused benefits of at-will employment are not borne out in practice.

As for the use of at-will termination, findings suggest that agencies use terminations mainly to deal with performance problems, but also for dealing with budget shortfalls and effecting agency downsizing goals. These fiscal and downsizing rationales should only fuel suspicion about government's motives in adopting at-will policies, that is, they play into the notion that employees are costs to be controlled. Importantly, there also was very strong agreement that the legal environment serves as a constraint on agency use of at-will termination. This finding suggests at least two things: first, that employees may have a measure of protection against abuses in at-will settings in the form of managerial/agency restraint relative to legal concerns; and, second, that the rhetoric suggesting that at-will employment and the threat of unfettered termination are the "cures" for government's "people problems" is both naïve and hyperbolic.

Finally, findings on the effects of at-will employment have a number of implications. Respondents generally agreed that at-will employment increases the insecurity employees feel about their jobs, but they disagreed that the threat of termination produces greater employee productivity. This, too, would seem to undercut a primary argument advanced by at-will proponents: the link between the threat of termination and enhanced productivity simply was not supported in Texas. On a broader level, the findings raise a number of red flags for those who fail to consider the broader effects of adopting at-will policies. For example, approximately 20 percent of respondents agreed that at-will employment discourages employees from taking risks that could lead to innovation, challenging management directives, and engaging in whistle-blowing. Similarly, results related to the deleterious effects of at-will employment decisions on the quality of other (non-HR) forms of organizational decision making are a source of concern. If, as some HR directors indicated, at-will termination decisions promote poor decision making and insensitivity to matters of procedural fairness, then the wisdom of such policies should be questioned on these grounds as well. In all, these findings suggest that governments who adopt at-will employment policies without taking into consideration their larger effects on essential aspects of good management may find that the costs of at-will employment policies outstrip their benefits.

Additional Perspectives

Aside from the survey data reported here, it is important to consider the larger context of employer-employee relationships. Given the current status of Texas, Georgia, and Florida as (in varying degrees) at-will employers, and given the push evident in some circles to expand at-will employment on a larger scale in the public sector, one might assume that the private sector's experience with the doctrine has been uniformly positive—at least from the standpoint of employers. In fact, there is a healthy debate in the private sector about the at-will doctrine. Researchers advise private employers to consider the "sensibility" of at-will employment in light of its potential disconnect from overall organizational strategy.[24] Others question the appropriateness of at-will employment on both moral and practical grounds, calling instead for the adoption of good cause policies and due process practices.[34, 40] And, as Bowman demonstrates, many leading private sector firms have done precisely that.[4] When these observations are coupled with the increasing number of legal exceptions to at-will employment, it is easy to see why some have gone as far as to suggest the "impending death" of the at-will doctrine.[43] Given this, it is ironic that some reformers are looking to a "dying doctrine" as inspiration for curing the perceived ills of the public service.

As suggested, a primary reason for the erosion of the at-will doctrine is the proliferation of legal exceptions created by state and federal law and by common law. In fact, it is the ability of public employees to seek relief through the courts for alleged wrongful termination or discrimination that serves as a way for advocates of at-will employment to offer assurances that employees will be adequately safeguarded once civil services protections are eliminated.[5, 27, 44]

In Texas, such a rationale was readily apparent in comments made by officials with the State Classification Office (SCO), the Texas Public Employees Association (TPEA), and the Texas Public Employees Union (TPEU). For example, an SCO official commented that state agencies are advised to "operate as if there is no such thing as at-will employment" and to "document, document, document." The obvious implication is that state agencies should handle all terminations as if they were going to wind up in court. The same official offered an example of an agency that came to the SCO looking for advice on how to execute an at-will termination. When the agency explained the reason behind the desired termination, the SCO official offered advice in the form of a question: "Are you comfortable telling that to a judge?"

Similar opinions were offered by representatives of TPEA and TPEU. For example, a TPEA official noted that the organization takes "at-will employment as a matter of fact" and that "[p]ersonally, I believe that there are ample protections of an individual's civil rights to provide recourse for termination." The individual went on to say that at-will employment is not even a peripheral issue for TPEA, which instead focuses on things like pay raises, health insurance costs, and retirement benefits. As for the TPEU, one official stated that employees are more concerned about meeting unrealistically high work demands created by staffing shortages than with losing their jobs through at-will termination. Another suggested that some agencies have instituted grievances processes (as allowed, but not required, by state law), but that the reason these agencies have done so has more to do with protecting themselves from legal claims than with promoting organizational justice. Regardless of the motive, the TPEU official stated that some agencies do offer grievance channels and, on occasion (i.e., when their prospects of losing a potential legal claim are great), will overturn a termination decision.

In all of these cases, the officials contacted gave the impression that at-will employment, per se, was not that great of a concern. On the one hand, the SCO essentially advises a good cause policy for termination as a means of protecting agencies from legal liability. On the other, organizations representing Texas state employees seem satisfied that adequate safeguards exist through the legal system or through agencies' voluntary internal grievance processes (even if the motives of these processes are less than altruistic).

To be sure, having the ability to seek redress through the courts for wrongful or politically motivated terminations may offer a measure of comfort for employees whose civil service protections are eliminated. But accepting this fact misses a larger point. If the legal environment has created a de facto good cause standard for employee termination, then the question arises as to what real benefit employers receive by adopting at-will policies. As demonstrated in this and other analyses, at-will policies can create anxiety among employees, erode the quality of agency decision making, eliminate one of the few real employment incentives (i.e., job security) that public employers have to attract workers, and require attacks on bureaucracy (e.g., "Civil service places protection over performance") to gain support for passage. This seems a high price to pay for passing a policy that may ultimately have only a marginal effect on government's ability to quickly terminate employees, not to mention the high costs of litigation, which likely far exceed the administrative costs of an internal civil service grievance process.

The point, then, is that public officials need to think more holistically about the effects of adopting at-will polices. Even if the conditions exist to support the passage of an at-will policy, that does not mean that it is in government's best interests to do so. As Roehling suggests, determining "whether it is organizationally sensible (i.e., wise) to adopt such a policy requires the strategic assessment of a variety of factors."[37, p. 122] For public employers, these factors include such things as the consistency of an at-will policy with espoused governmental or organizational values, the impact on employee attraction and retention, and the overall effect on litigation risk.

Given the "quiet crisis" in the public service, the second of these factors would seem particularly important. Schwoerer and Rosen argue that a critical element of contemporary HR policies is the guarantee of employee protection from arbitrary treatment.[29] As they discuss, such policies have been identified by some in the management literature as being key to attracting the "best and brightest." It is important to note here that the onus is on the organization—not the courts—to provide such protection. This does not imply that claims about the courts serving as an avenue for protecting employees from arbitrary action are wrong, but rather that such claims are irrelevant to the discussion about attracting, retaining, and motivating employees and achieving organizational excellence. Job security traditionally has been a major selling point for public employers. Rather than being viewed as an obstacle to meeting the challenges of the "quiet crisis," employers should view job security as embodied historically in civil service protections as a tool for competitive advantage.[30]

CONCLUSION

A holistic consideration of at-will employment cannot occur if the focus rests solely on the ease with which civil servants can be terminated. As this analysis has shown, there are important issues related to and affected by at-will employment. Although at-will employment does enhance executive control over government, it does nothing to attract new employees or to positively motivate existing employees. Moreover, at-will employment may discourage certain forms of desirable behavior (e.g., whistle-blowing and risk taking) and, at the same time, encourage undesirable behavior (e.g., poor decision making and insensitivity to procedural fairness). At a time when the United States' "best and brightest" opt not to pursue government careers, when those retiring from government do not recommend public service careers to others, and when antigovernment sentiment runs deep, government should be exploiting the competitive advantages it has—like job security—to meet its HR challenges. Far from helping curb the "quiet crisis," at-will employment may be helping to build a "perfect storm" in public sector employment.

REFERENCES

1. Osborne, D., and Gaebler, T., *Reinventing Government*, Addison-Wesley, Reading, MA, 1992.
2. National Commission on the State and Local Public Service, *Hard Truths/Tough Choices: An Agenda for State and Local Reform*, Rockefeller Institute, Albany, NY, 1993.
3. Horner, C., Beyond Mr. Gradgrind: The case for deregulating the public sector, *Policy Review*, 44, 34, 1988.
4. Bowman, J. S., At-will employment in Florida: A naked formula to corrupt public service, *Working USA*, 6, 90, 2002.
5. Walters, J., *Life after Civil Service Reform: The Texas, Georgia, and Florida Experiences*, IBM Endowment for the Business of Government, Arlington, VA, 2002.
6. Kettl, D. F., et al., *Civil Service Reform: Building a Government That Works*, Brookings Institution, Washington, DC, 1996.
7. Savas, E. S., and Ginsburg, S. G., The civil service: A meritless system? *The Public Interest*, 32, 70, 1973.
8. Cohen, S., and Eimicke, W., The overregulated civil service: The case of New York City's public personnel system, *Review of Public Personnel Administration* 24, 10, 1994.
9. National Commission on the Public Service, *Leadership for America: Rebuilding the Public Service*, Heath, Lexington, MA, 1989.
10. Barrett, K., and Greene, R., Grading the states '05: A management report card, *Governing*, 18, 24, 2005.
11. Barrett, K., and Greene, R., Grading the states: A management report card, *Governing*, 12, 17, 1999.
12. Condrey, S. E., and Maranto, R., *Radical Reform of the Civil Service*, Lexington, Lanham, MD, 2001.
13. Walters, J., Civil service reform tsunami, *Governing*, 16, 34, 2003.
14. Kearney, R. C., and Hays, S. W., Reinventing government, the new public management and civil service systems in international perspective, *Review of Public Personnel Administration*, 18, 38, 1998.

15. Kuykendall, C. L., and Facer, R. L., II., Public employment in Georgia agencies: The elimination of the merit system, *Review of Public Personnel Administration*, 22, 133, 2002.
16. Selden, S. C., Ingraham, P. W., and Jacobson, W., Human resource practices in state government: Findings from a national survey, *Public Administration Review*, 61 (5), 598, 2001.
17. Coggburn, J. D., The decentralized and deregulated approach to state human resources management in Texas, in *Civil Service Reform in the States: Personnel Policies and Politics at the Subnational Level*, Kellough, J. E., and Nigro, L. G., eds., State University of New York Press, Albany, 2006, ch. 9.
18. State Classification Office (SCO), *Texas Human Resource Management Statutes Inventory*, State Auditor's Office, Austin, 2004, http://www.hr.state.tx.us/Rules/HRInventoryFinal.pdf.
19. Muhl, C. J., The employment-at-will doctrine: Three major exceptions, *Monthly Labor Review*, 124, 3, 2001.
20. Dillman, D. A., *Mail and Internet Surveys: The Tailored Design Method*, 2nd ed., John Wiley, New York, 2000.
21. Bowman, J. S., et al., Civil service reform in Florida state government: Employee attitudes one year later, *Review of Public Personnel Administration*, 23, 286, 2003.
22. Daley, D. M., *Strategic Human Resource Management*, Prentice Hall, Upper Saddle River, NJ, 2002.
23. Lasseter, R. W., Georgia's merit system reform 1996–2001: An operating agency's perspective, *Review of Public Personnel Administration*, 22, 125, 2002.
24. Roehling, M. V., and Wright, P., Organizationally sensible vs. legal-centric responses to the eroding employment at-will doctrine, *Employee Responsibilities and Rights Journal*, 16, 89, 2004.
25. Green, R., et al., On the ethics of at-will employment relations in the public sector, *Public Integrity*, 8, 4, 2006.
26. Stephens, D. B., and Kohl, J. P., The "new" status of termination-at-will in Texas: Guidelines for employers in the aftermath of *Sabine Pilot v. Hauck*, *Southwest Journal of Business and Economics*, 6, 13, 1988.
27. Woodard, C. A., Merit by any other name: Reframing the civil service first principle, *Public Administration Review*, 65, 109, 2005.
28. State Classification Office (SCO), *An Annual Report on Full-Time Classified State Employee Turnover for Fiscal Year 2005*, State Auditor's Office, Austin, 2005, http://www.hr.state.tx.us/Workforce/Turnover2005/Default.html.
29. Schwoerer, C., and Rosen, B., Effects of employment-at-will policies and compensation policies on corporate image and job pursuit intentions, *Journal of Applied Psychology*, 74, 653, 1989.
30. Lewis, G. B., and Frank, S. A., Who wants to work for government? *Public Administration Review*, 64, 395, 2002.
31. Coyle-Shapiro, J. A.-M., and Kessler, I., The employment relationship in the U.K public sector: A psychological contract perspective, *Journal of Public Administration Research and Theory*, 13, 213, 2003.
32. Gossett, C. W., The changing face of Georgia's merit system: Results from an employee attitude survey in the Georgia Department of Juvenile Justice, *Public Personnel Management*, 32, 267, 2003.

33. Pfeffer, J., *The Human Equation: Building Profits by Putting People First*, Harvard Business School Press, Boston, 1998.
34. Radin, T. J., and Werhane, P. H., The public/private distinction and the political status of employment, *American Business Law Journal*, 34, 245, 1996.
35. Hindera, J. L., and Josephson, J. J., Reinventing the public employer-employee relationship: The just cause standard, *Public Administration Quarterly*, 22, 98, 1998.
36. Roehling, M. V., and Winters, D., Job security rights: The effects of specific policies and practices on the evaluation of employers, *Employee Responsibilities and Rights Journal*, 12, 25, 2000.
37. Roehling, M. V., The employment at-will doctrine: Second level ethical issues and analysis, *Journal of Business Ethics*, 47, 115, 2003.
38. Callahan, E. S., Employment at will: The relationship between societal expectations and the law, *American Business Law Journal*, 28, 455, 1990.
39. Jos, P. H., Hays, S. W., and Tompkins, M. E., In praise of difficult people: A portrait of the committed whistleblower, *Public Administration Review*, 49, 552, 1989.
40. Werhane, P. H., Justice and trust, *Journal of Business Ethics*, 21, 237, 1999.
41. Denhardt, R., *The Pursuit of Significance*, Wadsworth, Belmont, CA, 1993.
42. Kellough, J. E., Reinventing public personnel management: Ethical implications for managers and public personnel systems, *Public Personnel Management*, 28, 655, 1999.
43. Ballam, D. A., Employment-at-will: The impending death of a doctrine, *American Business Law Journal*, 37, 653, 2000.
44. Walters, J., Who needs civil service? *Governing*, 10, 17, 1997.
45. Dunn, K., Texas employers: Rest assured—your employees serve at will. *Corporate Counsel Review*, 19, 2002, http://www.stcl.edu/students/articles.htm.

ENDNOTES

a. State statutes prohibit terminations on a variety of bases (e.g., for employees on military duty, filing discrimination charges, filing workers' compensation claims, and joining an employee union), including a narrowly interpreted whistle-blowing law specific to public employees. In a number of cases, Texas courts have ruled that employer action can modify their status as at-will employers. Primarily, this comes in the form of written contracts or other explicit assurances.[45]

b. The Texas Public Employees Union (TPEU) is affiliated with the Communication Workers of America. Texas state law explicitly allows public employees to join unions (as the right to freedom of association), but it also explicitly states that the state will not recognize such unions for the purpose of collective bargaining.

c. Because at-will terminations can be made for no reason or any reason not contrary to the law, it would have been interesting to see how many HR directors agreed or disagreed with a statement about terminating employees "with no reason given." Unfortunately, such an item was not included in the survey.

8

THE ATTRACTION TO AT-WILL EMPLOYMENT IN UTAH GOVERNMENTS

Richard Green
Robert Forbis
Jennifer Robinson
Stephen Nelson
Jennifer Seelig
Angela Stefaniak
University of Utah

INTRODUCTION

The authors of this chapter have noted elsewhere that at-will employment seems to be emerging as a topic of some interest among politicians and public managers.(1) In its simplest terms, *at-will employment* means that employees may be fired for any reason or no reason at all. It is a common mode of employment in the private and nonprofit sectors, but has been uncommon in public employment since the Progressive era, when calls for reform of abusive patronage practices became widespread. However, the passage of the Civil Service Reform Act of 1978 prompted a series of changes at federal and then state levels that began reversing this trend. Increasing numbers and ranks of senior executive officials were converted to at-will status to enhance bureaucratic responsiveness.

The State of Utah followed suit as well, and by the early 1990s had converted many administrative positions down to the middle-management level to at-will status. Since then, politicians in Utah have made sporadic attempts to convert whole agencies at state and local levels. Most attempts were stymied or modified incrementally to affect only a small class of employees.[a] Notably, in 2005, the Utah state legislature, at the urging of newly elected Governor Jon M. Huntsman Jr., created a new information technology agency (ITS) that will centralize and house all state IT employees (about 900). One of the act's provisions requires that all newly created positions be at-will. Ostensibly, all transferring employees with job functions identical to their old job descriptions will retain merit status. However, another provision gives the new agency's administrators authority to redefine all existing IT positions, and thereby avoid retaining merit status for transferring employees. The law also stipulates that if an employee leaves a protected position in the new agency, it reverts to at-will status.

Advocates for this change in status claim that merit workers entail too many fixed costs that make ITS noncompetitive with the private sector, and further that some ITS employees and services have not kept pace with the times. Either at-will status will induce these employees to adapt, or they will be replaced. Moreover, these advocates insist that IT positions provide technical services and as a result will not be subject to political manipulation.[b] The new agency fits Governor Huntsman's reform agenda. He asserted that he would radically change how state government operates. It should be run like a business, and in so doing, no employee should take his or her job for granted. He reinforced this message by abruptly firing 40 top employees in the Divisions of Minority Affairs and Business and Economic Development. Though he was within his rights to do so (all were employed at-will), the manner of the dismissals broke with custom, and ignited significant controversy.

This and other recent actions taken by the governor and the legislature, such as folding the former Department of Human Resources Management into the Department of Administrative Services, set a tone that is conducive to changing the nature of public employment relations within the state system as a whole. Such efforts might simply be attributed to election-year zeal, but they fit a pattern of changes (or attempted changes) across all levels of government in prior years that suggest a readiness to embrace reforms that could be dramatic and long lasting.(2) This article attempts to provide better understanding about the mind-set among some influential Utah politicians and managers regarding at-will employment and related personnel reforms. A great deal of uncertainty exists about what they know concerning at-will employment, and what role they think it should play in public personnel policy. What attracts them to at-will conversion, and what rationales do they use to justify it?

METHODOLOGY

The research conducted for this study is exploratory and tentative, mainly because so little is known about at-will employment in the public sector. Only a few studies exist on the matter, and these tend to focus on specific instances where recent at-will measures are proposed or implemented.[cf. 3, 4] Moreover, no systematic data exists on the extent of at-will employment in the public sector, so it is also impossible to establish a baseline upon which to study its growth. Accordingly, it seems sensible to begin talking to public officials who have significant influence over personnel policy about at-will employment to learn more about their views on the matter, and to assess what factors make it palatable to them.

Discussions of this sort are interpretive in nature, and can yield new questions and insight to help guide subsequent and more systematic research.[5-7] The sensitive nature of this subject, however, presents some methodological difficulties. Public officials are extremely reticent to discuss at-will conversion openly for fear of starting rumors that might poison employment relations. Therefore, the interviews for this study were conducted with the promise of strict anonymity and an opportunity to review the article before publication. Remarks by interview subjects have been carefully edited, and no mention is made of their specific jurisdiction or agency. Coding of specific numbers and types of respondents and their views was also avoided for fear that some identities could be deduced. The small number of interviews and exploratory nature of this study also make precise, coded responses less significant.

The authors identified 30 state, county, and local government officials in the Salt Lake metropolitan region with extensive public sector experience, and who would likely be aware of efforts in their jurisdictions to make changes in personnel policy that include at-will provisions. Twenty interviews were successfully completed among the identified group. Interviewees were selected because of their ability to directly and significantly influence public personnel policy. They were chosen from elected, politically appointed, and career service ranks. Four have served in all three capacities during their careers. The appointees and career officials either are high-level managers in line agencies, or are highly experienced human resource officials.

The study targeted the Salt Lake metropolitan region, which accounts for more than 80 percent of Utah's population and reflects the widest diversity of public jurisdictions. It addresses only public employment practice in this urban and suburban context. Rural employment practices differ dramatically in character, and therefore deserve separate attention.

Officials were interviewed rather than surveyed to gain more understanding of the contextual nuances that influence their thinking about at-will employment.[8] Subtleties abound in the employment relations environment due to the complex nature of the public service, and due to constant political flux caused by elections, fluctuating budgets, and population shifts.(9) The interviews were semistructured, with interviewers (the authors) working from a prepared list of open-ended questions designed to stimulate conversation (see appendix A). Interviewers followed conversational leads or cues given by the respondents, and then weaved other prepared questions into the ongoing conversation. Opening questions addressed the interviewee's general understanding of at-will employment, and were followed with questions about whether it had been broached as a subject of interest or action in their institution, or if they knew of officials in other agencies who were considering or initiating at-will measures.

Subsequent questions probed more into the history of at-will employment within the interviewee's agency or jurisdiction, and then attempted to gauge the interviewees' own views about expansion of at-will employment. These included questions about what legal, managerial, or political advantages (and disadvantages) they believed resulted from the expansion of at-will employment, and for whom these accrued. The authors steadfastly avoided making any judgments about interviewee responses, but did ask for clarification or elaboration of responses that were vague or possibly misunderstood.

FINDINGS AND ANALYSIS

The interviews revealed a number of interesting and sometimes contradictory views on at-will employment relations, and these are organized into five themes that address the following issues:

1. How interviewees understand at-will employment, and what criteria they use to assess its benefits and drawbacks, and justify its use
2. The importance attached by interviewees to accountability of career service employees, and how this influences their thinking about at-will employment
3. The problems interviewees see with merit systems, with emphasis on the problems of discipline and dismissal
4. The role employee motivation plays in shaping their views on at-will employment
5. The interviewees' attitudes about expansion of at-will employment in Utah

The essential findings for each theme are briefly outlined in Table 8.1.

Table 8.1 At-Will Employment Relations: Interview Results

Topic	*Concerns/Views*
1. Understanding at-will public employment	Most respondents lacked a clear and common understanding of at-will employment. A few respondents were confused about their subordinates' employment status. Employment status and at-will is not a "front-burner" issue for most respondents. Attorney respondents gave divergent views on the employment status of Utah's public employees. Respondents differ on how to convert employment status. All agreed that traditional criteria for converting to at-will were vague and inconsistent.
2. Accountability and at-will employment	Political officials expect immediate responsiveness from career officials, with clear chains of command. Political officials also want a high level of expertise and institutional memory, and tend to ignore or not see the tension between these and immediate responsiveness. Political officials expressed frustration with some middle-management ranks (an at-will boundary) for resisting their initiatives. Elected officials generally believe experts should be merit-protected, though there are market-driven exceptions—such as IT workers. Career officials feel a need for insulation from politicians, more to avoid micromanagement. They see muddled lines of accountability among the superior branches.
3. Problems with merit systems: Discipline and dismissal	Local officials showed disdain for civil service systems for being mired in procedure and employee protection. Political officials expressed some frustration with executive merit system as well—still too difficult to discipline and dismiss employees. All interviewees perceive a general lack of courage and training among managers to use merit system to discipline and dismiss employees.

-- *continued*

Table 8.1 At-Will Employment Relations: Interview Results (continued)

Topic	*Concerns/Views*
3. Problems with merit systems: Discipline and dismissal	Some political officials believe cost of disciplinary processes is too high given the tight fiscal situation. HR officials see managers failing to start the disciplinary process early enough, and then overreacting later. Some officials noted that at-will systems rely more heavily on managerial competence. They have more power to make bigger mistakes. Thus, more training is needed, but is often sacrificed under tight budgets.
4. The role of employee motivation	Many interviewees believe at-will status drives employees to be more productive. A few see job security as better motivator over long run. Most believe public employees trade lower pay for job security. If they want more pay, then they should convert to at-will status. Lazy employees deserve at-will conversion. It will deter them from demotivating productive workers. A few officials emphasized intrinsic and professionally driven motivators in public employment that require more facilitation and support by managers than authoritarian leadership. Economic perks are insufficient to motivate in any case. Merit systems are thus better at fostering trust, institutional rather than personal loyalty, and communication. Job security enhances professional judgment and provides needed family and social stability—two powerful motivators.
5. Views on the expansion of at-will employment in Utah	No consistent awareness exists among interviewees of a trend toward public at-will employment. Conversions of positions from merit to at-will status are viewed as stemming from unique circumstances. Expansion of public at-will employment in Utah is sporadic and incremental rather than a matter of planning and strategy.

Understanding at-Will Public Employment

The interviewees' understanding of at-will employment status, as well as its implications within public agencies, varied considerably. Most officials did not articulate their understanding in any clear and concise manner. With the exception of attorneys and HR professionals—who all correctly observed that merit employees enjoy more extensive legal and managerial protections than do at-will employees—most elected officials and career managers provided examples or talked around the subject. They appeared to lack a shared language with which to discuss employment status, indicating that it was not a topic of frequent conversation. Nor did it appear to be a "front-burner" issue for most of the respondents. Among the attorneys interviewed, opinions differed on the status of public employees in Utah. One attorney concluded that all public employees in the state were at-will unless otherwise excepted, whereas the other attorneys thought that just the opposite was true. A few thought all city employees were covered under for-cause protections by state statute (Title 10), whereas others believed that this was contingent upon the class of city and that exceptions could be granted.

A few political officials misunderstood aspects of at-will employment in their jurisdictions, such as which employees were covered by at-will provisions, and how conversions of status were accomplished. For example, one elected official believed that the employees serving him or her and other colleagues were all merit-based, when in fact they were all at-will. This official formed this impression quite reasonably because the employees had worked for the office through several changes in elected officials, and this lent a sense of permanency to their status. Most non-HR officials displayed limited knowledge of the criteria and process for changing employees from merit to at-will status. All officials admitted that these criteria were difficult to sort out in practice, and were applied inconsistently as a result. The HR professionals confirmed that confusion about, and inconsistent application of, at-will status is prevalent throughout state and local governments.

All interviewees exhibited confusion about the criteria that had been applied to justify converting merit employees to at-will status. The majority of respondents believed justification existed whenever employees formally possessed policy-making as well as implementing powers. None clearly distinguish between "policy making" and other responsibilities, and few offered any insight as to why policy-making positions had been established as merit positions in the first place. As might be expected, the HR professionals attributed merit status to an earlier era that emphasized the minimization of direct electoral influence over professional managers. All sensed that this emphasis was changing. In addition, state officials believe that employees with responsibilities that coincide with the boundaries of an entire political jurisdiction are policy makers. For example, officials who supervise employees in all districts of the state must be policy makers, and are thus fair game for at-will conversion.

Accountability and at-Will Employment

Elected officials generally view themselves as governmental agents directly accountable to the public through the act of elections. The elected officials interviewed for this study think good government means, in part, that all government employees should be held similarly accountable. This type of accountability is demonstrated through immediate responsiveness to elected officials' requests or demands. Most believe that merit employees often do not respond quickly enough, and that at-will status changes that. When asked to which elected officials the employees should respond, these officials indicated that executive agency employees should respond to the elected chief executive, and legislative employees should respond to legislators. Most conveyed this sense of tidy and clear lines of electoral accountability. Only one raised the possibility, much less the right, of a competing branch to interfere with this arrangement.

Interestingly, these same officials also wanted a high level of expertise and institutional memory in their public employees. The elected officials viewed themselves and their policy preferences as living on borrowed time. They did not want to waste this time rehashing policy directions or solutions that had already proved unworkable. They want career employees to be knowledgeable of policy history, practice, and workability, and to advise them when proposals seem unwise in light of this knowledge. At the same time, however, most of the elected officials expressed frustration about some administrators resisting their agendas, especially at the middle-management level—where knowledge of workability is a critical function. As it happens, this is also where the line of demarcation between at-will and merit employment status now typically exists in Utah. Over the last 10–15 years, it is where politicians have attempted to convert managerial ranks to at-will status, asserting that these ranks are policy making in nature. Interestingly, one official thought this problem of bureaucratic resistance occurred more often in large agencies, and that scale might be a more significant factor than employment status.

Elected officials also consistently drew a distinction between experts and other employees. Experts in technical fields should be protected by merit status so that they can make expert decisions without undue political interference. The recent conversion of state IT employees to at-will status contradicts this point. Some saw this case as a market-based exception. Others saw it as an attempt to make some IT employees adapt quickly to new technologies or face dismissal. No one seemed to think these employees would be subjected to political manipulation, despite the fact that the previous administration (in 2003) had been excoriated by public employees and the press for its "political" hires in a state IT office.

Overall, both elected and appointed officials tended to downplay or even ignore the inherent tension between political responsiveness and managerial effectiveness. Effectiveness seems to mean responding quickly and favorably to the priorities of appropriate political superiors, while advising them of weaknesses or problems with policy prescriptions. Where administrators appear to play more than an advisory role in policy matters, they should be at-will to make them more responsive and loyal to political influence. Furthermore, it is their responsibility to ensure responsiveness and loyalty among the subordinate ranks.

Not surprisingly, the career administrators interviewed for this study expressed a need to be insulated from the political arena to properly manage their agencies and programs. They said they were acutely aware of, and attentive to, the priorities of elected and appointed superiors without need of a change to at-will status. Two career officials admitted that some career subordinates had resisted political agendas, but that this was rare. They reported concerns about the tendency of some politicians to micromanage agencies, and in some cases to politicize them. Micromanagement seemed more the common concern than partisan manipulation—and as much from legislators as from political executives. From their perspective, the lines of authority and accountability among the branches were not very tidy. Although this difference in perspectives is quite marked, it did not carry through to the problem of disciplining protected employees.

Discipline and Dismissal

In Utah, most public agencies have an executive-based merit system with a human resources office through which it is managed. In addition, some cities have a formal civil service system, primarily for police and fire employees, controlled by an independent commission. All of the local government officials interviewed for this study expressed complete frustration with civil service systems. They believed it near impossible for managers to hire the employees they want and to dismiss bad employees in a timely fashion. None felt that administrators could effectively manage civil service employees because of extensive rules and protections. They asserted that employment in civil service systems is a property right, and as a result, the disciplinary process is too structured and legalistic. Appeals are repetitive, constituting "de novo" proceedings at every level, and therefore requiring tremendous time and expense.

Most of the interviewees showed moderate frustration with executive-centered merit systems as well, but also admitted that they are significantly easier to deal with than civil service systems. All of the HR officials interviewed believe that merit systems have improved dramatically in terms of flexibility and timely support for public managers. All interviewees think, however, that too many administrators lack the courage to use existing merit system processes to discipline and remove employees who exhibit incompetence or poor performance. Most would rather reassign or transfer them out of their units. Many interviewees believe managers are neither adequately trained nor disposed to work with the existing disciplinary processes. Most officials think that disciplinary processes are too complex and lengthy, and therefore require a level of expertise and patience that most managers do not possess. Elected officials and political appointees complained that the cost of these processes per employee was too high given the tight fiscal constraints of local and state governments.

Many career officials interviewed maintain that merit systems are much more flexible than people realize, but that managers often fail to take action early enough when dealing with problem employees. HR officials described a common pattern of managers and supervisors failing to deal with problems at early stages, and then overreacting in frustration later on. In such cases, the manager's actions are usually a surprise to the employee, and often disproportionate to the nature of the problem. This passive-aggressive approach needlessly complicates the appeals process, and often works to the favor of the offending employee.

In this context, attempts to adopt at-will employment relations appear to result from a combination of exasperation, the desire to cut costs, and the desire to simplify or truncate managerial responsibilities. The assumption is that managers can then more easily identify employees who will work as a team.

On the other hand, a few interviewees, especially the HR officials, noted that an at-will system is only as good as the managers who run it. Their powers are far more acute, and the effects of their actions more dramatic as a result. Thoughtful managers could use such powers quite effectively, but less competent managers would only make bad situations much worse. One political official had witnessed this firsthand in a private sector organization, and believed that broad expansion of at-will employment would be disastrous on both political and managerial grounds. Ironically, the need for sustained and effective management training increases rather than decreases under at-will conditions. Unfortunately, this is highly problematic because management and professional training are among the first items cut under tight budgets.

One perceptive interviewee noted that employees in at-will systems also need to learn how to take care of themselves through the job-bargaining process during recruitment. Sophisticated at-will employees will protect themselves with contracts and severance packages, and some professionals, such as city managers, have learned to do this sooner and more effectively than others. This assumes, of course, that all employees possess skills valuable enough to induce the hiring agency to bargain with them. Most mid- and lower-level employees seldom do, which is why some join professional associations or unions to increase collective power instead.

A few officials firmly believe that merit systems are manageable and valuable, and that at-will employment causes a lot of cronyism, turnover, and difficulty in recruitment—especially when other public agencies in the area maintain merit protection. A few political appointees and career managers expressed strong preference for using merit employment to cultivate loyalty from employees. The threat of termination inherent in at-will status is ineffective over the long run. All but a few officials acknowledged that job security can be a positive motivating force. Many of them expressed satisfaction with the high quality of public servants overall, but were exasperated by the poor performance of a few. A couple of officials indicated that they would love to have the at-will prerogative just long enough to get the troublemakers out, and then revert to the for-cause standard.

The Role of Employee Motivation

The officials interviewed for this study displayed rather dichotomous views of motivation. Many embraced an economic model that emphasizes monetary incentives and competition for work as the primary motivators. Acceptable pay and the fear of losing one's job in a tight labor market combine as carrot and stick to drive productivity. These officials saw little or no difference between public and private work. As a result, some think agencies should adopt pay-for-performance systems. (Only one local jurisdiction in the metro region has done so.)

All interviewees recognized that governments tend to pay lower wages than in the private sector, and believe that job security is offered in lieu thereof. This is understood as a trade-off or bargain that should not alter the logic of economic incentives. If employees demand higher wages, then they should accept the risks that typically go with it in the private sector—meaning loss of job security. Some of these officials noted that recent (failed) attempts to convert attorneys on the state attorney general's staff to at-will status came in the wake of persistent requests by the AG for higher, competitive salaries. The positions deemed comparable in this case were attorneys in the legislative staff of the Office of Legislative

Research and General Counsel, who are paid closer to market standards but are employed at-will.

Additionally, employees who treat job security as an excuse to "slack off" rather than as a good-faith economic bargain deserve threats to privatize their jobs or efforts to convert them to at-will status. Most saw this as an aspect of employment justice and deterrence. If they are allowed to continue their slacking behavior for long, they will demotivate those around them. As one elected official expressed it, managers and fellow employees alike will be happier and more productive if they do not have to constantly work alongside poor-performing employees. Managers will be encouraged to manage effectively if they know that they can deal quickly with poor performers, rather than endure endless and expensive disciplinary processes.

About a third of the officials interviewed seemed to adhere to an alternative model of motivation that emphasizes intrinsic and professional motivation. That is, public work presents distinctive ideals, challenges, and conditions that attract and motivate employees. In many cases, they need stability, high levels of education and training, and long years of experience to do the work in a highly effective manner. Managers play more facilitative and maintenance roles, and rely on professional work ethic and institutional loyalties that they see most public employees display daily in getting the work done. As one HR official observed, public managers have very few external incentives to offer, and so cannot play the pay-for-performance game very effectively. These officials noted that such schemes usually fail in public settings.

These same officials believe that merit systems encourage loyalty and independence among employees, and thereby enhance their productivity. The looming threat of termination exhibited under at-will conditions is not an effective motivating tool over the long run. Rather, as one official noted, it can have a chilling effect on what they will say to their employers, which frustrates good communication and trust. It is "silly" to think that most employees cannot be trusted, and must constantly be watched. Several, including some political appointees, agreed that employees respond best to trust and rewards, not threats and punishment, and believe that job security provides an important motivational support for career employees at all levels of an agency or jurisdiction. As described, it serves at least two important functions.

First, it provides more room for independent judgment—an intrinsic motivator that also protects and enhances professional judgment. The attempt by some legislators to bargain with the attorney general's legal staff over higher pay for at-will status illustrates this. One of the officials interviewed indicated that the AG attorneys opposed such a bargain because their independence would be threatened, especially when they felt compelled to issue opinions on controversial legal issues, or prosecute highly contentious cases. They perceived the need for a protected zone of discretion that adds confidence to their decisions and supports their professional integrity in difficult public arenas.

Second, as another official observed, job security meets basic needs of many public employees for social stability and some indemnity against medical or other catastrophes. It was noted, for example, that the average age of state government employees is in the mid-40s, and new applicants are typically in their mid-30s, when most have growing families and corresponding ties to their neighborhoods and communities. The lack of stable jobs and adequate family benefits threatens these ties, and can seriously distract employees from their work.

However, most of the interviewees also see job security and stable benefits steadily eroding due to difficult fiscal constraints and privatization of many public services. The threat of at-will employment just adds to an already bleak public employment picture. Working in the public service is not as desirable or secure as it used to be. Moreover, the HR officials noted that the younger ranks of new workers seem less inclined to seek job security and stability in favor of job mobility and portable benefits. The expectation of stable benefits and careers seems to have diminished, and the commitment to a career in an agency or policy arena has weakened.

Overall, these observations about motivation suggest two things. The first is that more public managers and political officials seem ready to embrace, or at least to experiment with, at-will employment relations than in the past. The second is that younger employees may be more receptive to a wide range of employment relations, and share few concerns with older workers about at-will status. Conditions may thus be ripe for expansion of public at-will employment.

Views on Expanding at-Will Employment in Utah

Despite the potential for expansion of public at-will employment in Utah, there is no consistent awareness among the interviewed officials that it is happening. A few even have contrary impressions about this, and believe that merit protections continue to expand in the state. Most of those interviewed do not see a trend toward at-will employment. It is notable, however, that a couple of officials have witnessed discussions about at-will employment as an emerging trend at national conferences. Most, including these two, clearly believe that merit and civil service systems are increasingly subjected to reform efforts, though not necessarily resulting in at-will conversion. They characterize most of the changes in Utah public employment as marginal reforms of merit systems intended to improve managerial flexibility.

Second, the at-will conversions that have taken place are interpreted by many respondents as arising out of unique situations or events, even though they believe such situations are increasing in frequency. The events most commonly referred to occurred at the state level, though a few local officials did acknowledge that attempts at at-will conversion were desired, and in a few cases had been made. In most cases, the interviewees emphasized that the conversions did not target specific individuals, but were instead focused on the nature of the positions. Many acknowledged that rumors existed to the contrary, and some local officials admitted the desire for at-will conversion to go after specific "problem" employees.

Although there may be no general plan for at-will expansion, it is clear that at-will employment has expanded sporadically among the ranks of Utah state employees over the last 10–15 years. The movement is more a case of incremental fits and starts than steady progression. The efforts are narrowly focused, and viewed more as exceptions, with no apparent awareness among the actors of a movement or trend. Some of the interviewees believe these episodes have occurred more frequently in recent years, but this remains to be verified by subsequent study.

CONCLUSION

Conclusions drawn from this study are tentative at best. Nevertheless, they can be useful as points for subsequent study, and for posing questions and identifying dilemmas from what has been learned thus far. First, it appears that the expansion of at-will employment in Utah results from the slow erosion of public employment processes and protections due to the situational pressures of political and managerial expedience. Politicians demand immediate responsiveness from the administration and, in some cases at least, become quickly exasperated and ready to dispense with the protections typically afforded to administrative professionals. There is nothing new about impatient or exasperated politicians. What is different is the disposition to engage in structural reforms that drastically change employment relations for the sake of responsiveness.

There is a troubling dilemma involved with demands for immediate electoral responsiveness. To whom, and to what, should public administrators be responsive?[(10)] Contrary to the impressions of some political officials, the lines of accountability and influence in a system of blended powers are not amenable to tidy division of functions and authority. Legislators may, and at times do, micromanage agency programs and processes. Executives and independent commissions can and do get crosswise with intentions of legislatures and courts. To whom should administrative officials respond when these conflicts occur? At times, political officials want things done their way regardless of legal or ethical boundaries, or channels of authority. How should administrative officials respond? Should they follow legal or ethical principles, or take the safest path of political expedience? Such questions apply to any employment relation, but the implications become much more acute for at-will employees. For-cause protections provide a modest buffer against such pressures.

There are no happy solutions to the dilemmas of politics, but the system's ability to cope with them changes with the structure of employment relations. Professionalism has historically existed in tension with electoral responsiveness. What happens to the nature of professionalism when its protections are reduced or eliminated? Some of the political officials interviewed in this study believe professionalism will not be affected because politicians will restrain themselves from undue manipulation. In part, this stems from the belief that professionals should serve instrumentally and not govern in their own right. As long as professionals stick to instrumental roles, politicians will not be tempted to manipulate them. But a tremendous body of empirical research has demonstrated that even street-level bureaucrats shape policy—they govern on a daily basis through substantial discretionary powers.[cf. 11] And history indicates that political self-restraint, much like judicial self-restraint, seldom lasts for long. The founders designed the constitutional system of checks and balances because they distrusted such claims.

In this light, the dismissive attitude among many of the interviewees about possible political manipulation under at-will employment relations is one of the more remarkable and worrisome findings of this study. A general expectation exists that merit considerations will take precedence over politics regardless of employment status. As one official described it, spoils systems are now at an end, so such protections are no longer needed. Even a few career officials seemed ready to accept this conclusion. To what extent do elected, appointed, and career public servants as a whole share this view in Utah and nationally? Given the significant long-term implications, more systematic research on this question is clearly warranted.

Secondly, the impatience of career managers and political appointees with merit systems, and demands for more flexibility, present similar concerns. David Rosenbloom[12] has warned of the tendency in management thought and practice to neglect the "inherent politicality" of public personnel management. In public life, management can never be separated totally as an activity from politics. The system creates many bosses—some formally political, and some administrative. Any efforts at reform must anticipate the political dynamics of both. In this case, increased flexibility to discipline or discharge errant employees also means greater ease in sanctioning or removing employees for wrong reasons, including electoral partisanship, bureaucratic politics, personal vendettas, managerial intrigue, or even incompetence. And under at-will conditions, more rather than fewer superiors can acutely influence the situation with little or no justification.

The frustration about managers failing to use existing merit processes to discipline and remove employees further illustrates the problem. Interviewees cited a variety of reasons for this, chief among them a fear of conflict and lack of training. But this begs the question of whether lack of courage or training by some managers is a good reason to simplify or truncate their responsibilities to employees through at-will reform. What would their actions look like in the wake of such changes? Might this simply make it easier to hide the true reasons for expedited discipline and removal—which only increases the danger of arbitrary, unaccountable actions toward good as well as bad employees? Would this exaggerate rather than mitigate the passive-aggressive behavior pattern among some managers? Of course, these matters hinge mainly on the assumption that managers commonly do avoid using disciplinary processes when they think discipline or removal is called for. This may have more to do with strong impressions formed through a few bad cases than through systematic study to verify what is actually going on. The results of such study could have profound effects on this whole issue.

Finally, it is readily apparent from these interviews that the roles of professional administrators in relation to political officials need broader discussion, elucidation, and negotiation. The political officials sense correctly that administrators make as well as implement policy, but few of them seem ready or able to articulate the distinctive value that administrators, *as career officials*, bring in terms of legitimate democratic accountability and political efficacy. The tendency to drive at-will status down the administrative hierarchy stems at least partly from lack of understanding of these crucial matters. It is also apparent that career managers lack the ability or opportunity to discuss their roles as administrative politicians who must find ways to accommodate the agendas of elected politicians in a context of divided powers. Though normative scholars in public administration have devoted substantial attention to this subject,[cf. 13–17] their insights have not found a way into the forums that shape political minds. This presents a critical task that needs performing sooner rather than later. The stakes are simply too high to put it off much longer. Is it possible to engage career managers and politicians in constructive dialogue about their respective roles? That is perhaps the most important challenge of the day.

ENDNOTES

a. For example, Governor Mike O. Leavitt, early in his administration (1992–2004), talked of converting the entire state service to at-will status, but this was quickly dismissed in favor of converting only division directors who, arguably, possessed "policymaking responsibilities." Prison wardens were also converted on similar grounds. Though limited in scope, both efforts were quite controversial. Prior to these changes, the Department of Environmental Quality converted employees to at-will status. In recent years, attempts have been made in the legislature to convert attorneys in the attorney general's office to at-will in exchange for higher salaries. To date, the effort has failed.

b. State officials claim that the recently passed IT bill was not aimed at specific employees. They claim that many employees are motivated and excited about the change. To allay concerns about losing protected status, employees who lose their jobs will be offered training and first opportunity at other jobs in the state system. They also claim that employees who remain will likely be paid more competitive wages because their skills will be updated. Also, the new agency must provide quarterly reports to the legislature, and, before implementing any large-scale changes, must receive legislative approval.

REFERENCES

1. Green, R. T., et al., On the ethics of at-will employment in the public sector, *Public Integrity*, 2005, forthcoming.
2. Ibid.
3. Bowman, J. S., At-will employment in Florida government: A naked formula to corrupt public service, *WorkingUSA*, 6(2), 90, 2002.
4. Condrey, S. E., Reinventing state civil service systems: The Georgia experience, *Review of Public Personnel Administration*, 22(2), 114, 2002.
5. Berg, B. L., *Qualitative Research Methods for the Social Sciences*, 5th ed., Pearson, Boston, 2004, 7.
6. Neuman, L. W., *Social Research Methods: Qualitative and Quantitative Approaches*, 5th ed., Allyn & Bacon, Boston, 2003, 76.
7. Schwandt, T. A., Three epistemological stances for qualitative inquiry: Interpretivism, hermeneutics, and social constructionism, in *The Landscape of Qualitative Research: Theories and Issues*, 2nd ed., Denzin, N. K., and Lincoln, Y. S., eds., Sage, Thousand Oaks, CA, 2003, 296.
8. Leech, B. L., Asking questions: Techniques for semi-structured interviews, *PS: Political Science and Politics*, 34(4), 665, 2002.
9. Merriam, S., *Qualitative Research and Case Study Application in Education*, Jossey-Bass, San Francisco, 2001.
10. Saltztein, G. H., Conceptualizing bureaucratic responsiveness, *Administration & Society*, 17(3), 283, 1985.
11. Lipsky, M., *Street-Level Bureaucracy: Dilemmas of the Individual in Public Services*, Russell Sage Foundation, New York, 1985.
12. Rosenbloom, D. H., The inherent politicality of public personnel policy: An analytic introduction, in *Public Personnel Policy: The Politics of Civil Service*, Rosenbloom, D. H., Associated Faculty Press, New York, 1985.

13. Rohr, J. A., *To Run a Constitution: The Legitimacy of the Administrative State*, University Press of Kansas, Lawrence, 1986.
14. Cooper, T. L., *An Ethic of Citizenship for Public Administration*, Prentice-Hall, Englewood Cliffs, NJ, 1991.
15. Terry, L. D., *Leadership of Public Bureaucracies: The Administrator as Conservator*, Sage, Thousand Oaks, CA, 1995.
16. Cook, B. J., *Bureaucracy and Self Government: Reconsidering the Role of Public Administration in American Politics*, Johns Hopkins University Press, Baltimore, 1996.
17. Rosenbloom, D. H., *Building a Legislative-Centered Public Administration: Congress and the Administrative State, 1946–1999*, University of Alabama Press, Tuscaloosa, 2000.

PART IV

FUTURE REFORM ISSUES

9

DISSIN' THE DEADWOOD OR CODDLING THE INCOMPETENTS? PATTERNS AND ISSUES IN EMPLOYEE DISCIPLINE AND DISMISSAL IN THE STATES

Richard C. Elling
Lyke Thompson
Wayne State University

INTRODUCTION

Much of the public believes that governments tolerate the continued employment of far too many persons who would have been terminated were they employed in the private sector. They "coddle incompetents" and refuse to prune "deadwood." This problem is seen by critics to be the result of civil service practices gone awry. In response to such views, some jurisdictions have sought to tip the balance with regard to the disciplining or dismissal of employees more in favor of the employer. Defenders of traditional civil service and its "just-cause" standard for dismissal have often responded that such proposals assure a return to the bad old days of spoils politics. Advocates of change have often acted as if politicians and managers in the 21st century are unequivocally a better lot than their 19th-century counterparts.

This chapter presents new evidence to temper this debate, evidence that may help the public steer between the Charybdis of a knee-jerk defense of the status quo and the Scylla of uncritical embrace of at-will employment. The analysis begins with a look at the limited existing evidence on rates of public employee dismissal, followed by a more detailed discussion of a recent comparative analysis of state employee dismissal. Next, a second database explores whether state managers consider processes for disciplining or dismissing employees to seriously compromise their ability to manage. The chapter then seeks to account for interstate variation in state employee dismissal rates, and in managers' views of discipline and dismissal processes as a management impediment. Because extent of civil service coverage, extent of collective bargaining, and the degree to which a state's dismissal process had been simplified could account for little variation, other factors that might influence dismissals are then discussed. The analysis concludes by confronting the trade-offs in replacing the just-cause standard of dismissal with at-will provisions.

EMPLOYEE DISMISSAL EVIDENCE

Little data on public employee dismissal—especially for a number of jurisdictions and across time—exists. O. Glenn Stahl—drawing on the records of the U.S. Office of Personnel Management for federal data, as well as occasional articles on such actions in state and local governments—cites annual rates that range from "a little less than 1.0 to about 1.5 percent." [1] The U.S. Merit Systems Protection Board reports rates of 0.2 to 0.4 percent for civilian federal government employees. [2] Dresang asserts that dismissal rates for state and local governments are comparable to those found at the federal level. [3] Mercier reports that in 1976, California terminated less than 0.2 percent of its workforce of 110,000. [4]

Dismissal rates such as these appear to be lower than those in the private sector, although disagreement exists on this point. Stahl contends that the annual rate of dismissal "in American public jurisdictions as a whole is exceeded, if at all, only in certain categories of private employment, such as a few areas of manufacturing." [5] One of these categories may be the trucking industry, where Shaw, Delery, Jenkins, and Gupta found an average rate of dismissal for 1994 of 5.98 percent. [6] Hays states that "reported discharge rates for various categories of employees in the private sector ranged from 10.5 percent (among service employees) to 1.8 percent (a composite figure for industrialized employees as derived from a Bureau of National Affairs study)." [7] Steiber, however, reports the dismissal rate for *unionized* private sector employees to be only 0.9 percent. [8] Significantly, only unionized private sector workers enjoy job protections similar to those possessed by civil service employees.

PATTERNS OF STATE EMPLOYEE DISMISSAL: THE 20-STATE STUDY

An assessment of dismissal was part of a broader study of state government employee turnover conducted by Elling, [9] who collected data on forms of employee exit from employment for 20 states in 1993, 1994, and 1995. [10] Aggregate employee turnover was defined as consisting of voluntary resignations (or "quits"), retirements, dismissals, layoffs, and deaths. Half of the states distinguished between dismissals of probationary and non-probationary employees. Because not all of them did so, however, the figures for these two groups of employees were combined.

Termination rates were less than 1 percent annually across the 20 states for the period (see Table 9.1). Interstate variation in rates also existed. In 1993, rates ranged from less than 0.5 percent in Michigan and Wisconsin, to 1.5 percent or higher in Arizona, Missouri, and Ohio. Missouri had the highest dismissal rates in each of the three years. Michigan had the lowest dismissal rates in 1994 and 1995, and the state ranked next to last in 1993.

This data prompts several observations. First, these state dismissal rates are comparable to those reported by Stahl in the 1980s. Second, states appear to have consistent rates across time. Third, interstate variation is evident and suggests there is something about individual states that causes them to have differing results. Finally, whether one is a classified or an unclassified employee must matter. The statistics for three states—Missouri, Ohio, and Virginia—cover both classified and unclassified employees, and Missouri and Ohio are among the three states with the highest dismissal rates.

Because Ohio reported dismissals for classified and unclassified employees separately, the relevance of classified versus unclassified status can be approximated. Alas, the state did not provide data on the number of classified as opposed to unclassified staff. The actual proportion of total employment consisting of unclassified employees is, hence, not known. An Ohio personnel official estimated that "roughly ten percent" of total employment consisted of unclassified personnel, however. This proportion was applied to the total employment figure, and the resulting number of employees became the denominator used to calculate the dismissal rate for unclassified employees. The resulting rates were 2.4 percent in 1993, 1.6 percent in 1994, and 3.1 percent in 1995. This compares to a dismissal rate for the estimated 90 percent of Ohio employees who are in the classified service of 0.2 percent in 1993, 0.2 percent in 1994, and 0.4 percent in 1995.

Table 9.1 Number of State Classified Employees Dismissed, and Dismissal Rates, in 20 States, 1993–1995

State	*1993*		*1994*		*1995*		*Three-Year Average Dismissal Rate[b] (%)*
	Employees Dismissed	**Dismissal Rate[a] (%)**	**Employees Dismissed**	**Dismissal Rate[a] (%)**	**Employees Dismissed**	**Dismissal Rate[a] (%)**	
Alabama	169	0.6	190	0.6	141	0.5	0.5
Arizona	462	1.7	480	1.7	551	1.9	1.8
California	753	0.5	907	0.6	848	0.5	0.5
Florida	970	0.9	1261	1.1	1630	1.3	1.1
Idaho	66	0.6	69	0.6	64	0.5	0.6
Illinois	429	0.7	484	0.8	476	0.7	0.7
Iowa	132	0.6	152	0.8	166	0.9	0.8
Kansas	314	1.1	385	1.3	335	1.2	1.2
Michigan	196	0.3	135	0.2	200	0.3	0.3
Minnesota	175	0.6	196	0.6	239	0.8	0.7
Missouri	507	1.7	564	1.9	702	2.2	2.0
Nevada	137	1.2	152	1.2	165	1.3	1.2
New Hampshire	72	0.8	80	0.8	64	0.6	0.7
North Carolina	565	0.7	464	0.6	514	0.6	0.6
Ohio	876	1.5	680	1.5	1161	1.8	1.5
Oklahoma	147	0.5	167	0.6	205	0.7	0.6

Tennessee	216	0.6	275	0.8	338	0.9	0.8
Texas	1246	1.0	1278	1.0	1459	1.1	1.1
Virginia	765	1.0	753	0.9	647	0.8	0.9
Wisconsin	94	0.2	156	0.4	237	0.6	0.4
All 20 states	8291	0.8	8828	0.9	10,142	1.0	—
		(.50)[c]		(.44)		(.50)	

[a] The dismissal rate is the number of employees dismissed in a given year divided by the total number of employees in that state in that year. The total employment figures used to calculate dismissal rates are usually those for the beginning of the fiscal year. In a few states, the data is reported on a calendar-year basis. A handful of states used average employment for the reporting period rather than employment at the beginning of the period. This had little impact on calculations of dismissal rates because total employment rarely changed greatly over the course of a year.

[b] In the case of the three-year average dismissal rate, the total employment figure used is the total for the entire three years. This is divided into the total number of dismissals across three years in each state to calculate a three-year average.

[c] The figure in parentheses is the coefficient of variation (CV). This is calculated by dividing the standard deviation for a variable by its mean. A rule of thumb is that a CV greater than 0.30 indicates considerable variation.

Although formal rates appear to be low, a formal termination is not the only way an employer can rid itself of a low performer. Employees may be presented with the choice of going quietly rather than having a formal dismissal on their records. Alternatively, an individual may be encouraged to transfer to another agency. In the 20-state turnover study, internal mobility was not a focus. However, some states provided statistics on interagency transfers. This data indicates that the number of employees who move to jobs in other agencies is often as great as the number leaving government employ. Some of those transferring must be employees who have decided it makes more sense to switch jobs than to fight to hold onto their current ones.

Carolyn Ban's study of seven federal government units supports this line of argument. [11] Out of 128 instances where managers had to deal with "problem employees," only 15 percent were resolved by firing the employee. In another 17 percent of the cases, the person "voluntarily" resigned, "usually after he or she had learned that a dismissal was likely." [12] An additional 6 percent ended with the employee retiring. If Ban's findings are representative, the number of low-performing employees gotten rid of via coerced resignations or retirement may be again as great as the number who are formally dismissed.

Data from four states in the 20-state turnover study suggests that these "soft-core" dismissals are common. California, Idaho, North Carolina, and Texas each make use of an "involuntary" or "in lieu of dismissal" resignation category. In the turnover analysis, these actions were coded as resignations. If, however, such resignations are treated as functionally equivalent to formal dismissals, then—although dismissal rates remain quite low—they increased by anywhere from 20 to 40 percent in every state except North Carolina. In Texas, for instance, the formal dismissal rates were 1.0 percent in 1993 and 1994 and 1.1 percent in 1995, whereas the combined "formal/informal dismissal" rates for these three years were 1.4, 1.4, and 1.5 percent, respectively. Whether or not a state explicitly recognizes "coerced" resignations in their data, some of the resignations coded as "voluntary" must have been coerced. Hence, although formal dismissals may constitute most of the iceberg, they do not constitute all of it.

In sum, although formal rates of dismissal appear to be quite low in most states, variation is evident. It also appears that managers often use informal means to get rid of low-performing staff.

DEALING WITH PROBLEM EMPLOYEES: THE VIEWS OF STATE MANAGERS

Another way to gain perspective on dismissals is to see if managers who deal with problem employees consider the existing processes for doing so to present challenges. This is explored using data from two surveys of state managers in ten states that were conducted in 1982 and 2000. [13, 14] Hereafter, these studies are referred to as the 1982 Comparative State Management Study and the 2000 Comparative State Management Study. [15] The states included were Arizona, California, Delaware, Indiana, Michigan, New York, South Dakota, Tennessee, Texas, and Vermont. Although not a representative sample of all states, these states are a diverse lot and differ in population size and demographics, economic base, political culture, and ideological complexion. More to the point, these state bureaucracies differ in extent of civil service coverage and collective bargaining.

In both surveys, managers were asked whether one or another of a long list of conditions and practices hindered the "efficient and effective administration of the programmatic responsibilities" of the unit they headed. [16] In the 1982 survey, 12 of the 52 problems that managers were queried about were personnel related. In the 2000 survey, 18 of 65 potential problems were personnel related.

In both years, managers reported a number of personnel-related problems to seriously impede effective unit management. Moreover, some of these problems ranked among the most serious management impediments. Processes for employee discipline and dismissal were one such problem. In both 1982 and 2000, 34 percent of managers said dealing with problem employees seriously impeded their ability to manage their units (see Table 9.2). This problem was tied for fourth place as the most serious management issue in 1982 and ranked as ninth most serious in 2000.

In 2000, however, problems with uncompetitive salaries, adequately rewarding outstanding employees, filling key vacancies, personnel problems for recruiting candidates, and problems retaining staff were seen to be more serious than problems associated with employee discipline or dismissal. In recent years at least, difficulty in securing good employees and retaining them appears to constitute more of a challenge for managers than terminating nonperformers.

In a given state, the proportion of managers reporting discipline/dismissal to be a problem varied relatively little across the two surveys (column C, Table 9.2). But interstate variation was substantial in both years. In 1982 (column A, Table 9.2), the proportion of managers who considered problems disciplining/dismissing employees to be either serious or very serious varied from 17 percent in South Dakota to 41 percent

Table 9.2 Interstate Variation in Severity of Problems Relating to Employee Discipline/Dismissal, Ten States, 1982 and 2000

State	*Percentage of Managers Reporting Problems in Disciplining or Dismissing Low-Performing Employees to Be a Serious Impediment to Effective Management*[a]		*Change in Percentage Reporting Problem to Be Serious, 1982 versus 2000*
	1982	**2000**	
	A (%)	**B (%)**	**C (%)**
Arizona	37 (6)[b]	33 (10.5)[b]	–4[c]
California	41 (2)	41 (5)	0
Delaware	31 (7)	57 (2)	26
Indiana	32 (6)	27 (13)	–5
Michigan	39 (7)	32 (8)	–7
New York	41 (4)	44 (2)	3
South Dakota	17 (14.5)	35 (3)	18
Tennessee	40 (3)	36 (9)	4
Texas	21 (7)	18 (16)	3
Vermont	27 (4.5)	31 (5.5)	4
Overall	34 (4.5)	34 (9)	0

[a] Cell entry is percentage of managers in a state reporting that "difficulty in disciplining/dismissing low-performing employees" was either a *serious* or a *very serious* impediment to the management of the unit that they headed.

[b] Parenthetical figure is the rank in mean severity of employee discipline/dismissal in a particular state relative to the entire set of potential management impediments.

[c] A positive percentage indicates that employee discipline or dismissal was *more* of a problem in 2000 than it was seen to have been in 1982.

in California. The range in 2000 was from a low of 18 percent in Texas to a high of 57 percent in Delaware.

The extent of interstate variation should not be exaggerated, however. The proportion of managers who considered problems in employee discipline/dismissal to be a serious impediment was in the 30 to 40 percent range in all but two or three states in 1982 and 2000. [17] Disciplining/dismissing personnel ranked seventh or higher as a problem—out of a total of 52 potential impediments—in all but one state in 1982 (see parenthetical figures, column A, Table 9.2). In 2000—as the parenthetical data in column

B of Table 9.2 shows—disciplining/dismissing employees ranked seventh or higher in five states (out of 65 potential impediments), and ranked among the ten most serious problems in seven of them.

In short, state managers surveyed in 1982 and again in 2000 often saw processes for the dismissing of low-performing employees to be a problem. Other personnel-related problems were, however, frequently seen to be as severe if not more severe. This was especially true in the most recent survey.

DETERMINANTS OF DISMISSAL RATES AND THE SEVERITY OF DISMISSAL AS A MANAGEMENT IMPEDIMENT

State government dismissal rates during the mid-1990s were low. Moreover, managers surveyed in 1982 and 2000 frequently considered difficulty in disciplining or dismissing employees to be a serious impediment to effective management. But interstate variation was also evident. The next task is to identify some of the determinants of such variation.

Civil Service Coverage and Dismissal Rates

The procedural requirements associated with civil service are frequently criticized for constraining the ability of managers to dismiss low-performing employees. Data from the 2000 Comparative State Management Survey can be used to explore whether this is indeed so. The average proportion of unit employees covered by civil service in the ten state samples varied from more than 90 percent, in California, New York, and Michigan, to less than 60 percent in Texas and Indiana. Large coefficients of variation in several states indicated that coverage also varied substantially across the individual responding units in those states. [18]

Only a small positive correlation existed between the proportion of employees of an administrative unit who were classified civil servants and managers' views on the severity of discipline and dismissal as a management impediment (Pearson's $r = +.16$, significant at .05 level, one-tailed test). Nor was the association between the proportion of personnel in the classified service and the likelihood that the head of that unit considered discipline or dismissal to be a more serious management impediment strong or consistent for individual states. Significant positive correlations (at the .05 level, one-tailed test) emerged only in South Dakota ($r = .355$) and Tennessee ($r = .211$).

The impact of civil service coverage may be more evident in the case of actual dismissal data. Unfortunately, civil service coverage data for the 20 states in the dismissal study was unavailable. Data on dismissal rates for probationary as opposed to nonprobationary employees is, however, available for ten of these states. [19] Because the full panoply of procedural and substantive protections against dismissal does not apply to probationary staff, rates for such employees should be higher than for those who are no longer on probation. Probationary dismissal rates should, hence, approximate what rates might be in the absence of civil service coverage. [20]

Although ten states provided dismissal statistics broken down for probationary versus nonprobationary employees, the data was reported in a way that required that various assumptions be made to use them. When this was done, it was clear that probationary employees were more likely to be fired. [21] Under the assumption that 10 percent of a state's total employment consisted of probationary staff, in 1993 the dismissal rate for probationary employees in Arizona was 12.3 percent, whereas the rate for nonprobationary employees was 0.5 percent. In Illinois the probationary rate was 5.7 percent, whereas the nonprobationary rate was a meager 0.1 percent. Still, dismissal rates were not always much higher for the two groups. In 1993 the rates for the two types of employees varied by just 0.3 percent in New Hampshire and by just 0.5 percent in Ohio.

Simplification of the Disciplinary Process and Dismissal Rates

Discerning the impact of civil service arrangements on dismissal may require a more finely grained measure that focuses specifically on differences in dismissal processes. Sally Selden and her associates developed such a measure as part of the Syracuse University/*Governing* magazine Government Performance Project. [22, 23] They analyzed termination procedures in state governments and concluded that many states had streamlined their discipline processes, in some cases by cutting the number of procedural steps from 15 or 20 to as few as four or five. A number of states had sought to better integrate the disciplinary process with the performance appraisal process. Termination procedures were scored on a 0 to 20 scale, with a higher score indicating a simpler, more flexible process.

Do differences in termination processes matter insofar as employee dismissal are concerned? The procedural scores for 19 of the 20 states in the state turnover study (data for California was unavailable) exhibited considerable variability. [24] But such variation was not related to variation in dismissal rates. The zero-order correlation between a state's average dismissal rate across the three years of the study period and its procedural flexibility was not statistically significant (Pearson's $r = -.15$, $p = .28$). [25]

Collective Bargaining and Dismissal

A major objective of unions is to provide their members with job security. Recall that the dismissal rate for unionized private sector employees reported by Steiber was just less than 1 percent, a figure that is close to the average annual dismissal rate found as part of the 20-state turnover study. [26] Barrett and Greene contend that "[i]n Alaska and other states with extremely powerful unions, it's not the civil service laws that stand in the way of dismissals. Rather, it's labor leaders who will fight tooth and nail to defend every single employee." [27] The fact that the proportion of employees who collectively bargain is roughly three times greater in the public than the private sector may account for some of the difference in dismissal rates in the two sectors. Because public sector unionization also varies greatly, interstate or interunit variation in dismissal practice may reflect this fact. [28] This is not, however, the case. In the 20 states in the turnover study, although the relationship between unionization and dismissal rates had the expected negative sign, the Pearson's r of –. 276 was not statistically significant (p = –.12, one-tailed test).

The relationship between a manager rating discipline/dismissal as a "serious" or "very serious" impediment to effective management and the proportion of the employees of his or her unit who collectively bargained was also examined using data from the 2000 Comparative State Management Study. In contrast to the 20-state turnover study, however, in the 2000 Comparative State Management Study the extent of collective bargaining was measured at the organizational unit level in each state. The effect is to dramatically increase the number of cases in the analysis. Nonetheless, the correlation between a manager perceiving employee discipline/dismissal to be a more serious problem and the extent of his or her unit's workforce that was unionized—although positive and statistically significant—was weak (Pearson's r = .10, p = .01, one-tailed test). Within individual states, a significant (.05 level or better, one-tailed test) positive correlation emerged only in California. [29]

The fact that collective bargaining was not clearly or consistently related to lower dismissal rates, or to more complaints about dismissal processes, may surprise some. This pattern may exist, however, because unionization has consequences that reduce the number of employees who need to be dismissed. The next few paragraphs develop this argument.

To begin, it is important to note that the 2000 Comparative State Management Study found the most serious impediment to effective management to be "salaries that are too low to attract good employees"—with 58 percent of managers considering this to be a "serious" or "very serious" problem. [30] Moreover, in both the 1982 and 2000 Comparative State Management studies, more than half of the managers cited "adequately rewarding outstanding employees" as a serious impediment to management, and a third or more complained about difficulty in filling vacancies or retaining staff. Their unit's ability to attract and retain employees is as important for them as is being able to fire low-performing employees.

Here the links between collective bargaining, employee pay, employee turnover, and other personnel-related problems loom large. In the 2000 Comparative State Management Study, collective bargaining was negatively associated with concerns about uncompetitive pay (Pearson's $r = -.22$; significant at .05 level, two-tailed test). And this negative correlation is twice as large as the positive correlation between extent of collective bargaining and the severity of discipline/dismissal as a management impediment.

Various studies find unionization to be positively associated with pay and other compensation for public employees. [31–34] Attracting and retaining employees may be less of a problem in the more heavily unionized states in the 2000 Comparative State Management study, given that the correlation between the overall percentage of employees collectively bargaining and mean employee pay in these ten states [35] was a whopping .81.

Pay is also clearly related to levels of employee turnover—and to voluntary resignations or "quits" in particular. Elling found that the level of voluntary resignations ("quits") by government employees was strongly and negatively related to salaries. [36] Indeed, differences in average monthly earnings by noneducation state employees in 1992 could account for 60 percent of the variation in "quits." In a recent 44-state study, Selden and Moynihan found that both extent of collective bargaining and average pay were negatively associated with levels of voluntary turnover among state government employees. [37] In the case of the 20 states in the 1990s turnover study, the percentage of a state's workforce that collectively bargains is strongly correlated with average monthly earnings ($r = +.638$). States that pay better also have lower rates of dismissal, with the correlation between average pay and the three-year average state dismissal rate being −.418.

This latter relationship might be interpreted as meaning that better paying states fire fewer people because they are more highly unionized or because their termination procedures are more protective of employees. But higher paying states may also find it easier to retain good employees and may attract a higher quality pool of applicants from which to hire. If better paying states have better employees, then fewer of them may need to be fired. In short, unionization may sometimes be associated with lower dismissal rates because unions protect the less competent from being terminated. But lower rates may also occur because the presence of unions makes a jurisdiction more competitive in the labor market. As might be expected, collective bargaining was significantly and negatively correlated with the flexibility of a state's termination processes (Pearson's $r = -.47$, $p = .04$). So, although greater unionization did not depress dismissal rates, it was associated with a state having more complex processes of employee discipline and dismissal.

The analysis in this section of the chapter suggests that the "usual suspects" cited by critics as depressing dismissal rates—civil service provisions and union contracts—do not consistently have such effects, at least in those states for which data exists. Nor does it appear that efforts to streamline state dismissal processes have led to increases in dismissals. In the case of extent of collective bargaining, lower dismissal rates may reflect the fact that unionized states pay better and, hence, may be able to attract a higher caliber of employee.

IMPLICATIONS FOR DISMISSAL PRACTICES AND CIVIL SERVICE REFORMS

Although some interstate variation exists, formal dismissal rates seem quite low in the American states, averaging about one employee in 100 annually for a three-year period. Moreover, a third or so of the state managers surveyed in two other studies felt existing discipline and dismissal processes seriously impeded their units' performance. At the same time, neither variation in civil service coverage nor extent of collective bargaining could account for the interstate variation that existed.

Some might take the findings presented above as proof that state governments fire too few low performers. Other equally valid conclusions are possible, however. One complication is that no one has demonstrated what a "normal" or a "desirable" dismissal rate is. Specifying such a rate would, among other things, require knowledge on the proportion of a jurisdiction's workforce that is ill prepared, lazy, dishonest, or otherwise deficient. Second, the number of formal dismissals understates the frequency with which problem employees are replaced. Informal forms may occur through "coerced resignations," or the transferring of low performers to other units. Although perhaps distasteful to some, such practices do circumvent cumbersome formal processes.

Third, one must factor in the substantial levels of employee turnover—and the rather considerable "quit" rates in particular—that exist. In the 20-state turnover study, the average annual turnover rate from all sources for the 1993–1995 period was 9.5 percent. [38] But turnover varied from 5 percent or less in California, Michigan, and Wisconsin, to nearly 15 percent in Florida and almost 17 percent in Missouri. The "quit rate" (voluntary resignations) also varied greatly, from 3 percent or less in California, Iowa, Michigan, Pennsylvania, and Wisconsin, to more than 10 percent in Florida, Missouri, and Texas. Moreover, quitting is especially likely during the first three years of employment and for younger workers. [39, 40] Hence, those who find themselves unsuited for, or unhappy in, certain jobs—workers who might later become problem employees—may leave of their own volition.

The foregoing notwithstanding, the findings could be interpreted as demonstrating that "something" must be done to make it easier for managers to dismiss employees. What exactly that might be is not clear, however. States with higher dismissal rates did not necessarily have formal policies and procedures that made it easier to fire employees. Moreover, less extensive civil service coverage was only modestly associated with a decline in the likelihood that an administrative chief complained about discipline and dismissal processes as an obstacle to effective performance. States with less extensive collective bargaining did not necessarily fire more employees. Nor did extent of collective bargaining account for much of the variation in managerial views on discipline/dismissal processes as a management impediment.

These findings suggest that various other factors—including several that operate with equal force in both the private and the public sectors—reduce the likelihood that public managers will fire low-performing subordinates. These include the challenges of performance appraisal, limited training regarding disciplinary policies and procedures, organizational cultures that look askance at formal dismissals, and the human dynamics that make termination stressful and unappealing.

At least when a "just cause" standard is in force, the employer needs to have a well-documented case to sustain a dismissal. This means that valid systems of performance appraisal must exist. In addition, managers must be willing to honestly appraise their subordinates. Often neither the first nor the second condition obtains. [41, 42]

Carolyn Ban argues that formal discipline and dismissal policies are underutilized in part because governments fail to provide managers with sufficient training on those policies and their use. [43] Having "manager-friendly" disciplinary policies and processes may matter little if managers do not know what those policies and processes are or, even worse, think that they do know and believe the policies to be unworkable. Ban's argument is consistent with the findings of a study of disciplinary practices in four Puerto Rican organizations—two public and two private—to the effect that "if there was an organizational emphasis on training, then the supervisor was more likely to understand and use formal disciplinary approaches." [44]

Even when a supervisor has a well-documented case, even if the termination process is "manager friendly," and even if he or she is well acquainted with the process, firing someone remains an unpleasant business. A reluctance to dismiss employees may reflect solicitude for their personal circumstances. In a society in which access to health insurance is largely linked to employment, dismissing someone may mean leaving that individual and his or her dependents without healthcare. Moreover, supervisors who have fired employees have sometimes been physically assaulted, even killed. At the very least, the process is highly stressful for supervisors and employees alike, and may be viewed by managers as diverting attention from more fruitful ways of dealing with performance problems.

Hence, human dynamics may discourage dismissals far more than personnel processes and procedures. Glenn Stahl speaks of the "natural reluctance of executives to take such a drastic action as dismissal." [45] Recall that dismissal rates for unclassified employees in Ohio, although higher than the rates for classified employees, were still only in the 2 to 3 percent range. If increasing the number of public employees who are dismissed is deemed to be desirable, then the "natural reluctance" of which Stahl speaks must somehow be overcome. Nor is reluctance to fire low performers unique to government. Imundo argues that private sector managers are also hesitant to take disciplinary action. [46]

At some level, distaste for firing someone may be universal. But Ban's study of seven federal administrative units found that reluctance to fire was stronger in some units than others. Some units embodied a "clan culture" in which "the organization is seen as a family—a friendly, supportive environment in which to work, where organizational members have a voice in decisions, and where group cohesion, teamwork, and morale are highly valued." [47] Managers in such units were less likely to take formal disciplinary action against employees than were those in units that embodied a "market culture" in which "the organization values hard-driving competitiveness and achievement of measurable goals and targets." [48] Ban quotes a personnel specialist in a regional office of the U.S. Environmental Protection Agency—a unit that exemplified a "clan" organizational culture—to this effect:

> The people who are in charge here care about the people who work here, more than people even know. A question I'm always asked is the effect it would have on their [the problem employees'] personal lives. If I wanted to fire a single parent, it would be hard, because this place has too much of a heart. [49]

Ban concludes that greater aggressiveness in disciplining or dismissing low-performing employees requires changing the culture of many public agencies. But this is not easy. Moreover, is it necessarily wise to abandon a "clan" agency culture and replace it with a "market culture"? Although she cites certain disadvantages of a "clan" culture, Ban also notes the threat to various "contextual goals" in seeking to revise personnel processes so as to better embody the values of a "market culture." In the personnel realm, such goals include "the values of fairness and openness in hiring, fairness and due process in dealing with problem employees, and affirmative action goals, among others." [50] Are taxpayers badly served by an organizational culture that encourages managers to seek other ways to deal with problem employees than to dismiss them? Employers have a considerable investment in their existing workforces. Should they ignore those sunk costs by making it easier to fire those employees who are not presently performing well?

This section of the chapter has examined some of the implications of the findings for employee dismissal practices and the possible reform of those practices. Although formal dismissal rates were often low, the number of low-performing employees exiting state employment is undoubtedly greater when "soft-core" dismissals, and the high rate of "quits" in many states, are taken into account. Increasing dismissal rates will require more effective methods of performance appraisal, better training of managers in the use of existing disciplinary procedures, and, perhaps, fundamental change in organizational cultures. Even then, the fundamental unpleasantness of employee termination will continue to deter many managers from dismissing low-performing employees.

THE DILEMMAS OF AT-WILL EMPLOYMENT

For some, the only sure way to remedy low dismissal rates in public jurisdictions is to adopt an "at-will" standard for such actions. Rather than the employer having to make a case based on systematic evidence of an employee's failure to perform, that individual could be fired for any reason or for no reason at all. The failure of Selden's schema to account for variation in employee dismissal may mean that even the most employer-friendly dismissal policy is still not "friendly enough" if the goal is to increase dismissals dramatically. Evidence that this may be so is provided by the 2000 Comparative State Management Study. Of the ten states in that study, only Texas was reported by Coggburn to have an at-will employment standard in place as of 1999. [51] In Texas the proportion of managers who considered the disciplining/dismissing of low performers to present a serious problem was just 18 percent, although in the other nine states the average was 35 percent.

Instituting an at-will model of public employment may increase dismissals, but adopting such a model also likely has some serious negative consequences. Even if one ignores the potential for political abuse of the firing process inherent in such an approach, those who endorse it must understand that the ability of a jurisdiction to attract employees is a function of a number of factors, including whether applicants believe they have a reasonable chance of remaining with the jurisdiction. The greater job security of public employment has traditionally been seen as compensating for lower pay. There is evidence that better pay is strongly related to lower turnover rates and to less managerial concern about the retention of valuable employees. If an employer no longer offers reasonable security, then it stands to reason that this employer must pay better to attract or retain employees. Florida and Georgia are two states that have moved substantially in the direction of at-will employment in recent years. One has to wonder about the wisdom of their doing so, given that neither has historically paid its employees especially well. [52]

Because a plethora of factors are associated with effective administrative performance, a preoccupation with instituting "at-will" employment arrangements is very likely shortsighted. Employee dismissal cannot be considered in isolation from the other characteristics of a jurisdiction's personnel system that may impact on the quality and performance of those whom it employs. This argument can be buttressed using data for two states—Michigan and Texas—that were included in both the 20-state employee turnover study, and the 1982 and 2000 Comparative State Management studies (see Table 9.3).

Collective bargaining by Michigan employees is common, and virtually all of them have civil service status. Perhaps as a result, Michigan has a lower dismissal rate, and this may be why its managers are more likely than those in Texas to see unmotivated or lazy staff to be a problem, and also to complain that collective bargaining limits managerial authority (although only 5 percent of Michigan managers considered the latter to be a serious problem).

Managers in Texas state government are largely untroubled by unions, and many do not have to manage classified employees. As a consequence perhaps, although the dismissal rate is still quite low, it is three times greater than in Michigan. Moreover, Texas managers were less likely to see processes for dismissing low performers as seriously impeding effective management. This is the good news. The bad news is that Texas' managers were almost five times more likely than their Michigan counterparts to report that salary levels were too low to attract good employees. Furthermore, the proportion of employees quitting every year was four times greater than in Michigan and the proportion of Texas managers who considering retaining staff to be a serious problem was five times greater. In short, Texas state government must spend much more time and money replacing exiting employees and must cope with the loss in experience and competence that accompanies high turnover. A major cause of higher turnover in Texas is that it pays its employees less well than does Michigan.

Table 9.3 A Profile of Two State Personnel Systems: Michigan and Texas

	Michigan	*Texas*
Extent of collective bargaining[a]	62% (53%)	1% (11.5%)
Extent of civil service coverage[b]	98%	53%
Average monthly earnings of full-time employees in 2000[c]	$3,934 (3)	$3,095 (24)
Turnover Statistics[d]	%	%
Average turnover (1993–1995), all causes	5.2	12.8
Quit rate,[e] 1993	2.1	8.7
Quit rate, 1994	2.2	9.2
Quit rate, 1995	2.7	10.0
Quit rate, 1997	2.4	12.7
Dismissal rate, 1993	0.3	1.0
Dismissal rate, 1994	0.2	1.0
Dismissal rate, 1995	0.3	1.1
Severity of Selected Personnel-Related Problems in 2000[f]	%	%
Salaries too low to attract good employees	7	33
Retaining experienced staff	10	54
Adequately rewarding outstanding performance	45	52
Difficulty disciplining or dismissing low-performing employees	32	18
Filling key vacancies	41	46

Lazy or unmotivated employees	11	3
Security-oriented employees	7	2
Limits on managerial authority due to collective bargaining	5	0

a. The first figure in each cell is the average percentage of employees engaging in collective bargaining among the units headed by managers who responded to the 2000 Comparative State Management Survey. The figure in parentheses is the average percent of state employees for the 1994–1996 period with bargaining rights covered by a collective bargaining contract. In jurisdictions—such as Texas—in which employees do not have bargaining rights, the figure includes the percentage of workers represented by a union or employee association. See Kearney, R. C., with Carnevale, D. G., *Labor Relations in the Public Sector,* 3rd ed., Marcel Dekker, New York, 2001.

b. Average percentage of employees covered by civil service among the units headed by the managers who responded to the 2000 Comparative State Management Survey.

c. Average monthly earnings of full-time state employees in 2000. Figure in parentheses is state rank in average earnings. Source: U.S. Bureau of the Census, *State Government Employment and Payroll Data,* U.S. Bureau of the Census, Washington, DC, 2002.

d. Turnover data is from Elling, R. C., Slip slidin' away? Patterns of employee turnover in American state bureaucracies, paper presented at the annual meeting of the American Political Science Association, Washington, DC, August 28–31, 1997; except for the 1997 quit rate, which is from Selden, S., and Moynihan, D., A model of voluntary turnover in state government, *Review of Public Personnel Administration* 20 (3), 63, 2000.

e. This is the proportion of state employees in the indicated year reported to have voluntarily resigned their positions.

f. Cell entry is the percentage of managers in each state reporting a given problem to constitute either a *serious* or a *very serious* impediment to the effective accomplishment of the goals of the administrative unit that they head.

To conclude, the point is that—as in much of life—personnel reform is about trade-offs. Although it might seem that making it easier for managers to "'diss' the deadwood" is an eminently good idea, advocates of such a change also need to more explicitly acknowledge its costs.

ENDNOTES

1. Stahl, O. G., *Public Personnel Administration*, 8th ed., Harper & Row, New York, 1983, 305.
2. U.S. Merit Systems Protection Board, *Annual Report for Fiscal Year 1997*, Government Printing Office, Washington, DC, 1998.
3. Dresang, D., *Public Personnel Management and Public Policy*, 3rd ed., Longman, New York, 1999.
4. Mercier, D. K., Why California fires so few incompetents, in *Managing State and Local Governments*, Lane, F., ed., St. Martins, New York, 1980.
5. Stahl, ibid.
6. Shaw, J., Delery, J., Jenkins, G. D., Jr., and Gupta, N., An organization-level analysis of voluntary and involuntary turnover, *Academy of Management Journal*, 82, 511, 1998.
7. Hays, S., Employee discipline and removal: Coping with job security, in *Public Personnel Administration: Problems and Prospects*, 3rd ed., Hays, S., and Kearney, R. C., eds., Prentice-Hall, Englewood Cliffs, NJ, 1995, 147.
8. Steiber, J., Recent developments in employment at will, *Labor Law Journal*, 36, 557, 1985.
9. Elling, R. C., Slip-slidin' away? Patterns of employee turnover in American state bureaucracies, paper presented at the annual meeting of the American Political Science Association, Washington, DC, August 28–31, 1997 (hereinafter "Elling 1997").
10. Assuring comparability in the status of state employees was a major methodological challenge. Data was sought on turnover for full-time, permanent, classified employees. For most states, this is the data used in the analysis. A few states could not report turnover solely for such employees. In Missouri, Ohio, and Virginia, turnover was reported for classified and unclassified employees combined. Readers interested in more on the study's methods should contact the senior author of this chapter, or see Elling 1997; and Elling, R. C., Dissin' the deadwood? Patterns in the dismissal of civil servants in American state bureaucracies, paper presented at the annual meeting of the Southwestern Political Science Association, San Antonio, TX, April 1–3, 1999 (hereinafter "Elling 1999").
11. Ban, C., *How Do Public Managers Manage? Bureaucratic Constraints, Organizational Culture, and the Potential for Reform*, Jossey-Bass, San Francisco, 1995.
12. Ibid., 171.
13. Elling, R. C., *Public Management in the States*, Praeger, Westport, CT, 1992.
14. Elling, R. C., Thompson, T. L., and Monet, V., The problematic world of state management: The more things change, the more they remain the same? Paper presented at the annual meeting of the Midwest Political Science Association, Chicago, April 3–6, 2003 (hereinafter "Elling et al.").

15. In the case of both surveys, questionnaires were sent to all but the smallest or least significant state administrative agencies. In larger agencies a number of division and bureau chiefs were contacted in addition to the agency head. If an agency had field operations, the heads of some of its field offices were also contacted. A total of 847 managers responded to the 1982 survey, for a response rate of 40 percent. Individual state responses varied from a low of 35 percent for Vermont to a high of 50 percent for Arizona. A total of 683 managers responded to the 2000 Comparative State Management Survey, for a response rate of 37 percent. Individual state response rates varied from a low of 25 percent In New York to a high of 48 percent in Vermont. Studies that depend on the willingness of state managers to complete surveys have experienced declining response rates in recent decades; see Bowling, C., Chung-lae, C., and Wright, D. S., Exploring and explaining the preferences of state agency heads for governmental expansion—A typology of administrator growth postures, 1964–1998: Understanding minimizing as well as maximizing bureaucrats, paper presented at the annual meeting of the Midwest Political Science Association, Chicago, April 27–30, 2000; and Chung-lae, C., and Wright, D. S., The devolution revolution in the 1990s: Changing patterns and perceptions of state administrators, paper presented at the annual meeting of the American Political Science Association, San Francisco: August 29–September 2, 2001). Given this fact, response rates for the 1982 and 2000 Comparative State Management surveys are respectable. For more on the characteristics of the samples in these two studies, see Elling, 1992; and Elling et al.
16. The response options were *not a problem*, a *minor problem*, a *serious problem*, or a *very serious problem*.
17. In both 1982 and 2000, the state means in the severity of employee discipline/dismissal as a problem differed significantly (one-way ANOVA, F-test, significant at .01 level). Yet the absolute differences in the proportion of managers who considered this to be a problem were often quite small. So what is going on here? Significant mean state differences can result if only one or two states have scores that differ dramatically from those of the remaining states. Moreover, the F-statistic does not tell us *where* the differences lie. In each of the surveys, one or two states were often outliers with respect to the severity of the various management problems. This is true with respect to interstate means in the severity of discipline/dismissal. A multiple comparison of means test (Scheffe test) is one way to get at this. In the case of both the 1982 and 2000 data, no significant differences (.05 level) in the mean severity of employee discipline/dismissal existed between any given pair of states.
18. A rule of thumb is that a coefficient of variation (CV) greater than 0.30 indicates considerable variability. In the case of civil service coverage across the responding units, the CV was greater than 0.40 in four states: Arizona, Indiana, South Dakota, and Texas. Note that the average extent of civil service coverage for a particular state used here is for the *sample* of responding units. This proportion may differ from that which exists for all administrative units in a given state. The important point is to see whether—for the units in question in a particular state—variation in extent of civil service coverage matters with respect to dismissals.
19. These states were Arizona, California, Idaho, Illinois, Iowa, New Hampshire, Nevada, Ohio, Oklahoma, and Wisconsin.

20. One reviewer of our manuscript objected to the use of dismissal rates for probationary employees as an indicator of what might happen if the just-cause and due process aspects of traditional civil service dismissal processes were eliminated. This reviewer argued that "probation is part of the selection process and is not a disciplinary action. Passing probation is like passing an examination." This may be so, but the fact remains that—procedurally at least—probationary employees can, like at-will employees, be fired more readily. The reviewer admits this when she or he observes that probationary dismissal "has none of the substance of dismissal once one has 'permanent status' and none of the standards of just cause or due process apply." This is our point exactly. Yet why is a probationary employee dismissed? Is it not because of doubts that the employee will perform at adequate levels if granted permanent status? Hence, although we would grant that a dismissal of a probationary employee is not identical to the dismissal of an employee in the classified service, statistics on dismissal rates for the former do provide insight into the likely consequences of eliminating the just cause standard for dismissal.
21. For a more extended discussion of this data, see Elling 1999. A major shortcoming of the data was that although these ten states reported the number of dismissals of probationary and nonprobationary employees separately, none provided information on the *total number* of employees in each category in a given year. Hence we lack the denominator for the dismissal rate calculation. This is a very important point. Although discussions with state personnel officials suggested that a proportion of 5 to 10 percent of probationary employees was about right, these proportions likely varied from state to state in the same year, or across individual states in different years. For example, a state with high turnover would—assuming it filled those vacancies—have a higher proportion of probationary employees than would one with lower turnover, all other things equal. Hence, these findings should be interpreted with caution.
22. Barrett, K., and Greene, R., Pruning the deadwood, *Governing*, January, 42, 1999.
23. Elling 1999; ibid.
24. Florida, Texas, and Michigan were at the procedurally more rigid end of the scale, with scores of 2, 3 and 4, respectively. North Carolina, Iowa, and Virginia were at the more flexible end of the spectrum, with scores of 15, 16, and 18, respectively.
25. The Pearson's r between procedural flexibility and dismissal rates for individual years is .067 in 1993, .115 in 1994, and –.220 in 1995. Only the last correlation has a probability value that approaches conventional standards of statistical significance (p = .183). But the sign of the relationship is not in the hypothesized direction.
26. Steiber, ibid.
27. Barrett and Greene, ibid.
28. For the 20 states for which dismissal data is available, the average percentage of state employees for the 1994–1996 period that were unionized ranged from 8 percent in Virginia and 12 percent in Texas, to 61 percent in Minnesota and 73 percent in Florida.

29. Collective bargaining was significantly and negatively correlated with the flexibility of a state's termination processes (Pearson's $r = -.47$, $p = .04$). So, although greater unionization did not reduce dismissal rates, it was associated with a state having more complex processes for dismissal.
30. Managers were not asked about this potential problem in the 1982 version of the survey.

31. Belman, D., Heywood, J., and Lund, J., Public sector earnings and the extent of unionization, *Industrial and Labor Relations Review*, 50(4), 610, 1997.
32. Kearney, R. C., with Carnevale, D. G., *Labor Relations in the Public Sector*, 3rd ed., Marcel Dekker, New York, 2001.
33. Kearney, R. C., The determinants of state employee compensation, *Review of Public Personnel Administration*, 23(4), 305, 2003.
34. Kearney, R. C., and Morgan, D., Unions and state employee compensation, *State and Local Government Review*, 12(3), 115, 1980.
35. U.S. Bureau of the Census, *State Government Employment and Payroll Data*, 2002, http://www.census.gov/govs/www/apesst.html.
36. Elling 1997.
37. Selden, S. C., and Moynihan, D. P., A model of voluntary turnover in state government, *Review of Public Personnel Administration*, 20(3), 63, 2000.
38. Elling 1997.
39. Kellough, J. E., and Osuna, W., Cross-agency comparisons of quit rates in the federal service, *Review of Public Personnel Administration*, 15, 58, 1995.
40. Lewis, G., Turnover and the quiet crisis in the federal civil service, *Public Administration Review*, 51, 145, 1991.
41. Fox, C., and Shirkey, K., Employee performance appraisal: The keystone made of clay, in *Public Personnel Management: Current Concerns, Future Challenges*, 2nd. ed., Ban, C., and Riccucci, N., eds., Longman, New York, 1997.
42. Riley, D. D., *Public Personnel Administration*, HarperCollins, New York, 1993.
43. Ban.
44. Pagan, J., and Franklin, A., Understanding variation in the practice of employee discipline: The perspective of the first-line supervisor, *Review of Public Personnel Administration*, 23(1), 61, 2003.
45. Stahl.
46. Imundo. L. V., *Employee Discipline*, Wadsworth, Belmont, CA, 1985.
47. Ban, 24.
48. Ibid.
49. Ibid., 13.
50. Ibid., 271.
51. Coggburn, J., Personnel deregulation: Exploring differences in the American states, *Journal of Public Administration Research and Theory*, 11, 223, 2001.

52. In 2000 Florida ranked 23rd in average monthly earnings of full-time employees, and Georgia ranked 36th; U.S. Bureau of the Census, *State Government and Employment Payroll Data*, 2002, http://www.census.gov/govs/www/apesst.html. It is worth noting that, in the 20-state turnover study, Florida had the highest turnover rate—averaging almost 15 percent across the 1993–1995 period. Its "quit rate" was in the 11 to 13 percent range for these three years. Only Missouri had a higher quit rate.

10

AT-WILL EMPLOYMENT AND RACIAL EQUALITY IN THE PUBLIC SECTOR: THE DEMISE OF A NICHE?

George Wilson
University of Miami

INTRODUCTION

In the last several decades, social scientists have documented that the socioeconomic attainments of racial and ethnic minority groups vary across locations in the American labor market. [1–3] In this vein, "niches" designate relatively favorable locations where the socioeconomic attainments of racial/ethnic group members are favorable compared to other locations in the market. [1–2, 4–6] As such, a niche is not necessarily where a numerical majority of racial/ethnic group members work. Rather, a niche is a "segment of the labor market in which a disproportionate number of racial/ethnic group members in that segment achieve socioeconomic success" [1: 114] and where "minority group incumbents, particularly in favorable occupational slots, achieve relative parity in economic outcomes with members from other ethnic groups." [1: 117]

Scholars who have conducted empirical analyses of racial/ethnic labor market niches document that they may be produced by any combination of causal factors: (1) happenstance regarding the portions of the labor market that have available slots to be filled when minority groups first attempt to achieve social mobility, [1] (2) the kind of skills/talents minority group members have to sell, [2] and (3) the degree of discrimination/prejudice experienced, as well as levels and forms of state-sponsored assistance to redress these inequities. [2, 6] Further, the boundaries of niches may vary. For example, a niche may encompass particular occupations (e.g., Irish American representation in the police force in industrial cities in the Northeast and Midwest; [7] jobs (e.g., Jamaican and Trinidadian females as nurses in U.S. metropolitan areas; [8, 9] or, more broadly, sectors of the labor market (e.g., Latinos in small-scale entrepreneurship in metropolitan areas). [2]

This essay addresses evolving patterns of racial inequality of African Americans in the public sector, their labor market niche. In particular, it discusses several likely race-based consequences ensuing as the rules governing employment change in the public sector from the long-standing system based on tenure to one predicated on principles of at-will employment. [2, 10–11] On the basis of these consequences, the rise of at-will employment may negate the status of the public sector as the labor market niche for African Americans. Most importantly, the discretion of employers may increase susceptibility to discriminatory-induced job dismissals. In addition, the implementation of an at-will system may disproportionately reduce the social psychological benefits—job satisfaction and organizational commitment/loyalty—traditionally associated with employment in the public sector. These concerns are examined after documenting that the public arena is a niche for African Americans, outlining the traditional nature of work and benefits that accrue from working in the public service, and discussing the transformation from a tenure to an at-will system of employment in government.

THE PUBLIC SECTOR AS A NICHE FOR AFRICAN AMERICANS

The public sector has constituted the niche in the labor market for African Americans throughout the post-1965 civil rights era. [3, 12–13] In particular, the government—at both the federal and state levels—has made a concerted effort to overcome negative economic consequences associated with discrimination in the private sector by creating opportunities for African Americans to "find a haven in which to achieve a significant level of success." [6] Signs of the emerging niche can be seen as early as the end of World War II, when the federal government began to offer African Americans jobs in a range of midlevel positions upon completion of state-subsidized training programs. [13] However, it was not until the 1960s, when the welfare state expanded and issues of equality became a priority, that government assumed an activist posture in providing meaningful employment for African Americans. Since then, African Americans have been recruited into, and attained a degree of sustained economic success across, a range of occupations spanning the professions as well as upper- and midlevel managerial and administrative positions. [12, 13]

The record regarding the socioeconomic attainments of African Americans in the public sector is mixed. First, in an absolute sense, inequality exists in the representation of African Americans across different levels of the public sector. Analyses of state- and federal-level data indicate that African Americans continue to be underrepresented in middle- and upper-middle-class positions that include managers, executives, and professionals. [14–17] Second, in privileged positions across levels of the public sector African Americans tend to be disproportionately allocated into jobs that offer lesser rewards than those typically filled by Whites. Specifically, at both state and federal levels, African Americans are channeled into jobs that entail performing inferior-rewarded functions devoted to redistributing socioeconomic resources and serving as liaisons to community groups rather than more generously rewarded functions concerning regulating the scope and functions of government. [3, 18]

Nevertheless, despite these indicators of racial inequality, the criteria used to designate a particular segment of the labor market as a niche are satisfied in the case of African Americans in the public sector: first, a prominent source, the presidentially appointed Glass Ceiling Commission (1995), has found that African Americans achieve greater levels of representation in privileged positions at both state and federal levels of the public sector than in the private sector. Second, recent research demonstrates that for a variety of socioeconomic outcomes including income [19] and rates of promotion, [20] African Americans in privileged positions achieve greater levels of relative parity with similarly situated Whites in both the state and federal levels of the public sector than in the private sector.

Evidence that the public sector constitutes a niche for African Americans derives from the 2004 wave of the Panel Study of Income Dynamics (PSID). The PSID is a nationally representative data set that has tracked the labor market patterns of African Americans and Whites since 1968. [21] Table 10.1 presents descriptive analyses that identify the representation of African Americans and Whites in positions that offer reward-relevant decision-making responsibility in the public and private sectors. Three hierarchical levels of job authority are derived from the PSID: "none" if respondent did not supervise any workers on the job, "low" if respondent had supervisory authority but had no "say over the pay or promotion of others," and "high" if respondent had both supervisory authority and say over others' pay or promotion.

Table 10.1 illustrates that African Americans are more advantaged in terms of their distribution across the authority hierarchy in the public than the private sphere. Several findings stand out. First, the racial gap

Table 10.1 Levels of Supervisory Authority among African Americans and Whites

Authority Level	*Public*			*Private*		
	African Americans	**Whites**	**Difference**	**African Americans**	**Whites**	**Difference**
High	11.6	19.5	7.9	5.2	25.0	20.3
Low	21.4	24.5	3.1	14.5	22.5	8.0
None	67.0	56.0	80.3	52.5		
Total	100.0	100.0	= 11.0	100.0	100.0	= 27.8

Source: *Panel Study of Income Dynamics (PSID)*, Institute for Social Research, University of Michigan, 2004.

favoring Whites over African Americans in representation at the high level in the public sector (7.9 percent) is less than one-half the gap in the private sector (20.3 percent). The second derives from the index of dissimilarity (), which measures the proportion of people who would have to move to other levels in the table to achieve equality in the distribution of job authority. The dissimilarity index across sectors indicates that about two-and-a-half times the amount of people would have to change authority levels in the private sector (27.8) as the public sector (11.0) to achieve parity.

Table 10.2 presents income ratios for African Americans and Whites relative to Whites across selected levels of work experience in one working-class (*clerical/operatives*) and one middle-class (*managers/administrators*) 2000 U.S. Census–based occupational category in the public and private sectors.

Inequities favoring Whites are smaller across both categories in the public than the private sector. In particular, in both class categories in the public arena, African Americans earn between 80 and 95 cents for every dollar earned by Whites; in the private sector, the proportion earned by African Americans ranges between 68 and 75 percent of the amount earned by Whites.

In sum, the public sector emerges as the niche for African Americans. We now turn to an examination of the conditions of work that characterize the public sector and the benefits associated with working in the pubic sector.

Table 10.2 Annual Income Ratios for African Americans Relative to Whites at Selected Levels of Workforce Experience in Middle-Class and Working-Class Occupations

	Private Sector				
	Workforce Experience (Years)				
	(1)	*(3)*	*(5)*	*(7)*	*(9)*
Managers/administrators (middle class)	.72	.74	.77	.75	.70
Clerical/operatives (working class)	.68	.71	.73	.70	.69
	Public Sector				
	Workforce Experience (Years)				
	(1)	*(3)*	*(5)*	*(7)*	*(9)*
Managers/administrators (middle class)	.84	.86	.85	.83	.87
Clerical/operatives (working class)	.82	.80	.84	.85	.82

Source: *Panel Study of Income Dynamics (PSID)* Institute for Social Research, University of Michigan, 2004.

THE NATURE AND BENEFITS OF WORK IN THE PUBLIC SECTOR

Working in the Public Sector

Historically, the public sector niche for African Americans has been characterized by a unique set of working conditions. Perhaps most important is the extent to which tenure has governed the terms of employment. For example, in 1990 over 75 percent of full-time employees at both the state and federal levels worked in positions governed by tenure; [22] in the private sector, virtually no employees worked in positions governed by the same rules. [22]

In a tenure system, workers generally receive contracts to work for the duration of a probationary period until a decision is rendered regarding tenure. [14] If tenure is obtained, continuous employment is granted absent extraordinary circumstances such as institutional insolvency, financial exigency, or gross misconduct. [11] Further, tenure is associated with a range of detailed and formalized regulations designed to provide employees with protections and rights in the workplace. [11] For example, the structure of performance evaluations and the criteria used in evaluations are explicitly set forth. [11] Further, in a tenure system there are strict guidelines regarding the nature and timing of notice of inadequate job performance before a termination proceeding can take place. [11] Finally, workers have due process rights to contest issues related to their socioeconomic attainments and changes in work status. [23] In particular, at least two internal hearings to ensure adequate safeguards of the rights of workers are available in the majority of states and the federal government. [23]

Benefits of Working in the Public Sector

Social scientists concur that the most important benefit of working in the public sector derives from tenure—job security. [11, 23] It serves dual purposes. At the organizational level, security facilitates state responsiveness: it helps to ensure the efficient and uninterrupted delivery of services. [24] For workers, security facilitates uninterrupted material benefits and career status through protection from arbitrary job dismissals, namely, layoffs and firing without "just cause." [24]

A second benefit is social psychological in nature, namely, enjoying relatively high levels of job satisfaction and organizational commitment/loyalty. *Satisfaction* is defined as "a cluster of evaluative feelings related to the sense of gratification and enjoyment derived from the work one performs"; [25: 107] *organizational commitment* has been defined as "an attitude related to identifying with an organization's goals and purposes." [26]

A distillation of several studies addressing the distribution of satisfaction and organizational commitment across sectors documents that in the early 1990s, incumbents in both middle- and working-class positions in the federal government have higher mean rates along both experiential domains than workers in similar positions in the private sector. [25, 27–29] These sectoral differences have important repercussions. Levels of both job satisfaction and loyalty/commitment are related to workplace-based performance measures such as employee absenteeism and turnover, [30] worker productivity, [31] and workplace injuries and accidents; [31] they also impact on several socioemotional states that are experienced outside of the workplace such as stress [31] and depression. [32]

Literature in the social sciences has analyzed the dynamics of job satisfaction and organizational commitment. [25] This research indicates there is considerable overlap in the underlying determinants of both multidimensional constructs. In particular, "expectations for job certainty"

[25] and "intrinsic nature of work" [30] undergird satisfaction and commitment. The certainty dimension refers to "expectations for continued employment," [30] and the intrinsic work dimension refers to degree of routinization of job tasks [25] and—especially important for this analysis—engaging in work functions that serve the "broader public good." [32]

In sum, the traditional conditions of work in the public sector and the benefits—both socioeconomic and psychological—have been identified. Now, we discuss changes in the conditions of work in the public sector pursuant to the rise of at-will employment.

THE RISE OF AT-WILL EMPLOYMENT IN THE PUBLIC SECTOR

In the last decade, there have been increasing calls to reform the public sector workplace. One area of reform received favorably in political and policy-making circles involves altering public sector work to make it closer to the incentive-laden rationale governing employment in the private sector. [33] In particular, the "privatization" of work in the public sector is thought to enhance individual- and department-level productivity as well as increase the flexibility of employers to make efficiency-mandated personnel adjustments at a time when a more fluid public sector is perceived as a response to the rapid pace of social change. [33–34]

Perhaps, foremost in this agenda for increasing privatization is the move from a traditional tenure to an exempt or at-will system of employment. In an at-will system, employers have relatively wide latitude in determining the employment status of workers, as exemplified by the statement "Workers can be dismissed for any or no reason at all." Accordingly, absent a series of narrowly carved-out judicial exceptions (e.g., employee dismissed for refusing to do something that violates public policy) and legislative exceptions (e.g., protection from Title VII for illegal dismissal on grounds of race, gender, or age) to the at-will doctrine, [33] employers can alter the status of employees, including, for example, terminating or targeting them for layoff with no prior notice or justification including an assertion of substandard performance. [33] In addition, due process rights to contest policy and decisions by employers do not exist. [23]

The movement toward an at-will system has proceeded further at the state than the federal level. At the state level, workers in selected government agencies or in designated job titles in 27 states have been declassified as non–civil service workers, thus implementing an at-will system. [11] Of these states, Texas and Georgia appear to have moved the furthest in the direction of instituting at-will employment. In Texas, all workers have been declassified and work at-will; in Georgia, all new hires after 1996 have been declassified. [11] In addition, at least 15 other states have items forthcoming on legislative agendas to consider an at-will system. [11, 34] At the federal level, the newly created Department of Homeland Security and the more established Department of Defense have enacted reforms that move decisively in the direction of at-will employment, and the remainder of government agencies will formally consider declassifying their workers over the next several years. [35–36]

In sum, we have discussed the likely changing conditions of work in the public sector pursuant to the rise of at-will employment. We now discuss how these changing conditions impact on opportunities for African Americans to derive the traditional socioeconomic and psychological benefits associated with working in the public sector.

DISPROPORTIONATE IMPACT OF AT-WILL EMPLOYMENT POLICY BY RACE

At-Will Employment and Job Dismissals

There is a solid basis for arguing that the implementation of at-will employment in the public sector will have disproportionately negative consequences for African Americans. [11–12, 33–34] Most critically, the loss of job security will render African Americans disproportionately vulnerable to "the most glaring negative stratification-event in the workplace": [12: 55] job dismissal, which includes both layoffs and firings.

The possibility that African Americans are disproportionately susceptible to dismissals pursuant to the advent of at-will derives from research on its discriminatory underpinnings in the private sector, where at-will employment predominates. [37–38, 6] Accordingly, dynamics regarding at-will employment in business are a likely indication of their effect on the public sector. In fact, research in private sector firms has identified that subtle, institutional dynamics associated with "modern racial prejudice" [39] constitute the underpinnings of race-specific rates of job dismissal. Specifically, discrimination is manifested in its disproportionate impact on African Americans, rather than by individual ill will or malice, and tends to fall outside of the scope of legally enforceable guidelines instituted by the federal and state governments. [6, 12]

Specifically, research on dynamics in the private sector locates the source of racial inequality in dismissals in the discretion that employers exercise in formally evaluating employees. Discretion constitutes the primary basis of assessments, which, in turn, are the typical cause of firings, [40] and employers use them in determining who will be subject to layoffs. [41] Studies document that discretion takes the form of "particularism," [12, 42] that is, evaluations are based on a range of personal characteristics that are vaguely defined and difficult to measure directly—such as perceived loyalty, good character, sound judgment, and leadership potential. [12, 42]

Significantly, African Americans suffer from a relative lack of opportunity to demonstrate the requisite personal characteristics, which trigger discriminatory dynamics: for example, reduced access to crucial informal social networks exacerbates cognitive biases such as "statistical discrimination" [12, 39] and "attribution bias." [39] Consequently, African Americans tend to be assessed on selective bases that reaffirm negative stereotypes about capacity for, and levels of, productivity at work. Conversely, Whites have the opportunity to demonstrate the requisite personal characteristics on a relatively "meritocratic and individualistic basis." [12: 53] As such, they are more likely to be assessed on the basis of the "natural occurring distribution of relevant personal characteristics." [43: 1184]

Overall, the adoption of an at-will system in the public sector will likely produce a level of discrimination in job dismissals that approximates that in the private sector. Further, the adoption of at-will likely limits the ability to overcome this discriminatory practice. First, in an at-will system, there is no guaranteed probationary period, thereby limiting opportunities to demonstrate the "right stuff" to employers. In a tenured system, the probationary period provides opportunities to demonstrate relevant personal characteristics. Second, in an at-will system, the evaluation process tends to be diffuse and conclusions are often unwritten, [28] offering little basis for contesting its conclusions, even if a forum for challenging them existed. Third, in an at-will system, opportunities for appellate review are nonexistent; in a tenured system, opportunities to challenge the contents of employment evaluations for racial/ethnic minorities are formalized and relatively abundant, and job dismissals are legally required to be rationally related to job performance or the employer risks an employment discrimination lawsuit instituted by the government (Equal Employment Opportunity Commission or the Justice Department) or a private attorney.

Finally, an additional point bears mentioning: there is social science evidence suggesting that discrimination based on subtle dynamics associated with formal performance evaluations tends to fall outside of the purview of antidiscrimination law. In particular, discrimination deriving from performance evaluations constitutes an "affirmative defense" and is determinative as evidence in discrimination claims. [44–45] This is especially prevalent in individual charge/disparate treatment cases, which in recent decades have progressively become a growing proportion of EEO complaints at the state and federal levels that proceed beyond the investigative stage. [6, 46] Further, in similar types of EEO complaints, subtle discrimination based on seemingly objective performance evaluations does not often raise any "public policy exception" that may invalidate employment decisions predicated on principles of at-will. [47]

At-Will Employment and Social Psychological Benefits

There is also a foundation for believing the rise of at-will employment may handicap African Americans more than Whites in terms of the social psychological benefits, job satisfaction and organizational loyalty/commitment, traditionally associated with working in the public sector. First, African Americans are more burdened than Whites if the two groups experience similar levels of reduction in job satisfaction and organizational commitment pursuant to the rise of at-will. African Americans suffer a loss where they perform best in the labor market. As such, the negative impact on the most substantial concentration of the privileged among the African American population signals a significant loss for the group as a whole. Conversely, reduction in levels of job satisfaction and organizational commitment pursuant to the advent of at-will is, arguably, not as major a setback for Whites; they continue to disproportionately enjoy the benefits of incumbency in privileged positions in segments of the private sector, their labor market niche. [2]

Second, there is reason to suspect that African Americans will experience greater reductions in job satisfaction and organizational commitment than Whites if an at-will system is implemented. In particular, with the advent of at-will the sentiments of African Americans along crucial underlying determinants of both satisfaction and organizational commitment would be more adversely affected than Whites. For example, levels of perceived "job certainty," an underpinning of both experiential domains, would, presumably, decrease more for African Americans than Whites if they became more susceptible to discriminatorily induced job dismissals. Similarly, discrimination-induced dismissals disproportionately reduce beliefs among African Americans that working in the public sector is associated with an additional underpinning of job satisfaction and organizational commitment—"laboring for the public good." To the extent that the "public good" is social and racial justice, positive levels of satisfaction and organizational commitment, which are predicated on justice in the workplace, are undermined by discriminatory practices.

CONCLUSION

The merits of moving from a tenure to an at-will system of employment continue to be debated by scholars and policy makers. The scope of these debates, however, has not extended to considering the implications of this transition to at-will for racial inequality. Using the private sector, where at-will is prevalent, as a guide, it is argued that moving to an at-will system will likely increase levels of racial inequality in the public sector. In this vein, the increased discretion of employers will likely increase susceptibility of African Americans to discrimination-induced job dismissals.

Further, adopting an at-will system may disproportionately reduce the social psychological benefits traditionally associated with employment in the public sector.

Overall, it is maintained that these consequences may negate the long-standing status of the public sector as the labor market niche for African Americans. Accordingly, the decades-long commitment to equal economic opportunity will suffer a setback if at-will is implemented. It is in the segment of the labor market that has for generations served as a source of relatively stable and remunerative employment for African Americans that levels of inequality will come to increasingly resemble those in the private sector. Without the public sector serving as a "socioeconomic safety-net" [48: 78] for African Americans, the growing class differentiation that has been a hallmark of the African American population in the civil rights era will be reversed, making race a more fundamental cleavage that determines life-chance opportunities.

In sum, implementing an at-will system may well erode decades of socioeconomic gains made by African Americans. This possibility should merit the attention of policy makers when weighing the positive and negative consequences of implementing an at-will system of employment. Few concerns should be considered more fundamental in determining whether at-will in the public sector constitutes appropriate public policy.

ACKNOWLEDGMENTS

The author thanks Owen Dunham and Gleysi West for helpful comments on an earlier draft of this manuscript. Direct all correspondence to George Wilson, Department of Sociology, University of Miami, Merrick Building, Coral Gables, Florida 33124; e-mail: Gwilson1@miami.edu.

REFERENCES

1. Model, S., Economic niches among immigrants, in *The Historical Origins of the American Underclass*, 1st ed., Katz, S., ed., Harvard University Press, Cambridge, MA, 1985, 85.
2. Waldinger, R., *Still the Promised City: African Americans and Immigrants in Post-industrial New York*, Harvard University Press, Cambridge, MA, 1996, 272 pp.
3. Collins, S., *Black Corporate Executives: The Making and Breaking of a Black Middle Class*, Temple University Press, Philadelphia, 1997, 163 pp.
4. Portes, A., and Manning, R., The ethnic enclave: Theory and empirical examples, in *Competitive Ethnicity*, 1st ed., Nagel, J., and Olzak, S., eds., Routledge, New York, 1985, 73.
5. Fernandez, J., *Racism and Sexism in White Corporations*, John Wiley, New York, 1981, 235 pp.

6. Burstein, P., *Discrimination, Jobs, and Politics*, University of Chicago Press, Chicago, 1985, 234 pp.
7. Steinberg, S., *The Ethnic Myth*, Harvard University Press, Cambridge, MA, 1981, 212 pp.
8. Waters, M., *Black Identities*, Harvard University Press, Cambridge, MA, 1999, 270 pp.
9. West, J., Georgia on the mind of radical civil service reformers, *Review of Public Personnel Administration*, 22(2), 79, 2002.
10. Bowman, J., Gertz, S., Williams, R., and Gertz, M., Civil service reform in state government: Employees attitudes 1 year later. *Review of Public Personnel Administration*, 23(4), 286, 2003.
11. Green, R., et al., On the ethics of at-will employment relations in the public sector, *Public Integrity*, 2005, forthcoming.
12. Wilson, G., Pathways to power: Racial differences in the determinants of job authority, *Social Problems*, 44(1), 38, 1997.
13. Brown, M., and Erie, S., Blacks and the legacy of the great society: The economic and political impact of federal social policy, *Public Policy*, 29(5), 299, 1981.
14. Greene, V., Seldon, S., and Brewer, G., Measuring power and presence: Bureaucratic representation in the American states, *Journal of Public Administration and Theory*, 11(3), 379, 2001.
15. Riccucci, N., and Seidel, J., The representativeness of state-level bureaucratic leaders: A missing piece of the representative bureaucratic puzzle, *Public Administration Review*, 57(5), 423, 1997.
16. Sowa, J., and Seldon. S., Administration discretion and active representation: An experiment of the theory of representative bureaucracy, *Public Administration Review*, 63(6), 700, 2003.
17. Colvin, R., and Riccucci, N., Employment nondiscrimination policies: Assessing implementation and measuring effectiveness, *International Journal of Public Administration*, 25(1), 95, 2003.
18. Glass Ceiling Commission, *Good for Business: Making Full Use of the Nation's Human Capital*, Government Printing Office, Washington, DC, 1999, 176 pp.
19. Farley, R., and Allen, W., *The Color Line and the Quality of Life in America*, Russell Sage Foundation, New York, 1987, 345 pp.
20. Smith, R., Race, income, and authority at work: A cross-temporal analysis of black and white men, *Social Problems*, 38(1), 19, 1997.
21. Hill, M., *User's Guide to the Panel Study of Income Dynamics*, Institute for Survey Research, Ann Arbor, MI, 1985, 156 pp.
22. Hays, S., and Kearney, R., *Public Personnel Administration: Problems and Prospects*, Prentice-Hall, Englewood Cliffs, NJ, 1998, 243 pp.
23. Condrey, S., and Maranto, R., *Radical Reform in the Civil Service*, Lexington Books, New York, 2001, 283 pp.
24. Peters, B., *The Future of Governing*, University of Kansas Press, Lawrence, 2001, 285 pp.
25. Tuch, S., and Martin, J., Race in the workplace: Black/white differences in the sources of job satisfaction, *The Sociological Quarterly*, 32(2), 103, 1991.
26. Scholl, R., Differentiating organizational commitment from expectancy as a motivating force, *Academy of Management Review*, 6(3), 584, 1981.

27. Wright, B., and Soonhee, K., Participation's influence on job satisfaction, *Review of Public Personnel Administration*, 24(1), 18, 2004.
28. Pattakos, A., The search for meaning in government service, *Public Administration Review*, 64(1), 106, 2004.
29. Knudsen, H., et al., Downsizing survival: The experience of work and organizational commitment, *Sociological Inquiry*, 73(3), 265, 1994.
30. Hall, R., *Dimensions of Work*, Sage, Beverly Hills, CA, 1986, 188 pp.
31. Hanson, S., Martin, J., and Tuch. S., Economic sector and job satisfaction, *Work and Occupations*, 14(3), 286, 1987.
32. Kalleberg, A., Work values and work rewards: A theory of job satisfaction, *American Sociological Review*, 42(4), 124, 1977.
33. Kuykendall, C., and Facer, R., Public employment in state agencies: The elimination of the merit system, *Review of Public Personnel Administration*, 22(2), 133, 2002.
34. Lawthler, W., Privatizing personnel: Outsourcing public service functions, in *Public Personnel Administration: Problems and Prospect*, 1st ed., Hays, S., and Kearney, R., eds., Prentice-Hall, Upper Saddle River, NJ, 2003, 113–151.
35. Kaufman, T., and Sullivan, E., The future of civil service, *Federal Times*, January 31, 2005, 1, 6–7.
36. Kaufman, T., Overhaul at defense: Sweeping personnel authorities proposed for DOD secretary, *Federal Times*, April 23, 2003, 1, 11.
37. Fernandez, J., *Black Managers in White Corporations*, Lexington Press, Lexington, MA, 1975, 222 pp.
38. Reid, L., Occupational segregation, human capital, and motherhood: Black women's higher exit rates from full-time employment, *Gender and Society*, 16(1), 728, 2002.
39. Pettigrew, T., New black-white patterns: How best to conceptualize them? *Annual Review of Sociology*, 11, 329, 1985.
40. Zwerling, C., and Silver, H., Race and job dismissals in a federal bureaucracy, *American Sociological Review*, 57(4), 651, 1992.
41. Wilson, G., and McBrier, D. B., Race and loss of privilege: African American/white differences in the determinants of job layoffs from upper-tier occupations, *Sociological Forum*, 18(2), 301, 2005.
42. Kluegel, J., The causes and cost of exclusion from job authority, *American Sociological Review*, 43(2), 285, 1978.
43. Wilson, G., Race and job dismissals across the early work-career, *American Behavioral Scientist*, 48(5), 1153, 2005.
44. Burstein, P., and Edwards, M., The impact of employment discrimination litigation on racial disparities in earnings: Evidence and unresolved issues, *Law and Society Review*, 28(3), 79, 1994.
45. Skrentny, J., Pragmatism, institutionalism, and the construction of employment discrimination, *Sociological Forum*, 9(2), 343, 1994.
46. Malamud, D., The last minuet—disparate treatment after hicks, *Michigan Law Review*, 8(1), 2229, 1995.
47. Cunningham, C., Loury, G., and Skrenty, J., Passing strict scrutiny: Using social science to design affirmative action programs, *Georgetown Law Review*, 90(3), 835-882, 2002.
48. Edsall, T., and Edsall, M., *Chain Reaction: The Impact of Race, Rights, and Taxes on American Politics*, Norton, New York, 1991, 230 pp.

11

FEDERAL LABOR-MANAGEMENT RELATIONS UNDER GEORGE W. BUSH: ENLIGHTENED MANAGEMENT OR POLITICAL RETRIBUTION?

James R. Thompson
University of Illinois at Chicago

With approximately 1.9 million employees,[1] the federal government is the largest and most prominent public sector employer in the country. As such, the practices it engages in with regard to its employees achieve substantial visibility and serve to set a tone for labor relations practices in the public and private sectors more broadly. President John F. Kennedy's 1962 executive order authorizing collective bargaining in the federal government set the stage for a decade in which the proportion of public sector workers who became union members increased dramatically. President Ronald Reagan's confrontation with the air traffic controllers' union in 1981 set the tone for a decade during which unions were continually on the defensive.

Recent actions by the Bush administration may portend another era of adversarial labor-management relations. As discussed below, President George W. Bush has taken a series of aggressive, anti-union actions, canceling an executive order issued by his predecessor that directed federal agencies to cooperate with union representatives in addressing common issues, withdrawing collective bargaining rights from multiple groups of federal employees based on national security considerations, and significantly narrowing the scope of issues over which unions in two of the largest federal departments are permitted to bargain. These actions are justified on the basis of the argument that enhanced managerial control of the workplace leads to improved organizational performance. The Bush administration has not yet proposed "employment at-will" for all federal agencies, though that would be consistent with the logic of managerial control.

This chapter chronicles developments in labor relations practices in the federal sector for the period 2001–2005. Of particular interest is the design of the new personnel systems for the Departments of Homeland Security (DHS) and Defense (DoD). Soon to include approximately 850,000 of the government's 1.9 civilian employees, these systems may serve as a template for the Civil Service System of the future.[2] The labor-management relations provisions of the DHS and DoD models represent a significant departure from the status quo. A union lawyer describes the new DHS rules on labor-management relations as "a wholesale assault on the concepts of collective bargaining and grievance/arbitration."[3] This chapter probes the nature of those changes with a particular focus on whether and to what extent they are based on a coherent management strategy or, alternatively, are of a primarily political nature. Attention is also directed to the likely outcomes of the application of these new policies in the federal workplace. A detailed discussion of the Bush reforms is preceded by a brief review of the history of labor-management relations in the federal sector.

HISTORY OF LABOR-MANAGEMENT RELATIONS IN THE FEDERAL GOVERNMENT

Federal employees first gained the right to organize collectively under the Lloyd-LaFollette Act of 1912. They were not allowed to bargain collectively with management, however, until President Kennedy issued Executive Order 10988 in 1962. Even under EO 10988, the scope of issues over which the unions were permitted to bargain was extremely limited. Importantly, issues relating to pay and benefits were excluded from negotiation with pay and benefits determined unilaterally by the president in conjunction with Congress. In 1969, President Richard Nixon issued Executive Order 11491, which replaced EO 10988 and created an administrative structure for the bargaining process.

Not until the Civil Service Reform Act of 1978 was the right of federal employees to bargain collectively actually codified. Title VII of that law, the Federal Service Labor-Management Relations Statute (FSLMRS), incorporated the restrictive provisions of Executive Orders 10988 and 11491 by prohibiting negotiations over pay and benefits and by prohibiting strikes by federal employees. Masters and Albright comment on FSLMRS as follows: "Unions had a very limited scope of bargaining, no right to strike, no right to the arbitration of impasses (without management consent), no union-security protections, and a fearsome management rights clause emblazoned in statute."[4]

The consensus among observers is that the experience under FSLMRS has not been particularly positive; in the absence of authority to bargain over wages and benefits, discussions between unions and management, at least until President Bill Clinton's partnership experiment, tended to focus on peripheral matters. In a 1991 report, the General Accounting Office characterized the labor-management relations experience under FSLMRS as "adversarial and often plagued by litigation over procedural matters and minutiae."[5] Robert Tobias, former president of the National Treasury Employees Union, describes the somewhat dysfunctional relationship that evolved between unions and management under FSLMRS as follows:

> Unions feared that if they accepted a management proposal that constricted the scope of bargaining, it would set a precedent that could be used by managers in a subsequent or parallel negotiation. Conversely, unions aggressively sought to use the negotiation and litigation process to set a precedent that might minimally expand the scope of bargaining, crafting bargaining proposals that may or may not have addressed the real problem in the workplace. . . . Real issues were rarely addressed directly and were never finally resolved.[6]

The accession to the presidency of William Clinton in 1993 brought about a temporary change in the labor-management environment. As an element of his management reform initiative, the National Performance Review, Clinton issued Executive Order 12871, creating a National Partnership Council including both union and management officials "to advise the President on matters involving labor-management relations in the executive branch" (Clinton 1993).[7] The executive order further directed federal agencies to engage in partnerships with their respective unions. The partnership idea derived from the experience of some private sector companies that have engaged their unions at a strategic level, attempting thereby to gain union cooperation in strategy execution. In the executive order, Clinton (1993) states that "only by changing the nature of Federal labor-management relations so that managers, employees, and employees' elected union representatives serve as partners will it be possible to design and implement comprehensive changes necessary to reform government."[8]

The following seven-plus years were characterized by relative harmony in labor-management relations, and management in many agencies consulted with union representatives on issues that were technically outside the scope of bargaining. A 2001 evaluation of the partnership program by the Office of Personnel Management (OPM) listed, as issues that received the attention of partnership councils, quality of work life, human resource policies, customer service, and technology.[9] Although the OPM report concluded that partnerships had little impact on the "bottom-line" in the form of measurable improvements in productivity or service quality, the survey did identify improvements in the labor-management climate more generally as an outcome. Marick Masters of the University of Pittsburgh, author of the report, comments,

> It is precisely through improvements in labor-management communication, the labor relations climate, and opportunity for employee involvement and empowerment that the real tangible, long-term results of partnering in general and labor-management partnership councils in particular were to be realized.[10]

Sixty-three percent of the management and union officials surveyed by Masters agreed that labor-management relationships had improved either "some" or "very much" since the issuance of EO 12871.[11]

The improvement in "atmospherics" did lead to some cost savings by contributing to a reduction in the number of formal challenges to management made by employees or by unions. In a separate analysis, Masters summarizes declines in each of four major dispute indicators during the 1992–2000 period:

- Unfair labor practice charges declined from 8,848 to 5,638.
- Bargaining impasses declined from 253 to 167.
- Appeals to the FLRA declined from 115 to 65.
- Arbitration cases declined from 188 to 140.[12]

Upon taking office in January 2001, President George W. Bush took an aggressively adversarial stance toward the federal employee unions. After less than a month in office, Bush issued Executive Order 13203, formally revoking Clinton's EO 12871, dissolving the National Partnership Council, and rescinding agency directives in support of the order (Bush 2001).[13] In a subsequent memorandum, the head of the Office of Personnel Management elaborated on the executive order by stating that agencies were not prohibited from engaging in partnership with unions.[14]

In January 2002, using the authority granted him pursuant to the FSLMRA, Bush withdrew the collective bargaining rights of 500 employees in the Department of Justice, primarily in the offices of the U.S. Attorneys and in the Criminal Division.[15] In January 2003, the collective bargaining rights of the employees of the National Imagery and Mapping Agency were withdrawn on national security grounds, and the head of the Transportation Security Administration, James Loy, issued an order stating that TSA employees, "in light of their critical national security responsibilities, shall not . . . be entitled to engage in collective bargaining or be represented for the purpose of engaging in such bargaining by any representative or organization," on the grounds that "[m]andatory collective bargaining is not compatible with the flexibility required to wage the war on terrorism."[16]

CREATING A NEW PERSONNEL SYSTEM FOR THE DEPARTMENT OF HOMELAND SECURITY

President Bush's restrictive approach to collective bargaining in the federal government gained additional impetus subsequent to the September 11, 2001, attacks and the surfacing of a proposal to create a Department of Homeland Security (DHS). The new department was to consolidate under unitary control multiple agencies with missions relating to the protection of the American public from foreign threats. The administration's draft of legislation creating a DHS, released in June 2002, included a provision authorizing the new department to create its own personnel system. That provision, eventually codified, required adherence to some provisions of existing Civil Service Law such as those relating to merit principles, prohibited personnel practices, and veterans preference, but allowed DHS management a substantially free hand with regard to matters of compensation, performance management, and labor-management relations.

An attempt by Senate Democrats to include in the authorizing legislation a provision limiting the president's authority to waive collective bargaining rights for DHS employees became the focus of a major battle, ultimately resolved in the president's favor subsequent to the loss of two Democratic Senate seats in the 2002 elections. The final bill allowed the president to determine whether and to what extent collective bargaining provisions of FSLMRS would apply to DHS employees. Specifically, the legislation stated that "relevant labor subsections limiting [the president's] authority to exclude federal agencies, subdivision and units, 'shall not apply in circumstances where the President determines in writing that such application would have a substantial adverse impact on the Department's ability to protect homeland security.'"[17] The legislation did provide that DHS employees and their representatives be consulted in the design of the new personnel system, but the secretary of DHS, in conjunction with the director of the OPM, had the authority to impose a system unilaterally in the case of disagreement.

The draft regulations released in February 2004 elicited vocal opposition from the affected unions. Although some provisions to which the unions objected were modified in the final regulations released in January 2005, most were not. Among the provisions to which the unions have registered the strongest objections are the following:

1. A provision narrowing the scope of issues subject to collective bargaining. As noted above, Section 7106 (a) of Title 5 of the U.S. Code sets forth those issues over which management has exclusive authority. Under the law, although unions may not bargain over the substance of such matters, they can bargain over "implementation and impact." Under the new DHS system, such matters would no longer be subject to implementation and impact bargaining. Further, the new regulations reserve exclusively to management authority over "permissive" subjects of negotiation (see above); in other words, matters that (under FSLMRS) federal agencies *may* bargain over are now reserved exclusively for management at DHS.
2. A provision authorizing the creation of a new, DHS-only labor relations board to resolve collective bargaining disputes. The DHS board would take on many of the responsibilities performed by the Federal Labor Relations Authority and the Federal Services Impasses Panel under FSLMRS. Members of the board would be appointed by the secretary of DHS and would hence fall substantially under management control. The creation of the board was justified on grounds that the new board "would ensure that those who adjudicate the most critical labor disputes in the Department do so quickly and with an understanding and appreciation of the unique challenges that the Department faces in carrying out its mission."[18]
3. A provision limiting the scope of Merit System Protection Board review of adverse actions taken against DHS employees. For example, MSPB may mitigate a penalty "only if the penalty is so disproportionate to the offense as to be wholly without justification."[19] The regulations further streamline the appeals process by, for example, reducing from 30 to 15 days the amount of notice provided employees prior to the effective date of an adverse action, stating that "one of the fundamental objectives of the Homeland Security Act was to streamline the process for taking an adverse action."[20]
4. A provision creating a new pay-banding system to replace the General Schedule pay system. With pay banding, pay is based less

on seniority than on "performance." Pay determination will be a more subjective process than in the past, and hence grievances are likely to escalate. Further, annual pay increases will no longer be de facto automatic, with those employees whose performance rated as unacceptable no longer receiving any increase. The unions preferred to stick with the General Schedule on the ground that the benefits of pay banding and the associated pay-for-performance system are "unproven."

In general, the new personnel system at DHS vests line managers with considerably more authority over matters of pay, hiring, and discipline than is exercised by their counterparts at other agencies. Matters subject to collective bargaining, already severely constrained under FSLMRS, are further narrowed at DHS. Justification provided for the changes has relied largely on a claim that the agency's mission is unique. The final regulations include the following statement: "No Federal agency has ever had a mission that is so broad, complex, dynamic, and vital. That mission demands unprecedented organizational agility to stay ahead of determined, dangerous, and sophisticated adversaries."[21] Similarly, flexibilities incorporated into the personnel system being proposed for the Department of Defense rely heavily for their justification on that department's unique mission.

CREATING A NEW PERSONNEL SYSTEM FOR THE DEPARTMENT OF DEFENSE

Subsequent to the approval by Congress of a new personnel system for the Department of Homeland Security, the Department of Defense (DoD) requested and received the authority to create its own system. The National Defense Authorization Act of 2003 authorized the creation of a new National Security Personnel System (NSPS) for civilian employees in the Department of Defense. As at DHS, DoD was required to consult with employees and with the federal employee unions on the design of the system. Also similar to DHS, the secretary of defense was provided the authority to impose a new system unilaterally in the event that agreement with the unions could not be reached. The personnel system outlined in proposed regulations released on February 10, 2005, was similar to the DHS system and sufficiently adverse to union interests to warrant the immediate filing of a lawsuit by the major DoD unions in an attempt to forestall implementation.[22]

The proposed DoD personnel system is similar to that at DHS in most respects. Specifically, it incorporates the following:

- A reduction in the scope of matters subject to collective bargaining, similar to that at DHS
- A DoD-specific labor relations board
- Expedited processing of adverse actions
- A pay-banding system

DoD did gain flexibility, not provided DHS, in hiring and reduction-in-force (RIF) rules. DoD managers could, therefore, bypass competitive hiring procedures in some instances and make performance a factor in deciding who to let go during a RIF. Another difference is that whereas the DHS rules will apply to approximately 110,000 employees, the DoD rules will apply to approximately 750,000 employees.[23] The final DoD rules will not go into effect until after a comment period and the issuance of final regulations.

UNIONS AND ORGANIZATIONAL PERFORMANCE

The Bush labor-management relations reforms can be interpreted through either a political or a managerial lens. Politically, the federal employee unions have, alongside other major unions, been important supporters of Democratic candidates for president, including Al Gore against George Bush in 2000 and John Kerry against George Bush in 2004. The decision to repeal important collective bargaining rights for large blocks of federal employees may be, in part, political; to the extent that the unions play less of a role in the workplace, they are likely to be weakened and wield less electoral clout.

There is also a managerial agenda behind the dilution of collective bargaining rights for federal employees, a strategy that is encapsulated in the title of the Bush administration's first major piece of management reform legislation, the "Freedom to Manage Act." In support of this legislation, the administration commented,

> Federal managers are greatly limited in how they can use available financial and human resources to manage programs; they talk much of the discretion given to their private sector counterparts to do what it takes to get the job done. Red tape still hinders the efficient operation of government organizations; excessive control and approval mechanisms afflict bureaucratic processes. Micro-management from various sources—Congressional, departmental, and bureau—imposes unnecessary operational rigidity.[24]

In short, the Bush administration is operating on the premise that enhanced managerial control of the workplace is conducive to high performance. It is an idea that gains legitimacy from the New Public Management movement,[25] and taken to its extreme it can be used to justify a system in which employees hold their jobs "at the will" of their employers.

What data is there in support of or in opposition to this thesis? This section includes a review of available data with regard to union participation in the workplace as well as with regard to whether that participation enhances or detracts from organizational performance. Of interest is whether and to what extent the management literature provides support for the Bush management strategy, which includes as a central element the exclusion of unions from consequential decisions in the workplace as a means of enhancing organizational performance.

High-Performance Work Systems and Unions

President Bush's management reform program was presented in 2001 in the form of a report entitled "The President's Management Agenda" (PMA). The PMA included five main elements:

1. Strategic management of human capital
2. Competitive sourcing
3. Improved financial performance
4. Expanded electronic government
5. Budget and performance integration

The section of the report entitled "Strategic Management of Human Capital" makes no mention of the role of federal employee unions in the workplace and says little about employees themselves. The Office of Personnel Management's "Human Capital Assessment and Accountability Framework" does include the following statement: "Cooperation between employees and managers enhances effectiveness and efficiency, cuts down the number of employment-related disputes, and improves working conditions, all of which contribute to improved performance and results" (U.S. Office of Personnel Management n.d.).[26] On balance, however, it is clear that the Bush administration takes a management-dominated perspective on the workplace.

The "managers first" approach to enhancing performance runs counter to a well-established body of thought and practice regarding "high-performance work systems." In tracking the evolution of private sector collective bargaining in the United States, Kochan, Katz, and McKersie identify two distinct epochs.[27] The first epoch, lasting from passage of the

National Labor Relations Act of 1935 through the 1970, featured what Kochan et al. call "the New Deal industrial relations system." The underlying principle of this system, according to Kochan et al., "was the philosophy that management has the right to manage, while workers and their union representatives had the right to negotiate the impacts of those management decisions on employment conditions."[28] The system featured "job control unionism," with, "highly formalized contracts and a quasi-judicial grievance procedure to adjudicate disputes. . . . In this system, workers' rights and obligations are linked to highly articulated and sharply delineated jobs. . . . Strict lines of demarcation separate jobs within the bargaining unit from work performed by supervisors."[29]

For a variety of reasons relating to changing technology, globalization, and managerial ideology, an alternative model of workplace relations became prominent during the 1980s. Kochan et al. describe this as the "nonunion industrial relations system" on the grounds that many of the most prominent firms adopting this system did so as a means of evading union influence.[30] Importantly, however, research has shown that similar systems have been adopted in unionized firms in approximately the same proportion as in nonunionized firms. [31] Following Appelbaum et al., the term *high-performance work system* (HPWS) will be used here in referring to Kochan et al.'s "nonunion industrial relations system."

Kochan et al. identify the key aspects of that system as follows:

> The workplace changes being introduced jointly have two basic objectives: 1) to increase the participation and involvement of individuals and informal work groups so as to overcome adversarial relations and increase employee motivation, commitment, and problem-solving potential; and 2) to alter the organization of work so as to simplify work rules, lower costs, and increase flexibility in the management of human resources.[32]

Appelbaum et al. identify the distinguishing characteristic of HPWSs as being "that work is organized to permit front-line workers to participate in decisions that alter organizational routines."[33] The specific innovations employed as part of HPWSs include quality circles, worker attitude surveys, teams, work restructuring, skill-based pay, gainsharing, broader job definitions, team production, and increased training.[34]

Appelbaum et al. supplement the abundance of anecdotal evidence on the effectiveness of HPWSs in increasing organizational productivity and effectiveness (e.g., Walton 1980; Lawler 1986) with a rigorous study of their application in three separate industries; steel, apparel, and medical equipment, concluding that "in general, organizational changes at the shop-floor level make plants more productive and enable them to produce a greater volume of output or qualitatively superior or more varied output with a given amount of resources."[35]

Kearney and Hays also argue in support of "participative decision making" or what they call "the human resources model of administrative behavior."[36] Akin to the high-performance work system, this model features "training and employee development . . . worker security and long-term employment."[37] Consistent with the findings of the authors cited above, Kearney and Hays posit the importance of labor-management cooperation to the success of this model: "In the absence of unions, a collective employee voice is problematic. Where management itself designs a representational structure for employee participation in decision making, the employee response is likely to be a presumption of management insincerity, manipulation, or corruption."[38] Kearney and Hays further maintain that the FSLMRS, in placing unions at a disadvantage, inhibits cooperation. Under FSLMRS, they state,

> The power imbalance between management and labor often defies meaningful cooperation through participative mechanisms. Valiant efforts to develop collaborative mechanisms are being made, but where they succeed it is in spite of the CSRA [Civil Service Reform Acto of 1978] (Levine 1991). Disequilibrium in bargaining power is conducive to unilateral directives, not PDM [Participative Decision Making].[39]

The power imbalance identified by Kearney and Hays has been exacerbated under Bush, whose labor-management relations policy stands in particularly stark contrast to that of his predecessor.

The Clinton Management Strategy

President Clinton's labor-management relations strategy relied heavily on high-performance work system theory for its theoretical justification and as such stands in stark contrast to the Bush administration's approach. For example, the *Report of the National Performance Review* endorsed worker teams, work redesign, and employee involvement generally as well as both quality management and reengineering techniques specifically. It further posits that the success of these innovations is enhanced where management works in cooperation with unions: "Corporate executives from unionized firms declare this truth from experience: No move to reorganize for quality can succeed without the full and equal participation of workers and their unions."[40]

Some support for Clinton and Gore's position can be found in the industrial relations literature. For example, Eaton and Voos identify the following reasons why labor-management partnerships enhance the prospects of HPWS success.

1. "Unions provide workers with important protections against job loss, either for economic reasons or because of managerial reprisal, and this encourages involvement."
2. "Unions provide a mechanism whereby workers can utilize their 'collective voice' in the design and operation of a program on a long-term basis."
3. "Unions can play an important role in extending participation from the shopfloor to the entire enterprise. With unionism, it is possible for participation to become 'strategic', that is[,] allow workers to influence major corporate decisions like plant investment or technology."[41]

In his review of HPWSs, Levine (1995, 46) observes, "Successful cases of employee involvement often provide representative participation [i.e., through unions] to complement direct participation. Typical institutions include union-management committees, workers' representatives on the board of directors, and works councils." [42] Kochan et al. conclude that changes on the shop floor and in work restructuring will only have long-term, positive impact to the extent that they are linked with more formal involvement of the union at the strategic level.[43]

This view is by no means unanimous. In fact, Nissen (1997, 15) observes that the "majority view" is that "independent worker representation is [not] necessary for new forms of production to be successful."[44] Notwithstanding Nissen's comment, there is some basis in theory for the contention that unions enhance the prospects of HPWS success and some empirical support for that theory.

The Bush Management Strategy

What is the case for President Bush's more unilateral approach to labor-management relations? In contrasting the Bush strategy with that of Clinton, it is important to note that Bush, unlike Clinton, has not endorsed the application of HPWS ideas to the federal workplace. It may be happening on an incidental basis in some agencies, but HPWS ideas show up nowhere in the President's Management Agenda. Rather, the strategy for improving agency performance relies on (1) competitive sourcing, (2) the application of new technologies, and (3) performance incentives to increase the productivity and effectiveness of the federal workforce.

On competitive sourcing, the PMA states, "Recent competitions under OMB Circular A–76 have resulted in savings of more than 20 percent for work that stays in-house and more than 30 percent for work outsourced to the private sector."[45] There is an abundance of literature supporting the contention that contracting out or competitive sourcing can improve efficiency and reduce costs.[46] The contribution of new technologies to improvements in organizational efficiency is not really contested. The PMA (24) states, "A task force of agency personnel in coordination with OMB and the President's Management Council will identify E-government projects that can deliver significant productivity and performance gains across government."[47] Although not fully specified in the PMA, performance incentives are created in the new personnel systems at DHS and DoD through pay banding and the new pay-for-performance systems. The regulations provide for union representation on the "Compensation Committee" charged with designing the specifics of the DHS system, but the unions would fill only four of the 14 seats. Clearly, the Bush administration did not have a conventional partnership arrangement in mind when creating this process.

"TAKING CHARGE OF FEDERAL PERSONNEL"

Although there is ample theoretical support for Bush's management strategy, those theories do not preclude union involvement in its execution. In fact, as noted above, some theorists have argued that unions can play a positive role in the implementation of programs such as competitive sourcing. In Indianapolis, former Mayor Stephen Goldsmith effectively involved municipal unions in his competitive sourcing initiative despite the fact that the net result of the program was a substantial reduction in the number of municipal employees (Goldsmith and Schneider 2003; Osborne and Plastrik 1997).[48]

A case can be made that the Bush administration's exclusion of the federal employee unions from meaningful involvement in the workplace is premised on the adoption of a "political administration model" of management. The theoretical justification for this approach was presented in a Heritage Foundation policy paper entitled "Taking Charge of Federal Personnel" in January 2001. In that paper, George Nesterczuk, former staff director for the House Civil Service Subcommittee, and his coauthors argue that the president

> [m]ust be willing to call public attention to the weaknesses of the current system and to the importance of basing personnel management decisions on performance in carrying out the mission of the President. He must demonstrate a desire to eliminate duplicative programs and functions across the federal

> bureaucracy and to create a smaller, leaner federal workforce to manage the remaining functions. (2)[49]

According to Nesterczuk et al., "the permanent government, a network that includes the career civil service and its allies in Congress, the leaders of federal unions, and the chiefs of managerial and professional associations representing civil servants," stands as the primary obstacle to such a program.[50] To drive implementation of his program and to overcome the resistance of the permanent government, says Nesterczuk, the president needs to rely upon his political appointees. From the positions of leadership held, these appointees can impose the president's control on a reluctant civil service.

Nesterczuk is critical of the federal employee unions in obstructing change. He argues that Clinton's partnership initiative enabled the federal employee unions to "become a counterweight to the political management appointed by the President." Nesterczuk presages Executive Order 13203 in recommending, "The new President will need to revoke President Clinton's executive order [on partnership] and demonstrate from the outset that his approach to reforming the federal bureaucracy will emphasize political responsibility and accountability to the taxpayers."[51]

Nesterczuk endorses a "political administration model" that emphasizes "political responsibility—providing presidential leadership to committed top political officials and then holding them and their subordinates personally accountable for achievement of the President's election-endorsed and value-defined program."[52] This model stands in contrast to the more traditional "public administration model," which features "career public officials . . . who lead the political appointees."[53] Implicit in the political administration model are partisan considerations: members of the "permanent government" identified by Nesterczuk represent predominantly Democratic constituencies. To the extent these constituencies lose authority, Republicans presumably gain.

OUTCOMES OF THE BUSH LABOR RELATIONS STRATEGY

However viable the "political administration model" is as either a political tactic or a theory of governance, it also warrants examination as a managerial strategy. What are the likely workplace outcomes of such a model? Insights can be gained from several sources, including (1) conditions that prevailed in the federal workplace prior to President Kennedy's executive order; (2) testimony of union officials, past and present; and (3) a review of the state labor relations experience. This data points to the following likely outcomes: program implementation will be impeded, the labor-management relations environment will be characterized by extreme hostility between the parties, and, with little union trust in the dispute resolution process created by the Bush administration, litigiousness will increase, with more and more issues referred to the courts for resolution.

Problematic Program Implementation

Robert Tobias, former president of the National Treasury Employees Union, argues that a key flaw in the political administration model is the assumption that the hierarchical model works. Tobias comments, “Political appointees kept the hierarchies for decades, even after flatter organizations began proving more efficient in the private sector, because the appointees falsely believed that they could issue commands and the hierarchy would simply implement them.”[54]

The public administration literature is replete with reasons why orders from above are not blindly obeyed by bureaucratic subordinates. In the somewhat protracted chains of command that characterize most government agencies, there are ample opportunities for miscommunication, obfuscation, delay, resort to rules, and outright disobedience.[55] Tobias attributes the resistance of careerists to well-founded attempts to maintain stability in the workplace: “Political appointees’ attempts to impose changes in agency practices developed without employee influence not surprisingly generated resistance from career federal employees, fearful of the motives of appointees whose average tenure of 18 to 24 months would expire long before the appointee could implement the new practices.”[56]

To the extent that Tobias’s contention that political direction is inconstant and directed at short-term objectives is accurate, devices intended to enhance the responsiveness of the bureaucracy could create long-term damage. Workers being tugged back and forth by the shifting priorities of their political overseers will be distracted from their core purpose. Alternatively, they may persist with more traditional but increasingly subtle forms of resistance.

Hostile Labor-Management Environment

When unions are accorded only a limited formal role in the workplace, they find other means of making their presence felt. Slater comments that, in the era that preceded President Kennedy’s executive order, public sector unions engaged primarily in three types of activities: (1) political activities in an attempt to pressure policy makers to adopt policies favorable to public employees, (2) “they represented workers under other legal frameworks such as in civil service hearings" and (3) "they engaged in 'informal' bargaining, which in some cases led to quasi-collective agreements or at least understandings."[57] Adds Slater, "unions, "continued to organize and press management in ways that most parties involved ultimately decided were less efficient than giving the workers some collective bargaining rights."[58]

The Transportation Security Agency (TSA) has served as something of a test case for the new labor-management paradigm. As noted above, the legislation creating TSA provided the administrator with the authority to deny collective bargaining rights to its members. With that proscription in effect, the American Federation for Government Employees has nevertheless proceeded to organize TSA and represent TSA employees in grievance hearings and employment-related lawsuits. Slater contends that in the absence of a union check on management, workplace problems at TSA have multiplied:

> The TSA's employment problems were numerous, serious, and widespread. By March 2003, TSA workers around the country were complaining of low morale. They cited inadequate training (which they said had increased injury rates) and inadequate safety equipment (for example, no radiation detection badges for X-ray machine operators). They claimed that TSA managers showed favoritism toward screeners who formerly worked for private companies, and that the TSA had not disciplined supervisors guilty of sexual harassment.[59]

Although the federal employee unions retain some collective bargaining rights even under the new DHS regulations and the proposed DoD regulations, those rights are substantially curtailed. As noted above, Tobias attributes the adversarial and litigious nature of collective bargaining under FSLMRS to the diminished role accorded federal unions relative to their private sector counterparts. With the union role further curtailed under the new DHS and DoD systems, the dysfunctional aspects of the old system will be amplified if Tobias's thesis is valid.

Increased Litigiousness

Robert Tobias, former head of the National Treasury Employees Union, predicted an aggressive response from the federal unions to what at that time were only proposed regulations for a new personnel system at DHS. His prediction proved valid when, just days after release of the new DHS final and DoD proposed regulations, the federal unions went to court in an effort to stop both. Tobias anticipates an escalation of tensions and a new era of adversarialism in the federal workplace that will work to the detriment of the workers and the unions:

> Union combativeness will in turn lead to more aggressive responses by the Administration, creating reluctance among agency political leaders to collaborate with unions and employees. Local union leaders excluded from collaborative activities will revert to resistance. Labor and management will return full swing to their traditional adversarial dance. Excluded knowledge workers will feel dissatisfied with their jobs because of their more limited influence, and unions will have difficulty organizing new worksites and even maintaining membership, because unions will not have the ability to address worker desires."[60]

In reviewing the state labor-management relations experience, Malin (2003) finds that, in the absence of clear legislative guidelines, the courts play a prominent role in determining what is and is not negotiable. According to Malin, "virtually every management decision is arguably negotiable" (269).[61] Courts have therefore tried to develop rules for determining what has to be bargained. His conclusion however, is that the courts have met with little success in this area. Based on a review of key cases, Malin contends,

> There are no settled rules of general applicability that guide the parties' conduct. Instead, the law becomes what the labor board or court declares it to be in any particular case and the precedential effects of the declaration beyond that particular case are minimal. This approach encourages issue-by-issue litigation over bargaining rights and managerial prerogatives and discourages cooperative discussion of issues of mutual concern. It engenders the type of legal formalism identified by the Secretary of Labor's Task Force (U.S. DOL, 1996:65) as a significant barrier to labor-management cooperation.[62]

In Malin's view, a broader scope of bargaining facilitates issue resolution. He uses the Clinton experience with partnership in support of his contention that cooperation and attention to matters of substance are more likely when the two parties have roughly equal status. With the federal government now heading in the opposition direction, a reversion to a highly contentious and litigious period portends.

CONCLUSION

We are entering a new era of federal labor-management relations. The Bush administration has effectively pressed its political advantage to take a dominant position in the workplace. Although it is not "employment at-will," it represents clear movement toward providing managers with greater control over the workplace. The federal employee unions maintain enough of a foothold to serve as an effective adversary, however. The reforms, as noted, are limited to the Departments of Homeland Security and Defense; most of the rest of the government continues to operate under the provisions of FSLMRS. Even at DHS and DoD, however, the union presence will be felt. It will be felt both in the day-to-day processing of grievances and other employee actions and in court suits that will occupy lawyers but also impact managers. The primary impact is likely to be a more hostile, more contentious workplace. The employees, regardless of their attitude toward the unions, and the American public will likely be the losers.

It is possible that the new personnel systems will work, that pay-for-performance and the other innovations will enhance the quality of work life at DHS and DoD. There is some evidence of the success of these systems in other agencies that have experimented with similar systems. However, the very fact of union opposition is likely to impede successful implementation. Perhaps ironically, the most effective way that the unions can make their displeasure known about the labor-management relations provisions of the reforms is to inhibit successful implementation of other parts of the personnel package, indirectly injuring their own constituents. A more enlightened and less heavy-handed approach by the Bush administration toward the unions would likely have enhanced prospects for success of the system as a whole. It would, however, have been an approach at odds with the administration's political agenda.

ENDNOTES

1. The 1.9 million figure excludes the U.S. Postal Service, which had approximately 770,000 employees as of May 2004. See U.S. Office of Personnel Management, *Federal Civilian Workforce Statistics: Employment and Trends as of May 2004*, Office of Personnel Management, Washington, DC, retrieved February 19, 2005, from http://www.opm.gov/feddata/html/2004/may/.
2. In 2005, the Bush administration circulated a draft of a proposal to reform the civil service system. As of January 2006, the legislation, tentatively entitled the "Working for America Act," had not found a sponsor in Congress. See Ziegler, M., and Kauffman, T., Challenges won't keep White House from pursuing reforms, *Federaltimes.com*, January 3, 2006, retrieved January 3, 2006, from http://www.federaltimes.com.

3. Letter from the law firm of Minahan and Shapiro summarizing the proposed National Security Personnel System regulations. There is no date on the letter, which was distributed by the American Federation of Government Employees.
4. Masters, M., and Albright, R., Federal labor-management partnerships: Perspectives, performance, and possibilities, in *Going Public: The Role of Labor-Management Relations in Delivering Quality Government Services*, Brock, J., and Lipsky, D., eds., Industrial Relations Research Association, Champaign, IL, 2003, 171, p. 176.
5. U.S. General Accounting Office, *The Federal Labor-Management Relations Program*, GAO/T-GGD-92-8, U.S. Government Printing Office, Washington, DC, 1991, p. 2.
6. Tobias, R., Employee unions and the human resource function, in *Handbook of Human Resource Management in Government*, 2nd ed,, Steven Condrey, ed., John Wiley, San Francisco, 2005, 351, p. 355.
7. One element of Clinton's executive order proved highly contentious. FSLMRS sets forth two categories of items: (1) those that are reserved exclusively to management, including "to determine the mission, budget, organization, number of employees, and internal security practices of the agency" and "to assign work, to make determinations with respect to contracting out, and to determine the personnel by which agency operations shall be conducted with respect to filling positions, to make selections for appointments from among properly ranked and certified candidates for promotion any other appropriate source any other appropriate source." (5 USC 7106) and (2) those which management could, if it so chooses, bargain over. Included in this category are, "the numbers, types, and grades of employees or positions assigned to any organizational subdivision, work project, or tour of duty, or on the technology, methods, and means of performing work" (5 USC 7106). Clinton directed agencies to negotiate over these "permissive subjects" of bargaining. Management officials in many agencies, however, balked at putting items on the table over which they hitherto had unilateral control. For his part, President Clinton declined to force the issue by dismissing those officials who refused to abide by the executive order. See Clinton, W. J., Presidential Executive Order 12871, October 1, 1993, Labor Management Partnerships 1993, retrieved February 19, 2005, from http://govinfo.library.unt.edu/npr/library/direct/orders/24ea.html.
8. Clinton 1993.
9. U.S. Office of Personnel Management, *A Final Report to the National Partnership Council on Evaluating Progress and Improvements in Agencies' Organizational Performance Resulting from Labor-Management Partnerships*, Washington, DC, Office of Personnel Management, 2001.
10. U.S. Office of Personnel Management 2001, 48
11. U.S. Office of Personnel Management 2001, op cit.
12. Masters, M., Federal-sector unions: Current status and future directions, *Journal of Labor Research*, 25(1), 55, 2004.
13. Bush, G. W., Presidential Executive Order 13203, Revocation of Executive Order and Presidential Memorandum Concerning Labor-Management Partnerships 2001, retrieved February 19, 2005, from http://www.whitehouse.gov/news/releases/2001/02/20010221-1.html.

14. James, K., Memorandum for Heads of Departments and Agencies: Labor Management Relations, Office of Personnel Management, Washington, DC, 2001, retrieved February 19, 2005, from http://www.opm.gov/lmr/LMR_memo.asp.
15. See Slater, J., Homeland security vs. workers' rights? What the federal government should learn from history and experience, and why, *Journal of Labor and Employment Law*, 6, 295–356, 2004; and Tobias, R., The future of federal government labor relations and the mutual interests of Congress, the administration, and unions, *Journal of Labor Research*, 25(1), 19, 2004.
16. Slater 2004, 314. Also in 2003, employees in selected IT-related positions in the Social Security Administration were excluded from bargaining unit coverage on the grounds that their work directly affects national security. The justification provided was that if the agency's computers were disrupted, "40 million people would be delayed receiving their social security checks." See Slater 2004.
17. Masters and Albright 2003, 75.
18. U.S. Department of Homeland Security/U.S. Office of Personnel Management, Department of Homeland Security Human Resources Management System, Final Regulations 2005, 121, retrieved February 19, 2005, from http://www.nteu.org/DHS-OPM%20Regulations1.doc.
19. U.S. Department of Homeland Security/U.S. Office of Personnel Management 2005, 138.
20. U.S. Department of Homeland Security/U.S. Office of Personnel Management 2005, 148.
21. The mission statement of DHS is as follows: "We will prevent and deter terrorist attacks and protect against and respond to threats and hazards to the nation. We will ensure safe and secure borders, welcome lawful immigrants and visitors, and promote the free-flow of commerce." U.S. Department of Homeland Security, retrieved February 5, 2006, from http://www.dhs.gov/dhspublic/interapp/editorial/editorial_0413.xml.
22. American Federation of Government Employees, Defense workers' unions to sue Pentagon, press release, February 10, 2005, retrieved February 19, 2005, from http://www.afge.org/Index.cfm?Page=PressReleases&PressReleaseID=417.
23. Kaufman, T., DoD's personnel overhaul: More power for managers, less for unions, *Federaltimes.com*, February 10, 2005, retrieved February 19, 2005, from http://federaltimes.com/index.php?S=654817.
24. U.S. Office of Management and Budget, The President's Management Agenda, Fiscal Year 2002, 2001, retrieved February 19, 2005, from http://www.whitehouse.gov/omb/budget/fy2002/mgmt.pdf.
25. See Hood, C. A., Public management for all seasons? *Public Administration*, 69, 3, 1991, on New Public Management (NPM) doctrine generally; and also Thompson, J., Labor-management relations and partnerships? Were they reinvented? In *Handbook of Public Administration*, Peters, B., and Pierre, J., eds., Sage, London, 2003, 84–97, on the labor-management implications of NPM.
26. U.S. Office of Personnel Management, Human Capital Assessment and Accountability Framework, Washington, DC, no date, retrieved February 19, 2005, from http://apps.opm.gov/HumanCapital/tool/index.cfm.
27. Kochan, T., Katz, H., and McKersie, R., *The Transformation of American Industrial Relations*, ILR Press, Ithaca, NY, 1994.

28. Kochan, Katz, and McKersie 1994, 27.
29. Kochan, Katz, and McKersie 1994, 28.
30. Kochan, Katz, and McKersie 1994.
31. Eaton, A., and P. Voos., Productivity-enhancing innovations in work organization, compensation, and employee participation in the union versus the nonunion sectors, in *Advances in Industrial and Labor Relations*, Lewin, D., and Sockell, D., eds., JAI Press, Greenwich, CT, 6, 63, 1994.
32. Kochan, Katz, and McKersie 1994, 147.
33. Appelbaum, E., et al., *Manufacturing Advantage: Why High-Performance Work Systems Pay Off*, ILR Press, Ithaca, NY, 2000, 7.
34. Kochan, Katz, and McKersie 1994; and Appelbaum et al. 2000.
35. Appelbaum et al. 2000, 227. See also Lawler, E., III, *High Involvement Management*, Jossey-Bass, San Francisco, 1986; and Walton, R., Establishing and maintaining high-commitment work systems, in Kimberly, J., Miles, R., and Associates, *The Organizational Life Cycle: Issues in the Creation, Transformation, and Decline of Organizations*, Jossey-Bass, San Francisco, 208, 1980.
36. Kearney, R., and Hays, S., Labor-management relations and participative decision-making: Toward a new paradigm, *Public Administration Review*, 54(1), 44, 1994, 44.
37. Kearney and Hays 1994, 44.
38. Kearney and Hays 1994, 48.
39. Kearney and Hays 1994, 48. Levine, M. Legal obstacles to union-management cooperation in the federal service, *Labor Law Journal*, 43, 1991, 103–110.
40. Gore, A., *Creating a Government That Works Better and Costs Less: Report of the National Performance Review*, Government Printing Office, Washington, DC, 1993, 87.
41. Eaton and Voos 1994, 80.
42. Levine, D. I., *Reinventing the Workplace: How Business and Employees Can Both Win*, Brookings Institution, Washington, DC, 1995.
43. Kochan, Katz, and McKersie 1994, 204.
44. Nissen, B., *Unions and Workplace Reorganization*, Wayne State University Press, Detroit, MI, 1997.
45. U.S. Office of Management and Budget 2001, 18.
46. For example, see Savas, E., *Privatizing the Public Sector: How To Shrink Government*, Chatham House, Chatham, NJ, 1982; Goldsmith, S., and Schneider, M., Partnering for public value: New approaches in public employee labor-management relations, *University of Pennsylvania Journal of Labor and Employment Law*, 5(3), 415, 2003; and Osborne, D., and Plastrik, P., *Banishing Bureaucracy: The Five Strategies for Reinventing Government*, Addison Wesley, Reading, MA, 1997.
47. U.S. Office of Management and Budget 2001, 24.
48. Goldsmith and Schneider 2003; and Osborne and Plastrik 1997.
49. Nesterczuk, G., Devine, D. J., and Moffit, R. E., *Taking Charge of Federal Personnel*, Rep. No. 1404, Heritage Foundation, Washington, DC, 2001.
50. Nesterczuk, Devine, and Moffit 2001, 4.
51. Nesterczuk, Devine, and Moffit 2001, 4.
52. Nesterczuk, Devine, and Moffit 2001, 5.

53. The Bush White House was likely predisposed toward a "political administration" approach to governing even prior to Nesterczuk's exposition of the model. Many Bush II administration appointees were veterans of the Reagan and Bush I administrations, and as such were comfortable with the active role assigned political appointees in those administrations. See Ingraham, P., Thompson, J., and Eisenberg, E., Political management strategies and political/career relationships: Where are we now in the federal government? *Public Administration Review*, 55(3), 263, 1995.
54. Tobias 2004, 22.
55. See Pressman J., and Wildavsky, A., *Implementation*, University of California Press, Berkeley, 1973; Ingram, H., and Mann, D., Policy failure: An issue deserving analysis, in Ingram, H., and Mann, D., eds., *Why Policies Succeed or Fail*, Sage, Thousand Oaks, CA, 1980, 11–32; and Mazmanian, D., and Sabatier, P., *Effective Policy Implementation*, Lexington Books, Lexington, MA, 1981.
56. Tobias 2004, 23.
57. Slater 2004, 346.
58. Slater 2004, 346.
59. Slater 2004, 343.
60. Tobias 2004, 33.
61. Malin, M., Public sector labor law doctrine and labor-management cooperation, in *Going Public: The Role of Labor-Management Relations in Delivering Quality Government Services*, Brock, J. and Lipsky, D., eds., Industrial Relations Research Association, Champaign, IL, 2003, 269.
62. Malin 2003. U.S. Department of Labor, Secretary of Labor Task Force on Excellence in State and Local Government Through Labor-Management Cooperation, *Working Together for Public Service,* 1996.

INDEX

A

Alabama
Birmingham, 26
bureaucratic capacity, 87
civil service reform, 38–40
corruption, 85
employee dismissals, 198
government performance, 90
Jefferson County, 38–40
party competition, 88
personnel system, 8
reform readiness, 96
Alaska, 8
corruption, 84
government performance, 90
job security, 13
party competition, 88
reform readiness, 93, 95
unions, 205
American Federation of State, County , and Municipal Employees (AFSCME), 32, 61
Anti-unionism, 15
Antidiscrimination legislation, 48, 51, 126, 153, 227
Antiretaliation statutes, 51
Arizona, 8
corruption, 85
dealing with problem employees, 201, 202
declassification of civil servants, 11
employee dismissal, 197, 198, 204
government performance, 90
governor initiated reform, 15
party competition, 88
personnel system, 8
reform readiness, 94, 95
university system, 12
Arkansas, 66
abolition of merit system, 10, 124
corruption, 85
government performance, 90
party competition, 89
personnel system, 8
reform readiness, 93, 95
supervisor authority, 13
term limits, 17
At-will employment, 47–69
accountability and, 182–183
advocates for, 168
agency view of, 154
aim of, 27, 152
application of, 158–160
as a managerial tool, 157
calls for, 155
case study investigation of, 152
civil service abuse and, 166
criticisms, 54–57
defenders, 57
defenses, 57–58
defined, 175
description, 153
disadvantage, 164
dismissal and, 183–185, 226–227
disproportionate impact by race, 226–228
effects, 7, 125, 154, 157
perceived, 160–167
employee attitude toward, 32, 163, 165, 167
employee devaluation through, 147
employment relations, 178
exceptions to, 50–54, 168
implied contract, 52–53

implied covenant of good faith and fair dealing, 53–54
judicial, 51–52
public policy, 52
statutory, 51
antidiscrimination, 51
antiretaliation, 51
executive control and, 169
expansion of, 61–65
constitutional issues, 61–63
reducing transparency of government, 63–65
HR directors and, 154, 155, 162, 164
information dissemination and, 63
legal exceptions, 168
legal rights in, 60
limits, 16
misunderstood aspects, 181
opponents, 166
origin, 48–50
performance and, 154, 163
private sector, 168
proponents, 152, 164
protection in, 126
public sector, 177, 181–182
racial equality and, 219–229
rise of, 225–226
reforms protecting, 59–61
social psychological benefits and, 228

B

Blunt, Matt, 15
Boss Tweed, 79
Bungee cord management, 18
Bureaucratic capacity, 82–83
Bush, Jeb, 30, 31, 61

C

California, 8, 12, 58
at-will employment, 126
corruption, 84
dealing with problem employees, 201
employee
dismissal, 196, 198, 200, 202, 203
protection, 53
quit rate, 206
turnover, 207
government performance, 90
governor initiated reform, 14–15
party competition, 89
personnel system, 8
reform readiness, 93, 95
Carcieri, Donald, 15
Chapel Hill, North Carolina, 40–41
Civil service, 17
bureaucratic dysfunction, 20
centralized, 3
commission, 5
coverage, dismissal rates and, 203–204
current trends, 7–15
decentralization, 152
declassification in, 11
deprivileging, 16
deregulation, 124, 152
disaggregation, 125
disdain for, 179
experimentation at low levels, 26
federal, 78–80, 104, 127
framing innovations for, 25–43
grievance process, 170
guidelines, 7
impartiality, 136, 140
local, 80
management, 22
merit as defining feature of, 157
nonpartisan, 131, 133
politicization, 143
protection, 134, 170, 183
reduced, 77
removal of, 27, 67–69, 169
red tape, 129
reform, 12, 151
activist governors in, 14–15
arguments for, 78–80, 103
best and worst states for, 83–87
courts as initiators of, 38–40
dismissal practices and, 207–210
executives as initiators of, 36–38
federal, 104, 127
federalism and, 25
historical perspectives on, 101–102, 124
in Florida, 30–33, 123–192
in Georgia, 27, 30
in Jefferson County, Alabama, 38–40
in Louisiana, 36–38
in New York, 33–35
in Texas, 151–173
in Utah, 175–192

interest in, 25
justification for, 103
literature, 124
models of, 28–29
monitoring of, 42
news media and, 82
party machines and, 82
preconditions of successful, 87
state cases of, 123–192
Florida, 123–149
Texas, 151–173
Utah, 175–192
statutes, 62
traditional party organizations and, 86
spoil system, 81
state, 3–20, 80
tenure, 57, 77, 220, 223, 247
elimination of, 78, 96, 124
Georgia, 77
guidelines, 224
historical perspectives, 78–79
origin, 78
protection, 83
rights, 27
terms of employment and, 223
traditional, 225
tests, 33
transformation, current trends in, 7
violations, 12
Civil Service Commission, 5
Civil Service Reform Act (1978), 43, 175, 243
Clark and Stephenson v. State Personnel Board (1984), 62, 68
Collective bargaining, 19
Colorado, 16
corruption, 84
governor, 15
personnel system, 8
university system, 12
Connecticut, 8, 12, 16
at-will employment, 16
corruption, 83, 85
government performance, 90
party competition, 88
personnel system, 8
reform readiness, 94, 95
Contract theory, 52
Convergys, 31–32
Conway v. Searles (1997), 67
Corrections Officers Local 416, AFSCME v. Weld (1991), 67
Corruption, 83–85
Covenant of good faith, 535–54
Croslin v. Bush (2002), 61

D

Daniels, Mitch, 15
Declet v. Department of Children and Family Services (2000), 64
DeClue v. City of Clayton (2000), 63, 69
Delaware, 124
at-will employment, 16
corruption, 85
dealing with problem employees, 201
declassification of civil servants, 11
employee dismissal, 202
government performance, 90
party competition, 88
personnel system, 8
reform readiness, 92, 94, 96
Department of Aging, 11
Department of Corrections, 11, 61, 68
Department of Corrections v. Florida Nurses Association (1987), 61, 68
Department of Defense (DOD), 77
personnel system, 239–240
reforms, 78
Department of Homeland Security (DHS), 77
personnel system for, 237–239
Department of Juvenile Justice, 11
Department of Social Services, 11
Discipline, 183–185
Dismissal, 197, 198
at-will employment and, 183–185, 226–227
just cause, 19
practices, 207–210
rates, 203–204
soft core, 200
Downsizing, 143
Due process rights, 7, 224, 225
restrictions on, 12–14
violation of procedural, 68

E

Economic Development Office, 11

F

Federal Aviation Administration, 106
Federal Bureau of Investigation, 79
Federalism, civil service reform and, 25
Fletcher, Ernie, 15
Florida, 6, 7, 8, 16, 126, 148
  at-will employment, 48, 168
  civil service reform, 30–33, 123–143
  corruption, 84
  employee dismissal, 198
  employee quit rate, 208
  employee turnover, 207
  ending of civil service protections, 123–143
  governor's appointments, 12
  HRM model, 42
  Human Rights Commission, 147
  outsourcing, 148
  personnel system, 8
  Selected Exempt Service, 31
  Service First, 30, 31, 133–141
  union membership, 32
  Whistleblower's Act, 147
Florida Public Employees Council 79, AFSCME v. Bush (2002), 61
Fortune v. National Cash Register Co. (1977), 54

G

Gattis v. Gravett (1986), 62, 66
Georgia, 6, 16, 26
  at-will employment, xv, 16, 30, 36, 54, 61, 124, 211, 226
  civil service reform in, 27, 30
  corruption, 84
  government appointees, 12
  government performance, 90
  Merit Systems Reform Act (1996), 5, 27, 30
  party competition, 88
  personnel system, 8
  reform readiness, 93, 94
Gilmer v. Interstate/Johnson Lane Corp. (1991), 60
Government Performance Project, 151
Governmental Accountability Act (1993), 12
Guz v. Bechtel National , Inc., 126

H

Hawaii, 8
  corruption, 85
  government performance, 90
  party competition, 88
  personnel system, 8
  reform readiness, 94, 96
Health and Human Services, 11
Human resource management (HRM)
  administrative changes, 23
  decentralization, 3, 5, 10
  models of service delivery, 26–43
  outsourcing, 31–32
  reform interview template, 22–23
  splintered nature of, 26
  supervisors, 13
  telephone survey, 6–7

I

Idaho, 8, 19
  at-will employment, 16
  corruption, 84
  declassification of civil servants, 11
  employee dismissal, 198, 200
  government performance, 90
  job security, 19
  party competition, 88
  personnel system, 8
  reform readiness, 93, 95
Illinois, 16
  antipatronage policies, 115
  corruption, 83, 85
  employee dismissal, 198
  government performance, 91
  party competition, 88
  party organization, 86
  personnel system, 8
  probationary rate, 204
  reform readiness, 92, 94, 96
Indiana
  corruption, 83, 85
  dealing with problem employees, 201
  employee dismissal, 202, 203
  governor, 15
  governor initiated reform, 15
  party competition, 88, 92
  personnel system, 8
  recentralization, 8, 10

reclassification, 124
reform readiness, 94, 95
Iowa, 8, 92
corruption, 84
declassification, 11
employee dismissal, 198
employee quit rate, 206
employee turnover, 207
party competition, 88
reform readiness, 93, 94

J

Jefferson County, Alabama, 38–40
Job security, 5, 8, 9, 13, 17–20. *See also* Tenure
bargaining over, 53
compensation and, 164, 211
employee retention and, 164
for African Americans, 226
higher wages *vs.*, 57
legal challenges to elimination of, 61
motivation and, 161, 185
productivity and, 56
term limits and, 17
unionization and, 53, 56, 205
weakening of, 13
Just cause dismissal, 19

K

Kansas, 8, 16
corruption, 84
declassification of civil servants, 11
employee dismissal, 198
government performance, 90
governor initiated reform, 15
HRM model, 10
reclassification, 124
reform readiness, 92, 93, 94
university system, 12
Kentucky, 8
at-will employment, 16
corruption, 85
government performance, 91
governor, 15
governor initiated reform, 15
party competition, 88
reform readiness, 94, 95
Kulongoski, Ted, 15

L

Labor contracts, 126
Labor management relations, 13, 233–250
adversarial, 233
elimination of negotiations, 15
federal, 234–237
history of, 234–237
hostility in, 247–248
in DHS, 234
in DOD, 234
Louisiana, 8, 13, 26
civil service reform, 36–38
corruption, 83, 85
government performance, 91
governor initiated reform, 36–38
HRM model, 42
party competition, 89
personnel system, 8
privatization, 36

M

Maine, 8
corruption, 84
government performance, 90
party competition, 88
recentralization, 10
reform readiness, 93, 95
Marcy, William, 79
Maryland, 8
corruption, 85
government performance, 90
party competition, 89
recentralization, 10
reform readiness, 92, 94, 96
Massachusetts, 8, 102
at-will employment, 16
corruption, 83, 85
government performance, 90
party competition, 89
patronage in, 101–116
personnel system, 8
reform readiness, 93, 95
Massachusetts Bay Transportation Authority, 110
Massachusetts Low Level Radioactive Waste Management Board, 110
McMurtray v. Holladay (1993), 66
Merit system, 16, 62, 81, 184
abolition of, 10

aim, 57
arguments against, 19
at-will employment *vs.*, 157
characteristic, 124
criticism, 19
defined, 124
efficiency, 19
executive-based, 179, 183
executive-centered, 184
in Florida, 126
patronage *vs.*, 16
performance and, 19
protections, 167
recentralization of, 10
Merit System Act, 68
Merit System Protection Board, 238
Michigan, 8
collective bargaining, 211
corruption, 83, 84
dealing with problem employees, 201
employee dismissal, 197, 198, 202, 203, 211
employee quit rate, 206
employee turnover, 207, 211
government performance, 91
job security, 19
party competition, 88
personnel system, Texas personnel system *vs.*, 212
reform readiness, 92, 93, 94
Minnesota, 8, 19, 97
at-will employment, 16
corruption, 83, 84
employee dismissal, 198
government performance, 91
job security, 19
party competition, 88
reform readiness, 92, 93, 94
Mississippi, 9, 66
at-will employment, 11
corruption, 85
government performance, 90
governor initiated reform, 15
party competition, 89
reform readiness, 93, 95
Missouri, 9, 11, 19
abolition of merit system, 10
collective bargaining, 15
corruption, 84
declassification of civil servants, 11
employee dismissal, 197, 198
employee resignation, 207
government performance, 91
governor, 15
governor initiated reform, 15
party competition, 88
reform readiness, 94, 95
Model Employment Termination Act (1991), 59
Montana, 9, 16
at-will employment, 16, 59
corruption, 84
government performance, 90
party competition, 88
reform readiness, 93, 95
Moral panic, 102, 105–114
analysis, 109
criteria
concern, 109–110
consensus, 111–112
disproportionality, 112–113
hostility, 110–111
volatility, 113–114
Motivation, 185–187
Muldrow v. Bush (2002), 61

N

National Defense Authorization Act (2003), 239
National Partnership Council, 235
National Security Personnel System, 239
National Treasury Employees Union, 248
Nebraska, 9, 13, 19
corruption, 84
declassification, 11
government performance, 91
reform readiness, 93, 95
Nevada, 9, 66
corruption, 84
declassification, 11
employee dismissal, 198
government performance, 90
party competition, 88
reform readiness, 93, 95
New Hampshire, 9
at-will employment, 16, 51
corruption, 83, 85
employee dismissal, 198, 204
government performance, 90
party competition, 89

patronage, 109
reform readiness, 93, 95
New Jersey, 9, 53
corruption, 83, 85
government performance, 91
party competition, 88
reform readiness, 92, 94, 96
New Mexico, 9
corruption, 83, 85
government performance, 90
party competition, 88
reform readiness, 94, 96
New Public Management, 25
New York, 9, 26
civil service reform, 33–35
civil service web site, 34
corruption, 83, 85
dealing with problem employees, 201
Department of Civil Service, 33–34
employee dismissal, 202, 203
government performance, 90
HMO model, 42
modernization of civil service, 33–35
New Civil Service, 33
party competition, 88
reform readiness, 94, 95
traditional party organizations, 86
unions, 35
North Carolina
Chapel Hill, 26, 40–41
corruption, 84
employee dismissal, 198, 200
government performance, 91
party competition, 88
personnel system, 9
reform readiness, 93, 94
North Dakota
abolition of merit system, 10
corruption, 84
personnel system, 9
Nuclear Regulatory Commission, 79

O

Office of Information Systems, 11
Office Personnel Management, 236
Ohio, 16
at-will employment, 16
corruption, 83, 85
employee dismissal, 197, 198, 204, 209
government performance, 91
party competition, 89
personnel system, 9
reform readiness, 94, 95
unions, 97
Oklahoma, 9, 14, 17
abolition of merit system, 10
at-will employment, 16
corruption, 85
decentralization, 10
employee dismissal, 198
government performance, 90
party competition, 88
personnel system, 9
reform readiness, 94, 95
Oregon, 9
corruption, 84
government performance, 90
governor, 15
party competition, 88
reform readiness, 93, 95
Outsourcing, 31–32
Owens, Bill, 15

P

Pataki, George, 33
Patent Office, 79
Patronage, 126, 157, 175
demand variables, 81–82, 83
demonization of, 101–115
eradicating, 65, 81
folk devil, 103–104
for high-capacity public agencies, 83
merit system *vs.*, 16
policies against, 115
policy *vs.* spoils, 79
raid, 82
return, 65
reward-based, 80
spoils *vs.* policy, 79
spoils-based, 78
Patronage demand variable, 81–82
Pay-for-performance system, 18
Pendleton Act, 78
Pennsylvania, 9
corruption, 83, 85
employee quit rate, 206
government performance, 90
party competition, 88
reform readiness, 93, 95

Personnel function
reform, 4–6
Personnel reform, 4–6
Political environmental variable, 82
Privatization, 143, 187, 225
in Florida, 31, 32
in Louisiana, 36
trend toward, 33
Privatization/outsourcing model, 26, 28–29, 32
other reform models *vs.*, 42
Probationary rate, 204
Public policy statutes, 126
Public sector
as niche for African Americans, 220–223
nature and benefits of work in, 223–225
Public service career, 20

R

Racial equality, 219–229
Rhode Island, 9, 14, 52, 62
civil service statues, 62
corruption, 83, 85
employee dismissal, 19
government performance, 90
governor initiated reform, 15
job security, 19
party competition, 89
pay-for-performance system, 18
reform readiness, 87, 92, 94, 96
traditional party organizations, 86
unions, 97

S

Schwarzenegger, Arnold, 14–15
Sinnot, George, 33
Soft core dismissal, 200
South Carolina, 9
abolition of merit system, 10
as paragon of civil service reform, 12
at-will employment, 17
corruption, 85
decentralization, 10
declassification, 11
government performance, 91
Governmental Accountability Act (1993), 12
HR. model, 10
party competition, 88
reform readiness, 93, 94
South Dakota, 9, 201
corruption, 84
dealing with problem employees, 201
employee dismissal, 203
government performance, 90
party competition, 89
reform readiness, 93, 95

T

Tennessee, 9, 49
at-will employment, 16
corruption, 84
dealing with problem employees, 201
employee dismissal, 199, 202, 203
government performance, 91
party competition, 88
reform readiness, 93, 95
Tenure, 57, 77, 220, 223, 247. *See also* Job security
elimination of, 78, 96, 124
Georgia, 77
guidelines, 224
historical perspectives, 78–79
origin, 78
protection, 83
rights, 27
terms of employment and, 223
traditional, 225
Term limits, 17
Texas, 7, 9, 12, 152, 211
abolition of merit system, 16
annual turnover in government, 161
at-will employment, 16, 151–171, 210, 225
application of, 158, 160
doctrine of, 155–158
perceived effects of, 160–161, 163–167
civil service reform, 151–173
corruption, 84
dealing with problem employees, 201
declassification, 224
employee dismissal, 199, 200, 202, 203
employee quitting rate, 208
employee turnover, 211, 212
government performance, 91
party competition, 88
personnel system, 9

reform readiness, 93, 95
State Classification Office, 169
Texas Public Employees Association (TPEA), 154, 169
Texas Public Employees Union (TPEU), 154, 169
Tort theory, 52
Traditional Party Organization (TPO), 86
Tranportation Security Agency, 248
Transportation Security Agency (TSA), 124, 248

U

Uncovering, 11
Uniform Law Commissioners, 59
Unions, 19–20, 240–245
United States of America. *See also specific States*
bureaucratic capacity in, 87
corruptions, 85–86
government performance in, 90–91
media capacity, 86
party competition in, 86–87, 88–89
reform readiness indexes, 93–95
Universities, declassification and, 12
Utah, 9, 13
at-will employment, 175–191
bureaucratic capacity, 87
corruption, 85
government performance, 91
party competition, 89
reform readiness, 93, 95

V

Vermont, 9, 19, 67
corruption, 84
dealing with problem employees, 201
declassification, 11
employee dismissal, 202
government performance, 91
governor initiated reform, 15
job security, 19
party competition, 88
reform readiness, 93, 95
Virginia, 9
bureaucratic capacity, 87
corruption, 84
decentralization, 10
declassification, 12
employee dismissal, 197, 199
government performance, 91
HRM model, 10
party competition, 89
reform readiness, 93
turnover, 214
university system, 12

W

Washington, 9
at-will employement, 16
corruption, 84
decentralization, 10
government performance, 91
HRM model, 10
party competition, 89
reform readiness, 92, 93, 94
Washington, D. C., 78–83
Water town Police Department, 110
West Virginia, 9, 14
at-will employement, 16
corruption, 85
governor initiated reform, 15
party competition, 89
reform readiness, 92, 94, 96
Whistle-blower behavior, 165, 168
Wilkinson v. State Crime Laboratory Commission (2002), 62, 67
Wisconsin, 9
corruption, 83, 84
employee dismissal, 197, 199
employee quit rate, 206
government performance, 91
party competition, 88
reform readiness, 92, 93, 94
turnover, 207
Workers Compensation Agency, 11
Wyoming, 9
corruption, 84
government performance, 90
party competition, 89
reform readiness, 93, 96